1,000,000 Books

are available to read at

www.ForgottenBooks.com

Read online
Download PDF
Purchase in print

ISBN 978-1-330-27946-5
PIBN 10011390

This book is a reproduction of an important historical work. Forgotten Books uses state-of-the-art technology to digitally reconstruct the work, preserving the original format whilst repairing imperfections present in the aged copy. In rare cases, an imperfection in the original, such as a blemish or missing page, may be replicated in our edition. We do, however, repair the vast majority of imperfections successfully; any imperfections that remain are intentionally left to preserve the state of such historical works.

Forgotten Books is a registered trademark of FB &c Ltd.
Copyright © 2018 FB &c Ltd.
FB &c Ltd, Dalton House, 60 Windsor Avenue, London, SW19 2RR.
Company number 08720141. Registered in England and Wales.

For support please visit www.forgottenbooks.com

1 MONTH OF FREE READING

at www.ForgottenBooks.com

By purchasing this book you are eligible for one month membership to ForgottenBooks.com, giving you unlimited access to our entire collection of over 1,000,000 titles via our web site and mobile apps.

To claim your free month visit: www.forgottenbooks.com/free11390

* Offer is valid for 45 days from date of purchase. Terms and conditions apply.

English
Français
Deutsche
Italiano
Español
Português

www.forgottenbooks.com

Mythology Photography **Fiction**
Fishing Christianity **Art** Cooking
Essays Buddhism Freemasonry
Medicine **Biology** Music **Ancient Egypt** Evolution Carpentry Physics
Dance Geology **Mathematics** Fitness
Shakespeare **Folklore** Yoga Marketing
Confidence Immortality Biographies
Poetry **Psychology** Witchcraft
Electronics Chemistry History **Law**
Accounting **Philosophy** Anthropology
Alchemy Drama Quantum Mechanics
Atheism Sexual Health **Ancient History**
Entrepreneurship Languages Sport
Paleontology Needlework Islam
Metaphysics Investment Archaeology
Parenting Statistics Criminology
Motivational

SERMONS

FOR THE PRINCIPAL FESTIVALS AND FASTS OF THE CHURCH YEAR

BY THE

RT. REV. PHILLIPS BROOKS, D. D.

Late Bishop of the Diocese of Massachusetts

EDITED BY THE

REV. JOHN COTTON BROOKS

Seventh Series

NEW YORK
E. P. DUTTON & COMPANY
31 WEST TWENTY-THIRD STREET
1895

Copyright, 1895,
By E. P. DUTTON & COMPANY.

TO THE MEMORY OF MY BROTHER,
ARTHUR BROOKS,
MY COMPANION IN BOYHOOD AND IN MANHOOD,
I DEDICATE,
IN LOVING REMEMBRANCE AND PATIENT HOPE, THESE
SERMONS OF HIM WITH WHOM NOW HE WALKS
IN THE LIGHT OF THE GLORIFIED CHRIST,
WHOSE THEY ARE AND WHOM THEY SERVE.

J. C. B.

OCTOBER,
1895.

CONTENTS.

I.
PAGE

FIRST SUNDAY IN ADVENT.............................. 1

"Till we all come in the unity of the faith, and of the knowledge of the Son of God, unto a perfect man, unto the measure of the stature of the fullness of Christ."—EPH. IV. 13.

II.

SECOND SUNDAY IN ADVENT............................. 18

"He came unto His own, and His own received Him not. But as many as received Him, to them gave He power to become the sons of God."—JOHN I. 11, 12.

III.

THIRD SUNDAY IN ADVENT.............................. 35

"He was not that Light, but was sent to bear witness of that Light."—JOHN I. 8.

IV.

FOURTH SUNDAY IN ADVENT............................. 54

"But when the fullness of the time was come, God sent forth His Son."—GAL. IV. 4.

V.

CHRISTMAS EVE....................................... 72

"Because there was no room for them in the inn."—LUKE II. 7.

VI.

CHRISTMAS DAY.. 85
"And the Word was made flesh, and dwelt among us."
—JOHN I. 14.

VII.

SUNDAY AFTER CHRISTMAS 97
"And because ye are sons, God hath sent forth the Spirit of His Son into your hearts, crying, Abba, Father."
—GAL. IV. 6.

VIII.

ASH WEDNESDAY.. 110
"Blessed are they whose iniquities are forgiven, and whose sins are covered."—ROM. IV. 7.

IX.

FIRST SUNDAY IN LENT 130
"Then was Jesus led up of the Spirit into the wilderness to be tempted of the devil."—MATT. IV. 1.

X.

SECOND SUNDAY IN LENT............................... 150
"It is written, Man shall not live by bread alone, but by every word that proceedeth out of the mouth of God."
—MATT. IV. 4.

XI.

THIRD SUNDAY IN LENT................................ 167
"Again, the devil taketh Him up into an exceeding high mountain, and showeth Him all the kingdoms of the world, and the glory of them."—MATT. IV. 8.

XII.

FOURTH SUNDAY IN LENT.............................. 184
"And David said unto Nathan, I have sinned against the Lord. And Nathan said unto David, The Lord also hath put away thy sin; thou shalt not die."—2 SAM. XII. 13.

CONTENTS. vii

XIII.

FIFTH SUNDAY IN LENT.................................. 196

"Ye are they which have continued with Me in My temptations. And I appoint unto you a kingdom, as My Father hath appointed unto Me."—LUKE XXII. 28, 29.

XIV.

THE SUNDAY NEXT BEFORE EASTER 209

"And they that went before, and they that followed, cried, saying, Hosanna; Blessed is He that cometh in the name of the Lord."—MARK XI. 9.

XV.

PASSION WEEK 222

"Now is My soul troubled; and what shall I say? Father, save Me from this hour. But for this cause came I unto this hour. Father, glorify Thy name."—JOHN XII. 27, 28.

XVI.

THURSDAY BEFORE EASTER 239

"And He cometh, and findeth them sleeping, and saith unto Peter, Simon, sleepest thou? couldest not thou watch one hour?"—MARK XIV. 37.

XVII.

GOOD FRIDAY.. 255

"And I, if I be lifted up, . . . will draw all men unto Me."—JOHN XII. 32.

XVIII.

EASTER DAY.. 269

"That I may know Him, and the power of His resurrection."—PHIL. III. 10.

CONTENTS.

XIX.

ASCENSION DAY 286

"And a cloud received Him out of their sight."—ACTS I. 9.

"Then we which are alive and remain shall be caught up together with them in the clouds, to meet the Lord in the air: and so shall we ever be with the Lord."—1 THESS. IV. 17.

XX.

WHITSUNDAY 303

"The communion of the Holy Ghost."—2 COR. XIII. 14.

XXI.

TRINITY SUNDAY 318

"Again, He sent other servants more than the first. . . . But last of all He sent unto them His Son."—MATT. XXI. 36, 37.

XXII.

THE TRANSFIGURATION OF CHRIST 336

"And Peter answered and said to Jesus, Master, it is good for us to be here: and let us make three tabernacles; one for Thee, and one for Moses, and one for Elias. For he wist not what to say."—MARK IX. 5, 6.

FIRST SUNDAY IN ADVENT.

"Till we all come in the unity of the faith, and of the knowledge of the Son of God, unto a perfect man, unto the measure of the stature of the fullness of Christ."—EPH. IV. 13.

IF any entire stranger were to come to-day into our service and watch it as it moves along from step to step, one thing would become evident to him in it all. He would see that we were *beginning something.* Everything, apparently, is starting fresh. And if he looked along the services of the other Sundays that are to follow this he would see that it is a whole long year that we are commencing. A course that runs on through the next twelve months opens to-day. On through the deepening winter, on through the opening spring, on into the far-off warmth of next summer, until another autumn closes on us, is to run the course of services beginning on this Advent Sunday. It is the Church's New-Year's Day. And one thing more would strike him if he were observant. He would see that all this year is filled and shaped by the life of a *Person.* One man's biography sweeps through it all, and every season is colored with the aspect in which it finds the great pervading life of Jesus Christ. Men's fortunes and employments will change as they always do. Success and failure, health and sickness, life and death, will come with all the changing months around to next December; but through them all, as if it were something that lay deeper than their changes, as if it were the presence in which and even the power by which all men failed or succeeded, lived or died, will run the story of Him who was born in Bethlehem and ascended into heaven from the Mount of Olives. And the observant stranger who saw this would have thus found the central truth of Christianity. He would have seen represented that presence and power which all Christian life, whether of church or soul, is always trying to realize—the presence and power of the Incarnation; the truth that all of human life is lived in the presence of, is represented by, and may be filled with and inspired by the life of the great Son of Man, who in a hundred senses *lived for* all men; in whose experiences all human experiences ought to find their key and their solution; who became completely what we are that we might come in everything to be like Him.

Christ was both the Redeemer and the Type of human life, the Saviour and the Pattern of men at once. We too much separate His two great offices, which really are not distinguishable. He could not have been our Saviour without being our Pattern; and even in the most mysterious functions of this Saviourhood there is always something in which we can pattern ourselves by Him. It follows, then, that all this life whose story we begin to-day is not merely a remote inimitable transaction wrought for every man's salvation, but is also the type of every man's existence. It is the great representative existence. All that happened to

Christ's humanity belongs to the perfect ideal picture of every human life. As we stand, then, upon the height of Advent Sunday and look along the stages of the life of Jesus which the Church will one by one commemorate, we are really looking along the history of universal human life, and so the possible, the perfect life of every man. Each stage was perfect in its development in Him, but each stage, however imperfectly lived, belongs to all men. The Christian year becomes, then, in one very true view of it, the picture of a human life from its first suggested promise to its latest effective influence upon the earth. Let me lead you to this thought and its developments. Let us see how each season of the Church's year presents a true period in and experience of every truly human life, represented by and worked out in the pattern of the human life of Jesus. I hope that such a study may do something to bring the perfect divine and human life of Christ closer to these lives of ours; for that is what all our worship and preaching are for; that is the greatest happiness and blessing that can come to any man.

The Church's year begins with Christ's advent; then comes His epiphany, then His suffering and death, and then the giving of His Spirit. Through all of these we shall pass in these next few months.

1. Take first the *advent*. It was not suddenly and unannounced that Jesus came into the world. He came into a world that had been prepared for Him. The whole Old Testament is the story of a special preparation. The key to Jewish history is the anticipation of His coming. And we have not begun to understand

the vastness of His mission unless we know that not merely the education of Judea, but the education of the whole world, was and is aimed at the preparation for the time when Jesus Christ should come to be its Master. You go into some heathen island now and preach Christ, and every readiness of nature to appreciate and take Him, which has been wrought out by all their religious struggles, is but another sign and illustration of how God prepares the advent of His Son. And then inside of the Judean history we have the special preparation—the story which we read this morning, the mission and ministry of John the Baptist. Only when all was ready, only in the fullness of His time, did Jesus come.

And now what shall we say about the lives of other men—the men of whom He was the representative and the chief? Have they their advents too? It is easy to believe it about the greatest of them. It is easy to think that those who have gathered the richness of the world into themselves and turned its currents of action or thought—easy to think of Moses, Charlemagne, Luther, Bacon, Shakespeare—that God prepared the world against their coming and sent them when the world was ready. The ages seem to make their advents. But it is hard to think the same of common people such as you and I. It seems as if our lives might have been dropped anywhere—three thousand years ago as well as now, and on the banks of the Nile as well as on the shores of Massachusetts Bay. Hard as it is, great as the strain which it puts on all our low habits of thinking about ourselves, the Bible is a strong and glorious call to men to gird up the loins of their minds and believe that God had a place for them and put them in their own place. It has these two truths, which it insists upon everywhere: that God cares separately for every man, and that every man has his own individual personal character. Personal divine care and personal human character—these two ideas are bright in all the Bible; in both the Testaments, in David and in Paul alike. Take those two truths together and they would blend in the conviction that God surely could not send His souls at random into the world, but for each a place must be hollowed in the plain of time and filled with all that could bring that soul to its best completeness. And this conviction, gathered out of the Bible's whole treatment of humanity, is set forth with representative clearness in the story of the advent of the Son of Man.

This, then, is the beginning of a life. It goes back before the moment when the man is here, a visible fact upon the earth. It lays hold of the thought of God which runs back into eternity. God knew your nature. He had a plan and pattern of your being in His mind. As David says, His eyes did see your substance, yet being imperfect, and in His book were all your members written. Knowing you, He made ready a place for you, He shaped a cradle for you in the ages, and when it was all done He laid your new life in it—the advent before the nativity.

What influence shall it have upon a man for him to know all this about his life—to know that it was contemplated and the world made ready for it before he was born? Shall it not give him, first, *a deep reverence for his own life?* Shall it not shake him free from that moral laziness which cloaks itself in the disguise of modesty, and make him accept the responsibilities and duties of a being for whom God has made the earth and the ages ready?

And shall it not make him *docile*, teaching him to look not to his own self-will, but to the God who chose his place for him, to know what, living in just that place, he ought to be? Responsibility and docility—these qualities of which the life of Jesus was so full—must fill the life of every man who believes in his own advent.

2. After the advent comes the *nativity*. The promised Christ is born. We can see what that meant in the history of Jesus. No longer prophesied and anticipated, at last the great typal life was a real fact in the world—a visible fact with all its possibilities contained within it. It was, indeed, but a poor helpless child at Bethlehem, but in its being there was really wrapped up all that that child was to grow to and to be and do. No wonder that Christmas Day has been so sacred to all those who believed in Jesus Christ; for it has seemed to sum up in itself every association and meaning of His life. *Birth*, the second fact in existence, the actual appearing of a being planned in the thought of God, had first in Christ this deep and comprehensive value, but it has kept that same value always.

Carry it over now to other men. Why is it that we celebrate the birthdays of great men? Is it not because all that they were and did seems to be gathered up into that critical moment when their life first was present as a true, real fact among the lives of men? And remember, here, just as before, our distinctions between great men and common men are mostly arbitrary and accidental. We are all so little and all so great in God's sight. So that the birth of *any* man, the beginning of *any* new life, is a great and solemn thing. How hard it is sometimes to make it seem so to ourselves! With all this swarm of men about us, how in our lower moments we wonder, after all, whether it is more than the buzzing of a little wiser bees about their hive, or the clustering of a little bigger ants around their ant-hill! What matter whether there be one more or less? What matter whether one be taken away or one added to the uncounted number? What matter death or birth? That is the low way of looking at it all. The higher way, catching the spirit of the Lord's nativity, when the angels sang in heaven because a Man was born, and the very stars were conscious of His coming, sees the true dignity, the almost awful solemnity of a human birth. It wonders whether there is anything in the universe more critical and sacred than for a new human life to begin here on the earth. These other worlds about us may have the same mysterious, infinite event. In them, too, spiritual beings—beings with characters like men and women—may be born, and then there is in them the same solemnity that there is here. But if not—if they have no life of character, nothing corresponding to our personality—then no splendor or exquisiteness of physical life that they may have to boast can make them for a moment rivals in dignity and interest of this little planet that swims in their midst. For here men are born. Each from the moment of his birth has his own singleness and unity. Each may be saved or lost. Each may do right or wrong. Each may be like God or like Satan. Each has a capacity of happiness or misery as yet unfathomed. Each may become glorious or horrible—glorious with a spiritual luster that no physical brilliance of any brightest star can compare with, or horrible with a tragical destruction that no burned and blasted planet can begin to match. All this is wrapped up in every man's birth, his whole power of separate existence; and so every man who really knows the sacredness of his own birth, who has learned from the wonders that surrounded the entrance of God into our flesh what a wonderful thing it is for any man to begin to live in the life which the Incarnation illuminated, must go through life strong and alert, with a clear sense of his own personality, never losing himself in the mass and crowd, keeping his independence, thinking his own thoughts, and feeling his own feelings—*being a man*, as he never loses sight of his birth, the time when he *began* to be a man.

3. After Advent and Christmas in the Church's year comes the *Epiphany*, which celebrates the manifestation of Christ to those entirely outside of His own life and all its first associations. The world made ready for Him and His birth complete, now He must show His influence upon the world. The purpose of His coming must be seen, that men may be something different because He is here; may be drawn away from themselves to Him. I want you to see how this new stage in Christ's life represents the next stage in the fullest and highest life of man; for it is most important, and it is so easily forgotten and neglected. A man's place is made ready for him in the mind of God; the man's life is set here as a positive, clear fact; and what comes next? There is no doubt what ought to come. That life must *tell*. It must go out beyond itself. It must

have *influence*. It must testify and supplement the mere fact of its existence by making other existences be something which they would not be without it. This seems so plain. This is so clearly set forth in the great typical life of Jesus. Can you conceive of an incarnation in which it should not have been prominent? Can you picture to yourself God coming into this world and then living a perfectly self-contained life—one that recognized no relations with and exercised no power over other lives about Him? No! The epiphany followed immediately on the advent and the nativity. Not by an effort; it was the next natural and necessary stage. It was a true epiphany. He merely showed Himself. He let His life go forth on other lives. He let His great light shine before men. But how many there are who realize their advent and their nativity who have never conceived for themselves of an epiphany! There are so many men who believe in their own place in the world, and are conscious of their own personal nature with its capacities and needs, who never have gone any further—never have dreamed that they were put here *where* they are, and made to be *what* they are, in order that other men might be something else through them. This is one of the heresies of life which men are not ashamed to own. They put it into philosophic shapes. There are theories of self-culture which are printed in books, taught in our schools, given as very gospels to our children as they grow up, which would be just exactly the same that they are now if no such dream as a possible duty of usefulness and influence from that child to other people had ever entered into the thought of God or man.

Hear what a child is taught. Is not this mostly what is said to him? "You are born into this rich and gorgeons nineteenth century. You are the 'heir of all the ages.' All the thought, discovery, invention, progress of the centuries have been fitting this world for your coming. And now, when the world is all ready, here you are." That is the lesson of his *advent*. And then he is told: "*You* are born into this world; *you*, a separate, distinct, new being; *you*, with a personal life; *you* who are and can be something that no other being in the world can be." That is the lesson of his *nativity*. He takes them both, and the result of both as they sink into his soul is a conviction and a resolution full of selfishness: "I will study, I will work and think, I will claim my place here—all that I may be myself completely, that I may cultivate myself." It rings through all our books and colleges, through all our homes and stores, this gospel of self-culture. "Be strong, be rich, be wise, be good." What for? "Why, so that you may be wise and rich and strong and good." The endless circle with its bright monotonous round. No wonder that so many young men are asking in the bottom of their hearts questions of most terrible skepticism: "What is the use? Is it worth while to be wise and strong and rich and good?" Ah, you must find the use *outside yourself*. You must let your light shine *before men*, that they may see your good works, and glorify your Father which is in heaven. You must complete your advent and nativity with an epiphany of yourself. Then it will seem well worth while to light your human light most brilliantly and keep it trimmed most vigilantly. Do you ask me how? Do you not see that it is impossible for any one to tell you? The sun or the street lamp might as well ask *how* to light the passenger. Only shine *toward* your brethren's lives, only be your best in their direction. It must be a true epiphany, a real showing of yourself to other men. As different and characteristic as yourself is will be the light you give them. Perhaps you will illustrate for them some truth, perhaps you will inspire them with some hope, perhaps you will teach them how to do their work. The methods will decree themselves if only you, like Christ, are what you are, not for yourself, but for your fellow-men; if only, like Him, you have not only an advent and a nativity, but an epiphany. Put these two texts together, for they belong together; the same Christ spoke them: "The Son of Man came not to be ministered unto, but to minister, and give his life a ransom for many;" and "As Thou hast sent Me into the world, even so have I also sent them into the world."

4. But we must pass on. After the Advent, the Nativity, and the Epiphany in the Church's year comes *Lent*, with its preparation for and culmination in *Good Friday*, opening suddenly into the glorious light of *Easter Day*. What does this mean? The life of Jesus, prepared for before His birth, introduced into the world at Bethlehem, then brought into contact with and influence upon the lives of men, finally completes itself in suffering. Remember we are speaking now about Christ's life and death, not with reference to the mysterious redemptive efficacy that was in it, but as the great human life, the representative life that set forth the ideal experience and culture of a human soul. And surely it does not fail us here. Whatever else comes

to a life, there is a final grace and greatness which it cannot have until it has been touched by pain. I do not speak it sentimentally. I do not mean the mere pathetic romance which gives a charm to the story of the unfortunate. I mean the very stuff and qualities of our manhood—those things which make us really and completely men. They are not brought out in their manliest vigor until we have suffered. Often the suffering is of a kind men do not see. Physical pain, the sickness which makes one tremble as he walks, and takes the color from the cheek, is the most evident, but it is the smallest kind of suffering. But whenever you have seen a man leaving his crudity and childishness behind him and really growing mature, however men may say carelessly, " Oh, *he* has never known what it is to suffer," you may know better. That maturity of character is as sure a sign of some healthy experience of pain, however secret, as the brilliancy and clearness of a bit of glass is of the fire through which it has passed. The qualities which nothing but hard contact with suffering can make are not mere pleasing graces; they are the completing qualities of manhood, the very stuff and fiber of a man—self-knowledge, humility, patience, sympathy, and a constant consciousness of God. Can you have a complete man without these, and can you have these unless in some way the man has suffered? This is the reason why it is so universal. You think you know exceptions. But, my dear friend, what do you know about it? The men you call exceptions perhaps have been the very deepest in the sea of pain. You are pouring out your sympathy on some complaining grumbler who has lost a little money, and thinking how painless is the life of a brave man who refuses to grumble, but whose dearest hopes have been broken into fragments, and the ideals which were his very life all disappointed. You do not wrong him by denying him your petty sympathy, but you do wrong yourself in making too much of the little trouble and failing to see with what a great manly education of sorrow God is training *all* His children.

"It became Him, for whom are all things, and by whom are all things, in bringing many sons unto glory, to make the Captain of their salvation perfect through sufferings." When the vase is all shaped into its strong, beautiful form, when the artist's hand has lavished its best skill upon it, then it is quietly laid into the hot oven. By and by it comes out with its lines firm and bright, its surface clear and brilliant, its colors fixed forever. There is a glory after the pain, an Easter after the Lent; but no glory *without* the pain, no Easter without the Lent of character. And who are we that we should grow angry or miserable when we see that great universal treatment by which alone the Son of Man was made perfect, by which alone any son of man ever can be made perfect, drawing near to us or to any one we love among our fellow-men?

5. After the Lent and Easter comes one stage more —that which is represented by *Whitsunday*, the day of the giving of the Holy Spirit. You remember what Jesus said about the Holy Ghost: "He shall take of Mine, and shall show it unto you." It was to be the perpetuated work of Christ. After the suffering and death were over, and He was seen no more upon the earth, then His power was really to have but just begun.

It should go out and touch men wider and deeper than He had ever done when He was present on the earth. The epiphany was the influence of the visible Christ; the Whitsunday is the influence of the invisible, ascended Christ. Would you call any man's life a great life, even a true life, whose influence stopped the moment his personal, seen presence was removed? It seems to me as if there were hardly any surer test of the reality or unreality, the depth or superficialness of human power. One man seems strong. Here in our community it appears as if he were deciding what men should do or be, which way events should turn. Some day we read in the papers that that man is dead, and from that moment on his power is all gone. It is as if he had never lived. It is as if some hand had with a single touch shifted the machinery so that not the smallest or most insignificant wheel thereafter owned his influence. "None so poor to do him reverence." Another man dies, and it is as if death were the revelation of his force and the beginning of his influence. Men did not know how they loved him till he was taken away. Men did not see the stores of motive and impulse that were in his character till the shell of circumstances was broken through. In his own circle, in the city where he lives, it seems as if he were more powerful when he is seen no more upon the streets than when men met him every day. There has been, as it were, a descent of his spirit, a Pentecost of his departed presence. Oh, there are households among you where some son or daughter who is dead is stronger in the shaping of the daily life than any of the men and women who are still alive. His character is at once a standard and an inspiration. You do what would please him more scrupulously than when he was alive. He conquers your sluggishness and corrects your wilfulness and refines your coarseness every day. To say that he is not *with you* is to make companionship altogether a physical, not at all a spiritual thing. To say that he is absent from you, and that the neighbor of whom you know nothing, for whom you care nothing, and who cares nothing for you, is present with you, is to confuse all thoughts of neighborhood, to put the false for the true, the superficial for the deep.

This is the difference of men—those whose power stops with their death, and those whose power really opens into its true richness when they die. The first sort of men have mechanical power. The second sort of men have spiritual power. And the final test and witness of spiritual force is seen in the ability to cast the bodily life away and yet continue to give help and courage and wisdom to those who see us no longer; to be, like Christ, the helper of men's souls even from beyond the grave.

I must stop here. After Whitsunday in the Church's year there come certain Sundays not nominally but really connected with the life of Christ—Trinity Sunday and those that follow it. They represent, I think, the way in which a great life opens into all the various lessons of absolute truth and fills with its influence every field of duty, till it is absolutely world-wide in its range.

Thus I have traced along the Christian year the history that runs through it. It sets up the great human life. The building of the perfect man is the noblest work that can go on in the world. The seasons come and go, the harvests ripen and are gathered in, the mountains are built up and decay; but all these are sights that cannot match in dignity and interest the spectacle of a full, strong man's life. First God prepares for him the place where he is to live. Then his life comes and takes its place, a strong and settled fact. Then it puts forth its power and influences other men. Then suffering comes to it and matures it, but finally it issues out of suffering, refined and triumphant. And at last, when it has passed away out of the world into new regions of activity and growth, it leaves its power behind it to bless men after it is dead. There is nothing so round and perfect as such a life in all the world. It is the very crown of God's creation.

Such a complete life is pictured in the Church's year. It has its Advent, Nativity, Epiphany, Lent, Easter, Whitsunday, Trinity Sunday. It fills the year with its increasing, slowly maturing beauty. This is the true meaning of the year, with all its sacred seasons. Let us be true Churchmen and give it all its richness. Only, dear friends, we do not really honor the venerable beauty of the Church's calendar when we make it a badge of our denominational distinction, or deck its seasons out with all the trickery of colored altar-cloths, purple and white and green, but when we see in it the story of a human life slowly ripened from God's first purpose to the full-grown, glorified manhood standing before God's presence and sending forth God's power to its fellowmen.

We do not dishonor the humanity of Jesus when we

thus make it the type of what ours may be. He wanted and He loves to have us use it so. "As I am, so are ye in this world," He declared. Only remember He is not only pattern, but power. We must be like Him, but we cannot be, save as He makes us. We must come to Him, but we can only come to Him by His grace and help.

Standing at the beginning of the Christian year, remembering how He came to redeem us all unto Himself, let us pray for ourselves and one another that the perfect manhood which we see stretching down that year may be complete in each of us; that we may be led as our Lord was led through every stage of growth, till we too enter into the glory of God and leave the spirit of our life behind us to be a live blessing to our brethren when we are what they call dead. This be our Advent prayer.

II.

SECOND SUNDAY IN ADVENT.

"He came unto His own, and His own received Him not. But as many as received Him, to them gave He power to become the sons of God."—JOHN I. 11, 12.

WHO was it that came? Who was it whose coming is thus described? Everybody knows who, as child or man, has read the first chapter of St. John, in which these words occur. It was the "Word," which "was made flesh, and dwelt among us." It was the Word which was "with God in the beginning," and which "was God." It was Jesus Christ. The words, then, take us instantly into connection with an event with which no other can compare. Whatever our growing wisdom learns that is marvelous about the past history of our planet, of the tremendous forces that have been at work upon its structure, and the strange, splendid deeds that men have done upon its surface, this one event in its long life—that God came here, that divine feet trod upon its ground, and a divine voice spoke with its breath—must forever stand out bright and high above everything. Just as in an old nobleman's palace, where all kinds of life have flowed along for centuries, where men and women have lived and loved and worked, been born, married, and died, where splendid deeds have been done and splendid lives been lived, there still shines out above all others one day, centuries ago, when a king was its guest, so in the world's history there can be no time to compare with that in which Divinity came here. The whole world that knows about the coming dates its whole life from it. Such is the splendor and importance of the *advent* of Jesus Christ.

In speaking of Christ's advent to-day I should like to be led by the verse of St. John which I have quoted: "He came unto His own, and His own received Him not. But as many as received Him, to them gave He power to become the sons of God." And it will lead me to speak first of the *fact*, then of the *purpose*, and then of the *result* of the Incarnation. What is there that a man can speak to men about that can come to and take hold of the soul of him who speaks and them who hear like the story of God manifest in a human flesh and life like ours? I bespeak your attention and interest.

1. First, then, we speak of the *fact* of the advent. *God came to man.* What do we mean by that? Evidently, I answer first, something separate and peculiar; evidently something definite and different from anything that there had been in the world before. We mean some preëminent and distinctive coming. For God had not been absent or foreign before. He had labored in every way to make men know that He was with them. And He had come to them with clear and certain exhibitions of Himself. Always, at the very outset let us say, when we speak of God's coming to man it is not in any sense which implies that He had not been with them always. It is a coming, not of *ap-*

proach, but of *manifestation;* not such an approach as the sun makes when it rolls up in the morning from the under-world, but such as it makes when it scatters the cloud and shows us where its glory shines. And even in this sense of *manifestation* God had come to men before. Some people ask about the Incarnation. What does it mean? You say it was God speaking to man. Had not God always been speaking to man? Are there not two eternal voices which have never been silent for an instant—the voice of God in His works and the voice of God in the soul of man? Many people, I believe, peculiarly alive to these great voices of God, hearing them all the time, listening to them always, think it strange when the Incarnation of Jesus is set forth as *the* utterance of God to man. It seems to them almost to dishonor and insult those rich and constant messages which they have always been receiving from the works around that told them of the Maker, and the child-heart within that told them of the Father. These messages of God we want to assert most strongly. They are very real. We cannot listen to them too devoutly. But it does seem to me that very often just the man who listens most devoutly to these messages is the man who comes to feel the need of another message out beyond these, the man who sighs and cries for something more. You are impressed with the truth that all the world is an utterance of the Almighty. Its countless beauties, its exquisite adaptations, all speak to you of him. You sit and listen, and it seems, now that these lips have been opened and all the universe is vocal, as if there were nothing left between you and God to desire. Listen and listen on and you will learn

SECOND SUNDAY IN ADVENT. 21

everything. But by and by you certainly come to an end of that utterance. By and by you have reached the limit beyond which you are sure that there is something which sky and land and ocean cannot tell. The message is imperfect. It gives you glimpses of *Purpose*, *Wisdom*, even *Benevolence*, and a profound impression of *Power*, but all is inarticulate and stops far short of perfect knowledge of the *Person* of the God who speaks. And then you seem to discover another fuller voice of God. He speaks to you through *great men*. Prophets and sages and saints are His utterances. Their lives transmit His being. That is a vast discovery. It opens the ear and sets the heart to quicker beating. "Now," you say, "I shall know God." But there, too, comes disappointment. No great man is quite great enough. No good man is quite good enough. Each mixes himself with the message that he brings. His own partialness and imperfectness is in it. You have not fully heard God yet. And then comes one hope more. Disappointed outside yourself, you are sitting despondent, perhaps, when suddenly the voice begins to speak *within* you. Here it is right in your heart. What is true, what is good, is being uttered from the oracle within. A solemn awe and a deep delight in himself come to the man who hears that voice. *Now* let the world be as disturbed and disappointing as it may, how can it harm him? He carries the voice with him. It is the clearer the more solitary he is. At last God certainly has come. Alas! I need not tell you of *that* disappointment. You have not come to doubt the voice of God within you—God forbid that you ever should. But you have learned that your own inner self is full of confusions and contradictions. You have been deceived. You have taken your own passions for the voice of God until you are afraid to trust implicitly even that conscience which you reverence. You know yourself too well to think that through that self the highest and richest voice of God can utter itself to you. And what then? Listening to all these voices, we have not yet heard all that God has to say. Opening all these doors, it has not wholly come to us. The soul, as I said, that has most tried and so most known the insufficiency of all these other ministries is the readiest to welcome the new mercy as just that which it needs, when at last there is another coming, an objective and historic fact, something recognizable and clear, the visible appearance of Divinity itself, so that those who had seen God's works and heard some of His words and felt some of His movements now saw *Him* not merely speaking *to* humanity, but present *in* humanity—God manifest in the flesh.

I think that we can understand how the Incarnation was something new and different in the relationship of God and man if we think about our own relations to our friends. My absent friend comes to me every day in very true, important senses. The works that he has done are all around me. I see his hand in every arrangement for my comfort which his care and money have provided. That is *one* coming. And every day when the door opens and some mutual friend comes in, some one who knows him and loves him and has caught his character, it is as if my absent friend himself stepped across the threshold. That is *another* coming. And yet again, when I look into my own heart and find my friend there, when he speaks to me in tastes that he has cultivated and standards that I have learned from him, when he speaks to me out of my own self filled with him by love, there is *another* coming. But with all these still he is dim to me; I cannot feel him, I cannot find him. But some day, as I sit there trying to apprehend him, the door opens and *he himself* comes in— with the face I know, with the smile I love, with the step that always made my heart beat. There he is himself; now he has really come. Not that the old comings do not help me still; not that I do not see new meaning in his face because of all the study I have given to his works and all the hours I have talked with my own heart about him, trying to find him there; but here he is himself—no longer through a glass darkly, but now face to face. Now if the Incarnation is really as separate and new a method of knowledge as that, then it is not strange that it should stand out so in history. "He sent unto them other servants more than the first, but last of all He sent unto them His Son." It is not merely a fuller and easier way to receive the old messages—not merely an improvement of machineries so that they could more perfectly communicate the person who stood behind them. It was a getting rid of messengers. It was the sweeping of machineries aside, and by a new and living way bringing those whom the very methods of their communication had separated from one another, God and man, close together, face to face and heart to heart.

I have been anxious thus to state the true character and show the real importance of the Incarnation because only so can we properly understand and believe, by getting into the spirit of, that circle of miraculous events which group about the coming of our Lord. There are two things about the whole history of the advent of Christ which will be constantly presented to our thoughts during these next few weeks. One is its *miraculousness* and the other is its *quietness*. He came girt round with wonders, and He came so gently, so unnoticed save by the few who clustered nearest to His life, that the great surface of the world's existence was hardly rippled by the wonderful touch that had fallen upon it. Of the first of these characteristics of the advent—its miraculousness—we are sure that the credibility will be more clear to us if we have really felt how vast was the importance and how great was the necessity of the event. If ever miracle might be let loose out of the rigid hand of law, when should it be but now, when the King of all the laws is coming in his personality? If there are angels, now certainly is the time for them to appear. If the stars can ever have a message and lead men, now is the time when their ministry can plead its strongest warrant. If ever the thin veil between the natural and the supernatural may break asunder, it must be now, when the supernatural power enters into earthly life and God is present among the sons of men. To any one who believes in the possibility of miracle at all, and who knows what the meaning of the Incarnation is, the wonder would be if it had no miraculous accompaniment. The breakage through the ordinary laws of nature's life seems natural and fitting, as when a king passes through a city we expect to hear trumpets and cannon replace the common sounds of trade and domestic life which are all that its streets commonly echo. But then along with the miraculousness comes an impressive quietness. Quiet even to homeliness will be the simple scenery on which the supernatural light is thrown. The village inn, the carpenter's household, the groups of peasants —all is as simple as the story of a peasant's childhood. With wonderful power, but with wonderful stillness —no noise, no tumult. Surely such a description falls in with the *spiritual* intention of the event. It is a spiritual miracle, and the miracles of spiritual life are always as still as they are powerful, as powerful as they are still. So the whole nature of the advent was written in the historical circumstances that were grouped around the great historic fact.

In speaking thus of the *fact* of the Incarnation I beg you to observe that I speak only of its manward aspects. It is what it does for man and how it seems to man that we are able to consider. All the other side of it—of how it seems to God, of what it *is* in the nature of the Godhead—of all that who can say anything? If any man begins to tell me anything about all that I turn away from him without interest. He cannot *know*, and it is a subject on which I do not want his speculations. I can see the sunlight in its wonderful works. It may bring me messages, as it has brought to our newest science, about the nature of the sun; but of how the sun issues the sunlight and sends it forth no eagle eye has looked near enough upon the sun to see. Men talk, sometimes, about the difficulties of the Incarnation. I do not know what difficulty means to an Omnipotence to which nothing is impossible save what is wrong. I do not know but incarnation is the easy and natural effort of Divinity toward humanity. Whatever is loving and good is easy enough to God. Whatever is wrong only is impossible. And so the loving redemption of his world, the coming to His children that they might be able to come to Him, cannot have been hard. I do not know how to stagger at its difficulty.

2. And this leads us to speak not only of the *fact*, but of the *purpose* of the Incarnation. Let us pass on to that. St. John says of the divine Word, not merely that He came, but that He came " unto His own." Those words, as it will come into our way to say by and by, have primary reference to the Jewish people. But those Jews were typical. Christ came to them only as to the doorway through which He might enter into humanity. And so when it is said that Christ came to *His own*, it is *all* humanity that stands crowded in behind the Jews and claims the name. And it is in this statement that all humanity is *Christ's own* that the real meaning and purpose of the Incarnation lie involved. That statement that all men are Christ's own seems to me to contain two truths, both of them full of loftiness and inspiration. What are they?

The first truth is the essential unity of man's life and God's, and so the essential glory of humanity. Christ came not merely to man, but *into* man; and that was possible because the manhood into which He entered was "His own," had original and fundamental unity with His Godhood, was made in the image of God. Here was man, made in God's image, separated from God, trying spasmodically to struggle back, failing and falling so continually that the consciousness that he belonged with God was well-nigh lost. That it might not be lost, that it might be a real and living thing, it must be asserted from the other side. Man and God had the capacity of entrance into each other. Since man would not, and, as it almost seemed now, *could* not enter into God, God would enter into man. Man had failed of being godlike; God, then, would be manlike, and so the first truth—that God and man belonged together —should not be lost for want of assertion. Is not this a noble and inspiring value of the Incarnation? I cannot help thinking that the man to whom it seems incredible that God should have been made man is not so likely to have been misled by a peculiar reverence for God as by an unworthy estimate of man. He has seen the degradation of everything. He has seen how low the passions grovel. He has taken things as he sees them and lost sight of their ideals. He has seen the mercenariness of friendship, the squalor of home, the animalness of love—everything sunk down out of its nobleness; and he has said, "There is no place for God here. It would degrade Him to become man, man being thus." Ah, brethren, if we could only begin at the other end! God *did* become man, and therefore manhood must be essentially capacious of Divinity. He lived in a human home, and so our homes must be capable of a Divinity they do not have. He entered into friendships, and so friendship must be sacred. He worked, and so work must be honorable. He cared for the body that He lived in, and so the body cannot be so vile as men have called it and as we make it. If *this* could be the way the Incarnation came to us, then surely it must be a constant inspiration to us that it was "His own" to whom Christ came.

I cannot stop to tell you what I am sure that many of you must know—how real this belonging between God and humanity becomes to a man at the time of his own conversion. God stands far off from you, and you think that you have nothing to do with Him. You send Him duty-prayers as if you shot arrows into the darkness, toward a voice which you are not wholly certain that you hear. By and by that God comes to you; and the surprise of all surprises in conversion is to see how your heart knows Him and opens and lifts itself to take Him in. "My beloved is mine, and I am His," it says, with surprised and sudden recognition. Christ has come "unto His own."

But there is a yet closer and tenderer meaning of these words, I think. They mean that Christ came in answer to a most urgent and pressing *call of need.* That is what it signifies when it is said that "He came *unto His own.*" For in a true sense everything is a man's own which *needs* that man; not everything which he needs, but everything which needs him. Do you not know what that is? Your child is yours not merely by the claim of birth and nature, but by the tie of continual dependence. He is most yours when he needs you most. He is never so much yours as when he requires your forgiveness for some sin. He ceases in part to be yours as he outgrows his most urgent need of you. So the charitable man or woman talks about "*my* poor." So the teacher talks about "*my* boys." Everywhere that is yours which needs you. I pity the man who does not know the responsibility and privilege of that high sort of ownership. It is a most sacred claim upon another to go to a poor helpless creature and say, "You need me. I will help you. You are mine." Now when it is said that Jesus came *to His own*, is not this at least part of the meaning? He came to those who needed Him; most of all to those who from the stricken earth held up to Him the deepest of all needs, the need of sin that craved forgiveness; and that was what made them His. Certainly no level-eyed intercourse of sinless man with sinless Christ could have wrought in us such a profound and precious sense that we belong to Him as this simple knowledge that we *need* Him. Need has its sacred rights. Because we want forgiveness and help, and He only can forgive and help us, therefore we are His.

How clearly this shines out in those typical men and women of the Gospel stories! How closely they became Christ's by merely needing Him! How He acknowledged their claim! The sinning woman who crept in and touched the hem of His garment was completely His; she commanded with a perfect freedom His sympathy and time and care simply because she was so wretched and could not do without Him. The poor man to whom He gave sight, and whom the Pharisees turned out of the synagogue, laid hold of Christ immediately, and Christ acknowledged him as one of His because he could not do without Him. And who among the apostles was more perfectly Christ's own than Simon Peter, whom Christ was always answering and saving in extremest need?

Need I say more about the meaning and the purpose of the Incarnation? Put these two ideas together. Jesus "came unto His own." To men forgetful of their godlike nature He came to tell them that they were the sons of God; and to men who could not do without Him He came because they needed Him. Oh, my dear friends, by what high warrants does the Saviour claim us for His own! Because we are His Father's children, and because we are so needy, therefore our divine Brother comes. He comes to you and says, "You called Me." And you look up out of your worldliness and say, "Oh no! I did not call. I do not know You!" But He says, calmly, "You did, although you do not know it. That power of being godlike which is in you, crushed and unsatisfied—that summoned Me; and that need of being forgiven and renewed which you will not own—*that* summoned Me. And here I am! Now wilt thou be made whole? If thou canst believe, all things are possible to him that believeth." Just as all through the crowds of Jerusalem there must have been many who walked with a sense that they peculiarly belonged to the great Healer—one with his healed arm that once was withered, another with the new-given sight in his eyes, another with his body yet missing the long possession of the demon who was cast out yesterday, each with some need which had been recognized and supplied—so through this congregation there are many who rejoice that they are Christ's. They needed Him and He owned their need. He took them, He forgave them, He holds them, and nothing shall pluck them out of His hands.

3. We turn, then, in a few last words, to describe, if we can, the *result* of the Incarnation as it is pictured in

this great descriptive verse. There are two classes. "He came unto His own, and His own received Him not. But as many as received Him, to them gave He power to become the sons of God." Those who received Him and those who refused Him. Here we are come to a division in the multitude, which so far has been all one. All sons of God and all needing Christ, He came to them all, and some of them rejected Him. Here, as I said, there is a primary reference to Jewish history. In these ten words, as if with one broad dash upon the wall, is sketched that tragedy which surpasses any other tragical passage in national history. It is the story of the Jewish people, chosen, privileged, obstinate, rebellious, ruined. But here again they are only representatives. These words, "He came unto His own, and His own received Him not," are an assertion of the awful ultimateness of the power of free will in man. Behind everything else that settles a man's destiny there lies the power of his own decision whether all that is done *upon* him and done *for* him shall be effectual or not. How absolute and terrible that power is! Not even God's coming to a soul that belongs to God is so necessarily powerful that the man may not resist and in his obstinacy turn away. Men have discussed this very much indeed. They have taken their sides. Some have constituted themselves champions of God's power. Some have buckled on their armor in defense of man's free will. The battle has gone on, and all the time, as it so often is the case, the question that men were quarreling to settle theoretically was working itself out practically everywhere without their aid. The fight goes on and the field lies calm under the fighters' feet. For always these two, God's power and man's will, have lived along together, God's power yielding to nothing *but* the rebellious will of man, and man's will able to set itself even against the will of God. Certainly, as I look round on men and see the signs which I am always seeing—signs of divineness and signs of brutishness, signs of heavenliness and signs of earthliness, movements of God and movements of self all mixed up together—when I see man tempted everywhere by God to better things, yet everywhere able to bind himself down to what is low, it seems to me as if no words were ever written which so completely told the story as these old words of John : "He came unto His own, and His own received Him not." Not a soul unvisited of God—truly man is not that; a soul always claimed by the highest, and only by its own choice giving itself away to the lowest. That is the seriousness and solemnity of Advent-time. Christ's invitations force us to self-decisions. He comes to us, and we must accept Him or refuse Him. "For judgment I am come into this world," He declared.

But turn to the other side: "As many as received Him, to them gave He power to become the sons of God." There is no time here, at a sermon's very end, to tell what the whole blessing of the Incarnation is to those to whom it brings its richest fruits. But there are some texts in the Bible which, if you simply let them rest in your mind, floating on the waves of your experience, will open their meaning gradually to your consciousness. This text is one of them : If you receive Christ, you shall be a son of God. "Ah, but," you say, a little puzzled, "I always *have been* God's child. I was made so. I always have been so." Have you, my dear friend?

Were you indeed God's child in those unchildlike hours and years when you went your own proud way without humility and without a prayer? Were you God's child when you forgot your Father and lived as if your own will were your only law? Were you God's child then? "Yes," you say. "Rebellious as I was, rebellious as I am, I am God's child still. Nothing can disinherit me. He is my Father." And you are right. The privileges of your creation, the possibilities of your relation to Divinity, nothing has destroyed. But oh, my friend, if some one were to come and bring that Father to you with such convincing evidence of His love that all your indifference and rebellion should go down, and you should find yourself thoroughly at your Father's feet, claiming your long-neglected sonship, calling Him "Father," and begging Him to take and rule and lift your life—tell me, would it not be right and just to say of him who did this for you that he gave you power to become a son of God? Would you not say of him that he gave you back your Father? This is what the Redeemer does. He takes the native capacity and trains it into a live and active fact. He rebuilds the broken bridge. So He is our great Pontifex, our great High Priest, bringing God and man together; once more opening a channel through which the hindered and impatient love of God may flow, and once more opening the powers in man that can respond to that love; so reconstructing the family in heaven and earth; giving back the Father to the children and the children to the Father; making God man's Father, giving man the power to become the sons of God.

The sons of God—that is what we want to be. We

can be that by the power of the Incarnation. If we accept Christ He will teach us His truth, He will give us His law, He will help us to obey it. To us, become obedient, He will unfold His nature more and more. He will show Himself to us. We shall see Him, and, as He said Himself, he who has seen Him has seen the Father. That is the salvation of the incarnate Christ.

III.

THIRD SUNDAY IN ADVENT.

"He was not that Light, but was sent to bear witness of that Light."—JOHN I. 8.

"WHERE does the power come from?" is the natural question always when we are watching any strong effect. "Where did it begin?" we curiously ask as we stand by the side of any process and watch its steady flow. What pleasure is greater on a summer's day than to trace a mountain brook back along its bed, keeping up-stream, seeing it grow thinner and thinner, until at last we find it issuing from the hidden spring under the high crest of the hill; or to track a mechanical process back through a great factory, from the hammer that strikes the anvil to the boiler that makes the steam; or, most of all, to follow a series of human activities along the chain of influences that bind each man's action to the one before it as lakes are strung upon a silver stream, until at last we come to some strong man whose act seems to have had no father-act behind it, but to have started out of the creative fountain of his own strong will? Such search for the seats of original power is among the first instincts and the keenest pleasures of the human mind. And when such a source of power is found, then the human soul bows down before it and pours out its reverence. All idolatry is merely the giving to some secondary cause that virtue and regard which can belong only to the Highest and First Cause: to worship the sun instead of the God who makes him shine; to deify a hero or sage into the place of the God who makes him brave or wise; to glorify an abstract virtue until it sits cloudily in the place of the distinct personal God in whose nature all virtue has its being— these are the great types in which idolatry has prevailed among mankind. And to-day the man who is looking to his money or his education or his good repute or his family for the satisfaction and the culture which God gives us through them all, but which neither of them gives us of and by itself, he is the modern idolater. He, like all the idolaters of old, has cut the channels of life off from the source of life, and sits with his thirsty lips pressed to their dry mouths, getting no real refreshment, however he may delude himself.

The words which I have made my text were written about John the Baptist. His life was certainly one of the most original in the whole New Testament. It must have seemed so to his contemporaries. To the multitude of Pharisees and Sadducees, men and women, rich and poor, good and bad, who went streaming from Jerusalem down to the banks of the Jordan to hear him preach, how new and refreshing it must have seemed! So different from all the people who said what other people told them and were what other people made them, here was a man who was himself and spoke things of his own. It must have seemed as if that light that shone with such a new and piercing luster were certainly a light that burned by its own radiance;

as if the fountain that their old prophets had said should be opened for sin and for uncleanness had really burst the ground at last, so clear, strong, new, and independent, like a spring of fresh water bursting up in the very middle of a brackish pool, the life of John the Baptist must have dashed in among their ordinary experience of scribes and Levites.

We can see such a feeling. They evidently wanted to worship him. There were all the materials for a full-made idolatry; and the nobleness of John the Baptist's character is shown most of all in the way in which he swept it all aside. He said of himself again and again, what John the Evangelist says of him in this verse, that he was not an original source of light or power, but that all the force of his life consisted in the way in which he reflected upon men the Light that came on him from above: "He was not that Light, but was sent to bear witness of that Light." The life of the Baptist does furnish us the completest study of the truest "originality." In that way I want it to point our subject to-day. But at the very outset he tells us, and the Evangelist tells us of him, that his originality consisted not in the structure of his own life or its ability to send out power from itself, but solely in the way in which it caught the life of Christ and made that influential in the world.

Here is the figure. I see what seems to me to be a sun burning in the distance. I go up to it and find it is no sun, but only a mirror, and looking up at the angle which the mirror points, there is the true sun blazing overhead. The power of the mirror is only that it has caught the sun on a peculiar surface and flashed it in a new direction, on a new level, in the eyes of men. Is there anything in a theory of human greatness and effectiveness like this that helps explain any of the commonest phenomena we see? At the very first statement of it I think there is. When we look at our fellow-men there is much that bewilders us. In the first place, their *inconsistencies*. They are such strange mixtures. At one moment we are ready to fall down before them for something that they do, and almost worship them; and the next moment something else occurs that makes us almost hate to think that we are men. This double nature is always turning its different sides upon us. What shall we think of this brother man of ours (and what we think of him we must think of ourselves, for we know that we are like him)? Is he gold or clay, precious or worthless? And there is also the strange look of only *half-appropriation, half-ownership*, in the best things that they are and do, which we have all seen in other men, and felt something of, also, in ourselves. When a man does an act of higher purity or unselfishness than usual he seems to be at once vaguely impressed with the sense that it was not he that did it; that some higher power has but used him as an instrument; that it was the act of God in him. Now, taking these two phenomena, not to speak of any other—this blurred and mottled life, with its double natures, and this strange misgiving that the best that is in us does not belong to us—two facts of universal human consciousness—what theory could explain them like this: that no man is a separate, rounded character, independent of any other, carrying his own qualities included in himself; that every man is a medium through whom God expressed Himself with more or less of clearness and effectiveness, according to the transparency or dimness of the character on which His life falls? We are like windows through which a higher light is always falling; but the window is blurred and mottled because at some places it is stained deep and will not let the light through; and where it does receive it, it is always conscious of *receiving*. The radiance with which it shines comes to it from without—not *it* shines, but the light shines through it.

This is the fundamental idea of the dependent, the related, humanity. We learn to count men, thus, not by the witness that they bear of themselves, but by the witness that they bear of God. Not merely these notable phenomena of human life which I have suggested, but many others of the most subtle and perplexing, become clearer to us when we have once reached this conception of the unity of the universe, of the way in which man exists and manifests himself only in relation toward God. "Christ is *all*, and *in all*"; or, in Paul's phrase, "None of us liveth to himself, and no man dieth to himself. Whether we live, therefore, or die, we are the Lord's."

And yet let us not think that this limits or impairs the sacred and precious truth of personality. It might seem at first as if it led on to a horrible idea—to the idea that our personality consisted only in those elements of our own selfhood with which each of us obscures the divine light that is trying to express itself by each of us. It would, indeed, be a horrible idea to hold that our individuality lay only in our sin and imperfection; that if you could cleanse every man of sin and lift every man to perfect harmony with God, then men would be all just alike; that this separateness from one another which makes every man himself would all be lost, and one uniform divine life blot out and supersede this multitudinous variety of human character. It is a groundless fear. The substance of these single mirrors which each of us would hold then in their perfect purity to God is still so different that each must reflect God in its own way. None of them could utter Him completely. Each must catch and send forth that part of Him for which it had most fitness; and so still in a world of saints, as in this world, all stained and mangled with its sin, the beautiful variety of character must be preserved, and each man be himself more evidently the more evidently that he shone with God.

It must be so, surely. Holiness does not make men monotonous. The dimmer the light the more things look alike. Increase the light and then you see how different they are. Childhood with its bright hopefulness, and manhood with its enterprise, and womanhood with its tenderness—each grows more specially itself at the touch of grace. The old man and the young man, the thinker, the artist, the worker, the merchant, the doctor, and the lawyer—out of each comes up to the surface a profounder individuality when they all begin to live to God. And the subtler differences which distinguish man from man and woman from woman, making each being a separate thought of God, unlike any other—these become clearer as the idea of God in the creation of each becomes more fully realized. The pebbles lie dull and dead and all gray alike in the dry bed of the brook till with the spring freshet the water comes pouring down and wets them all alike and brings

THIRD SUNDAY IN ADVENT. 41

out their beautiful variety of color and makes them all different.

Here, then, I think, we have the *religious* conception of originality. How strangely men talk about being original! They are always passing on, as they grow to be more and more of men, to deeper and deeper sorts of originality. First we have the mere boy's notion of being original, which some men who never deepen seem never to outgrow. It is the mere originality of dress and habits. To look different from other people, to wear other clothes, to live in some strange house, to adopt some strange set of phrases, some peculiar style of talk, to be somehow eccentric, to separate one's self somehow from this great indistinguishable crowd, so that men may distinguish our figure from the multitude as we sweep by, and say something about us or ask somebody who we are—this is the most superficial form of the desire for originality which, perhaps, almost all young men feel at some time, but pass out of and outgrow, but which now and then some poor old creature lives in all his days. Beyond this mere originality of habits runs the desire for originality of opinions and ideas. Not to think over again what all the common herd are thinking, to start some new idea, to send forth something that shall show our fellows that this machinery within us does not work just the same with all the mental machinery in all the world—this is the higher ambition of a higher man. Both of these are struggles. They are the efforts of a man to make himself original. They have their origin and their limit in his own self-esteem. Different from both of them is that religious consciousness which the devout man has that God made him special, for a special purpose, for a special exhibition of himself; and so the desire to *be himself* completely, in order that no purpose which God had in his creation may fail through his being distorted or obscured. This is a desire for the divine originality of *character* which God intended, and is far above the lower desires for mere originality of *look* or of *opinion*. Many men try to be John the Baptists by wearing the skins and eating the locusts and wild honey. Others would be John the Baptists by preaching strange doctrines to the Pharisees and the people. Very few seek to live the life that he lived by recognizing that they are sent into the world, not to shine themselves, but merely by some way of their own to bear witness of the Light of God.

But, once having reached this idea of human life, it would seem certain that a man must make very little of the lower and more superficial ways of emphasizing his own personality and seeming to be original. The mere effort to look different from other people or to be the utterer of new and startling thoughts must seem very insignificant to a man who has come calmly to the knowledge that God meant something separate and special by his life, that God made him for something, and who is therefore trying to be so pure and obedient and truthful—in one word, so truly *himself*—that God *can* say and do by him all that He designed. Such a man will resent any interference with the truthfulness and obedience of his life no matter whence it comes, but he will easily conform himself to the ordinary indifferent ways of living that he finds about him. The higher view that a man gets of life the more able he will be to distinguish just where he ought and where he ought not to conform his individuality to the standards and habits of his fellow-men. The cheap and superficial aspirant for originality is apt to be rebellious in small and insignificant details and to be servile all the while before the worst requirements of social life. The true disciple of God will be yielding enough in indifferent details, but firm as a rock against the most time-honored abuses or iniquities. He will dress like his neighbors and use no unfamiliar phrases when he talks with them, but he will stand out, even if he stands out all alone, against the most reputable fallacy of business or the social lie which all the parlors in the town are telling. He will be like a healthy plant that does not care about the color of the pot it grows in, but does care very much about the quality of the earth out of which it has to feed its roots.

Just think how different from what we ordinarily see would be the society thoroughly informed with this idea of life. Instead of the dreary monotony of the many, and the eager, nervous search of the few after some superficial sort of singularity, we should have our houses and streets full of men and women each simply doing his separate duty, and so unconsciously bearing his separate witness of the Light of God. We should not be asking whether we were like one another or not —not trying *to* be and not trying *not* to be—but only asking always whether we were like that special type of love and duty which God designed for us to be. Such a society I can picture to myself, full of activity and yet free from restlessness, having the same beautiful charm which fascinates us in nature, where every tree and shrub and brook, every wing of bird and stretch of sky and patch of snow, shines with its own color, which is merely its translation of the universal sunlight, in a variety which has no restless jealousy, and a peaceful harmony which cannot become monotonous.

And to my mind this thought of life involves a very noble and satisfying conception of God and what He is to us. It puts Him in the center of all life, and all life revolves around and lives by Him. We are so apt to make our God either careless or servile. Our reverent feeling toward God is always in danger of setting Him afar off, as if He did not care for and had little to do with these lives that He had made. And, on the other hand, many efforts to make God familiar, to feel how close He is to, and how He is always helping the lives of, all His children, have seemed to make Him but the Servant of His universe, waiting at men's beck and call to bring them what they need. How many people's idea of special providences labors under this difficulty, as other men's awe of God seems to make their souls orphans by putting their God so far away! And then, again, we are always localizing God—bringing Him down to our own land or sect, narrowing Him even to our own single experience, and thinking that all the ministrations of help or revelations of duty that He makes to others must be the same, in the same shape, that He has made to us. But here He takes His kingly and fatherly place in the center of mankind, and all men, with their different capacities of uttering Him, are gathered around Him. Upon each He flashes some portion of Himself. Out from each some witness of His love and power is sent into the universe, not for the amazement of other worlds, perhaps—we cannot say how that may be; rather, I think, out of the absolute need of utterance that belongs to all the highest existence. He bears witness of Himself through the obedience of all His children. Thus He Himself is glorified in helping them. Here is a kingliness that does not need to be withdrawn in order to maintain its majesty. It is the more majestic the nearer that it comes to needy lives. Here is a ministry to man that does not lower, but glorifies the God who renders it, making man, after all, only the humble minister of the God who serves him.

If we want to bring this truth out of its vagueness and make it very real, we must look at the manifested God in the life of Jesus Christ. I look back to the story of the Gospels, and as the men and women there stand around our Lord, the account that must be given of them all, as they catch their character and their immortality from Him, seems to be this: they were not that Light, but they were sent to bear witness of that Light. Mary, John, Peter, Zaccheus, the Magdalen, Martha, Nicodemus, and the dying thief—how they shine like stars in the firmament of the gospel, not by their own light, but by His who shone upon them all! How clear their personality is as He walks among them and charms them out of their artificialness and makes them be themselves! Have you a servant in your house who serves you as meekly as the Son of God served those poor men and women? And yet how, by the service that He rendered to each of them, He translated His eternal nature into some new glory of helpfulness, and was more manifestly the Son of God!

And so the highest object of a man's life still is that it may give forth some new and characteristic expression of the life of God. As the sun shines upon a bank of snow no two of all the myriad particles catch his light alike or give the same interpretation of his glory. Have you ever imagined such a purpose for your commonplace existence? If you have you must have asked yourself what the quality is in a man's life which can make it *reflective* of God—capable of bearing witness of Him. There is some quality in the polished brass or in the calm lake that makes it able to send forth again the sunlight that descends upon it. What is it in a soul that makes it able to do the same to the God who sheds Himself upon its life? The Bible has its one great name for such a great transforming quality, and that is "*love.*" Love in the Bible is not so much an action of the soul as it is a quality in the soul permitting God to do His divine actions through it. "If any man love God, the same is known of Him" (1 Cor. viii. 3). That is the profound expression of St. Paul, and it includes this idea. The love of God is a new nature, a new fiber, a new fineness and responsiveness in the soul itself, by which God is able to express Himself upon and through it as He cannot when He finds only the medium of the coarse material of an unloving heart. Do we not know something of this? I live with a crowd of people who love nothing better than the world and the things that are in the world, or I keep company with some unloving men who call themselves Christians, hard men of the commandments, to whom the work of God is always an unremitting task; and from all that I see of them I get no knowledge of God;

THIRD SUNDAY IN ADVENT.

I am as ignorant of Him as ever. But then I spend an hour with a man who has the fine and subtle quality, who really does love God, and I come away feeling that I have been in God's very presence, and that I know more of Him. This saint has borne witness to me "of that Light." And think how independent the soul humbly conscious of such a task as that must be of the ordinary judgments of mankind! Ah, my friend, you know very little how like the harmless wind your critical sneers sweep by the man whose soul is only set on serving and manifesting God. His only care concerning his fellow-men must be a noble anxiety lest he should *mis*interpret God to them—not lest he should *offend* them, but lest he should *harm* them or mislead by his imperfect reflection of the life of God.

For there are imperfections enough. What does it mean? Here is a man who, I know, loves God, and I am sure that, reflected from his love, I do get, when I am with him, some true impression of what God is. His life is a revelation. He does bear witness of the Light. And yet how full the light that he sends to me is of motes and blotches of darkness! I am sure that when I hear him pray or talk of his religion, though much of what I get is God, yet much is the man's self and is not God at all. What is the reason that very often your religion seems to men selfish and vain and insincere? They call it *cant*. It may be that it is their obstinacy, but certainly part of the reason is that you are flinging yourself at them and not casting on them the pure light of God. It is as if the surface of the brazen mirror were crumbled and disintegrated and covered with a sort of thin dust of itself which blurred every image that it tried to cast. So we mix ourselves with what we tell men of God—a sort of dusty, superficial selfhood, not the true transparent self from which He wishes to shine. Certainly we all know that there are other reasons besides men's native wickedness, besides their blindness and obstinacy, to account for their not being convicted and comforted by what we try to show them of God in our Christian lives.

I hope that with all this definition I have succeeded in putting before your minds what seems to me to be a very distinct and high conception of the purpose of this life which we are living in this world. It puzzles us so sometimes. What are we here for? What does it all mean? What is it all about? We are not facts of consequence enough to account for ourselves. Our lives are not beautiful enough to be their own "excuse for being." Nor, in full many moods, does it seem to us even as if our fellow-men were of so great importance that we should exist solely for helping them. To think so sometimes seems merely an effort to account for insignificance by piling up other insignificance which it is made to help. But if any such idea as this be true—that we are here to manifest God, to make Him glorious by opening ourselves to every inflow and outflow of His perfect will—then it is not unaccountable. At least with this idea we shall have gained several important things which have seemed almost impossible to get before.

We shall have discovered a possible harmony between a profound value of our own existence and a complete humility. As soon as you spur a man on to do any good work in the world by making him think that there is a work that he can do better than anybody else, almost always you find your new-made worker growing full of self-consequence, until you are disgusted with the way in which you yourself have pushed him on, and wonder whether it would not have been better to have left him in his idle uselessness, which at least was free from the poison of conceit. How very rare it is to find an exceedingly useful and hard-working man whose energy and devotion are not tainted by self-satisfaction! But here, if all we do is but to make ourselves channels through which the power of God shall flow; if when a man stands up and calls a whole city out of corruptness, or a whole race out of slavery, he is deeply and genuinely conscious that it is not he that speaks, but God (as Jesus, you remember, told His disciples it should be with them), then that is won which is so rare in the great workers (or in little ones either): all self-satisfaction disappears. The man is lost in the cause; nay, the cause itself is lost in joy that God, whom to know is life, has made Himself hereby a little more known to men.

And again, here is this continual conflict between the sense of responsibility and the desire of repose which we find more or less in all the more faithful lives. I know that there is such a thing as *peace* to seek and find. But here is my work to do, to worry over whether I am doing it right, to keep myself restless over how it will turn out. "*My work*," I say; but if I can know that it is not my work, but God's, should I not cast away my restlessness, even while I worked on more faithfully and untiringly than ever? Ah, there was mighty and blessed truth in all the old theologies, hard and mischievous as they often grew to be, that magnified God and made man the humblest of instruments; that aimed to lose the man in God as utterly as possible. If I could pour through all the good plan over which I am laboring the certainty that all that is good in it is God's and must succeed, how that certainty would drive the darkness out of it! and while I worked harder than ever, my work would have something of the calmness with which He labors always. This must have been what Jesus promised when He said, "*My peace* I give unto you." This must have been what Paul meant when he said, " Work out your own salvation : for it is God which worketh in you." "*Fear and trembling*" still, but no dismay, no hastening or discontent.

But, more than all, this truth seems to me powerful because it so brings out the wickedness of sin. It is so easy for us to make our sins seem insignificant. What are they? "The perversions of good passions—that is all." Lust, cruelty, even falsehood, the meanest and most confessedly contemptible of sins—how readily we find apologies for all of them! Men may make them of little account from every point of view excepting one. Only when men have dared to think of themselves sublimely, as possible reflections of the life of God on earth—only then does sin become essentially and forever horrible. Be sure of this in all your thinking about yourself and all your preaching to your fellow-men : that you can never make them see their sins aright except by seeing rightly the very highest idea and possibility of their existence. If you could see the divine life which that sin of yours yesterday hindered and blurred, how you would hate it! We never shall be as glad as the angels are that a sinner is forgiven (be that sinner ourself or some poor brother) till we first see as the angels see what sin interferes with and destroys—how idleness blurs like a cloud, and selfishness covers with great spots of blackness, and impiety breaks with a blow that pure human life which was made to reflect God, to bear witness of the Light.

And, once more, this truth seems to me to throw a flood of light upon the whole work of the Lord Jesus Christ. What was He doing in those hard three and thirty years? "Redeeming us," we say. Yes, at great cost, bringing us back again to what He made us first to be; cleansing the clouded mirror; making man once more fit to be the witness of God. Men ask wherein the virtue of his Atonement lay. Was it in His life? Was it in His death? And we must answer, "*Everywhere!*" Wherever any cloud was swept away, any stain loosened so that it could fall off from the mirror soul, any restoral made in the injured substance of the soul itself, any power used to turn back again the soul's face which had been turned away from God—wherever that marvelous Being, living and dying, wrought any restoral in man, or made clearer the atmosphere between God and man, there was, there *is* in His continual work, the perfect Atonement which He came to make. And this we are sure of: that so long as men will keep in mind and heart what the final purpose of Christ's Redemption was—to restore a pure humanity that could receive and utter God—so long there is no serious danger that anything unworthy, anything too mercantile or brutal, can come into their theories about the method of the

Redemption; or, if it finds its way there through any wrong teaching, its harm must be neutralized.

I hope I have not seemed to-day to take too large and vague a view of human life; to talk about the architecture of the heavens when you were trying to learn how to build your house-roofs. I believe in these larger conceptions of life which men call vague. I must have some notion in general of what I am alive for, or I cannot live rightly from hour to hour, this evening and to-morrow morning. Much that seems petty and paltry in our ordinary life can only be exalted and made tolerable by being taken up and lost in some great idea of life—as the tawdrinesses and poor work that abounds in a great building like St. Peter's Church at Rome is all harmonized and subdued and made of use in the mighty vastness of the whole great building. Ten thousand men become machines, I believe, from too narrow, where one man becomes a visionary from too large, theories of life.

This be our thought of life, then. It is not for what we are that we are living, but that something more of what God is may become evident and effective in the world. *There* is a purpose of life which we never can outgrow. We shall go up to heaven some day, and as we stand before His throne still there will be witness of God for each of us to bear—some witness, I believe, which no other soul in all the universe could bear but we. The heavens will be telling the glory of God forever; and though our star may be indistinguishable, somewhere in all the flood of radiance shall be the light it sheds—a witness special and different in color from all the others which are reflecting that Light which is to lighten every saint.

Until that comes, the same truth is true here on the earth. To every poor sufferer, to every discouraged worker, to every man who cannot think much of himself and yet is too brave to despair, this is the courage that the gospel gives. Not what you can do, but what He can do in you; not what you are, but what you can help men to see that He is—that is the power by which you are to work. I beg you to think, in the light of this truth we have been studying to-day, of the deepest meaning of these words of St. Paul: "Ye are not your own. Ye are bought with a price: therefore glorify God in your body, and in your spirit, which are God's."

IV.

FOURTH SUNDAY IN ADVENT.

"But when the fullness of the time was come, God sent forth His Son."—GAL. IV. 4.

No event ever happens in this world of ours until the fullness of its time has come. This belief must go with any true belief in a real governing and guiding God. No wind blows and no child is born, no old man dies and no bush flowers, no avalanche tumbles and no revolution bursts, no error is exploded and no truth discovered, until the fullness of its time has come. If a great crime make the whole world tremble and grow pale with horror, it came because its time was full. If an angelic deed of piety or mercy lights up the world like sunshine, and makes men's hearts sing for triumph and for very joy in being men, it came because its time was full. If we could open the frozen ground to-day and read the history of every buried grain of wheat, of every sluggish root which is hiding in the warm earth with its next year's blossoms folded up within it; if we could know the whole nature of their latent forces, and see their possibilities entirely, then we should be able to tell of each of those forces when its time would be full, and we could prophesy just when the ground would break, and just how the color in the flower-leaves would deepen, and just at what moment the fruit would stand finally and perfectly ripe; and next spring and summer would bear witness to our prophecies and confirm them all. And so if we could open the surface of the world's moral and spiritual life, and read all that is hidden there, and understand the nature of every impulse and the powers to which it will respond, what should we need more? Should we not see at once the whole moral and spiritual future of the world revealed to us? We should see just when each force would reach the fullness of its time, just when the harvest of all the struggles that are in tumult here about us would be peacefully ripe, just when the world would be converted and human nature would be free from its sin and the millennium would open on the redeemed, regenerated earth. For all those things exist now. They are with God in the secrets of his counsels. He is withholding them until their times are full, and then He will send them forth into the light.

If, then, any one could get into those secret counsels of God, he would see all these wonders of the future now. The glory that the Church of Christ is to wear by and by, when she is pure enough to conquer her enemies—he who went into God's treasuries of grace would see this, kept there by God until the Church is ready for it. The delight and peace and joy of Christianity, for which, it may be, you have prayed and struggled and contended long, and at last have made up your mind that there is no such thing anywhere for you—he would see that dream of all your days and nights lying carefully folded away until your struggles and prayers had made your soul large enough to take it and to wear it. God has the world's best robes, the heart's best graces, safely kept in the great treasure-room of His own intentions, as a parent keeps rich garments for his child till he grows worthy of them. Whoever, then, can enter into the intentions of God can see for himself what the world and the heart will be when, after long delay and tribulation, the fullness of the time shall come.

Does not this let us know in part what is the true character of prophecy, what it is that makes a prophet? God knows the future by knowing the present perfectly; He knows the future *in* the present, sees it folded up within the present's transparency, waiting for its full time. Whoever, then, can see the present as God sees it will see the future as God sees it too. Foresight is insight. The two are one. And so it is because David and Isaiah are in such profounder sympathy with God's government than other men that they are able to look forward as other men cannot, and know what the results of that government will be. In this truth, we are sure, must lie the key to at least a part of the mystery of prophecy.

I am well aware that there is much in all this statement which must sound like fatalism. But it is very possible for providence and fatalism to sound alike, and yet they stand as far apart as the two poles, as heaven and hell, as light and darkness. The truth that no event can come until its time is full is based, not upon any iron necessity in the order of things themselves, but in the wisdom of an overruling Father who knows that to send any gift to man out of its true time would spoil its character and ruin His gift altogether.

This fullness of time consists of two parts, is of two kinds; it is both external and internal. It is *internal* in so far that no event can happen except as the result of a certain logical process of preparation which must come first. The life of Moses, let us say, could never have been lived, the character of Moses could never have existed, till first there had come the patriarchs and the Egyptians, the famine and the captivity, which all added something to the character which was then born into the son of the bondwoman who was found among the bulrushes upon the Nile. And then there is the *external* preparation, which consists in such an ordering of surrounding events as makes it possible for a certain character, when it *is* born into the world, to do a useful and efficient work there. Pharaoh and the Israelitish brethren of Moses had reached, in their relations to one another, just that point which needed such a man as he was, and *so* he came in the fullness of time. Or take another case. America was discovered, as we can see, in the fullness of time. First there had to come the long education of the world which made possible the energy and patience and skill that achieved the task. And then *we* can see how it had been kept until the pressure of the crowded life and the fermentations of the new activity of the Old World called for another continent to work out to greater issues the problem of human history. Then the great curtain was withdrawn —then, in the fullness of time. Or, yet again, take the more personal case of which I spoke: a man, a Christian, after long struggles and doubt, attains to peace and faith. Is it not true that God *could* not give him that peace except by the slow stages of an education which made him ready for it, and also that God would not give it to him till it was the best thing for him to have with reference to the circumstances about him, in the midst of which his Christian life had to be lived? There was both an internal and an external reason. And it is because both reasons, the necessity of internal education and the necessity of external circumstances, will be there perfectly satisfied that *heaven* alone, the future life, is the perfect fullness of time for man's full peace and joy.

This truth is very precious to us because it puts any such idea as accident out of the universe entirely. And the love for an accidental government is far too common among men. How strange it seems! You hear so many people talk as if a *process*, a slow development from evident cause into evident result, so that you can see how the blessing comes, somehow makes the blessing less and lightens the burden of our gratitude—as if the things we ought to be most thankful for were those that came with least apparent cause, most unconnected and unassociated with the great continuous current of mercy that fills our lives. We have a word that expresses this. We talk about a *godsend*, and a godsend means an unexpected and, so far as we can see, an uncaused blessing. It is about the same as what we mean by that other word which we use, with only a touch less of reverence, under the same circumstances, when we speak of a *windfall*. It means an *accident*. How strange it seems! It is as if a child thought that his father sent him, and thanked his father for, the crumbs that he found dropped upon the floor, which fell there with no design of food, and never thought of

FOURTH SUNDAY IN ADVENT.

being grateful for the orderly, long-devised, patiently earned meal which in the system of the household his father was accustomed to set before him at a certain hour of the day. Neither the godsend nor the windfall is an accident, because law is the very nature and method both of God Himself and of the wind that He "bringeth out of His treasuries." And if we looked aright we should feel that law did not hamper or forbid the return of personal gratitude; that the God whom we could come the nearest to and feel our God most fully was the God who wrought out His benefits for us under the dominion of the largest and most eternal laws. If you and I could perfectly investigate and measure the causes that produced it, certainly we should see that the discovery of the art of printing came just at that one point in the world's history where it was necessary that it should come; just in its true fullness of time—no earlier, no later. If we saw perfectly, our eyes and minds would recognize a certain impossibility that it should have come a century before—an impossibility just as impossible in its own way as that the sun this morning should have risen at six instead of seven. But would that sight anyway weaken the certainty that when the time came it was God that enlightened the ingenuity of the inventors of the great art and guided their hands to the discovery that was waiting for them? Would it not rather intensify and multiply the sense of God's presence by all the length of time in which He would be seen to have been at work? Or if I saw the causes of my own inner spiritual life, and saw a law of growth there, saw that I could not reach any high height of Christian life except by slow development, that it is as impossible for the soul to be all at once what it will be some day, when it stands perfected in the full glory of the throne of God, as it is for the gray dusk of the morning to be clothed at once in the splendor and luxuriance of noon, what then? Would that sense of the necessity of growth *exclude God?* Would it make me turn away and say, "Ah, this soul of mine is a self-growing thing—a thing with its own laws and fates wrapped up within itself. I need not pray or thank or love or fear about it, but let it go its own necessary way"? Why, this growth *is* God—God ever at His gracious, loving work; and the longer and more orderly its processes may be, so much the more steady and serene and determined on its end, I know, is that great love of God which has me in its charge.

So let men work away with their statistics and their averages and prove how beautifully under all our life there run the great necessities of God. Let them show with their marvelous exactness how truly everything waits for its full time and then comes, and will not be delayed, as it could not be hastened. Let us learn how in history and science and character—everywhere—*cause* is the method of the universe. The curse or blessing causeless *cannot* come. And into the clear light of all such speculations we may look to get a clearer and more loving understanding of our God. I see Him now as He stands holding back the inventions and discoveries and institutions, the great schemes for man's elevation and education and relief, that are to make the next generation glorious, more glorious than ours— holding them back until their time is full. The home of the future, the republic of the future, the Church of the future—they must be built upon the present, and they must wait until their foundations shall be laid. I see Him laying His hand upon some bright, impatient joy that is eagerly leaping forward to go out and bless some poor, dark, sorrowful heart, and He says, "No, not yet! My child is not yet ready for the joy, with that readiness which can come only by the discipline of sorrow. Wait till the fullness of time has come." I see Him gently holding back the shrouded shape of a dark-robed sorrow that with slow, reluctant steps is leaving the great council-room of His designs where they all abide, to enter like a heavy shadow into some happy home of hitherto unbroken joy. Again He says, "Not yet! Your time will come. But now wait till My children grow a little stronger by happiness; till they win in the sunlight a little more faith and clear-sightedness to find Me in the darkness. Wait till joy has made them more fit to use sorrow—then you shall go, then will be the fullness of your time." How many households there are here where the sorrow thus will come in its full time! and God grant you the clearness, when it comes, to know that it is not the destruction and contradiction, but merely the completion and development, of the joy that went before it, carrying you on to a higher life, perfecting you for the kingdom of heaven. Shall we say more? Shall we dare to say that *death* comes to no man except in the fullness of his time; that God holds back His angel and will not let him speak that word which no man can resist—so strong it is and so persuasive—till He sees that the man's time is come? What! with so many deaths about us that seem premature, with a world full of children's graves, with the strong man eager for labor and doing it so well swept in a moment, in a fiery whirlwind, from his unfinished work? Shall we dare to say in the face of all this that no man's death is premature, that each is ripe with what ripeness is best for him in *this* garden of the Lord's vast culture before God calls him to the next? Ah, my dear friends, we must know more of that next garden and its cultures before we can say it is not so. If, indeed, the children's graves are not the ends, but the starting-points of lives, and if the strong man only proves his hands *here* for work—of who can say what magnitude and importance?—that he is to do forever *there*, then, as surely as the body cannot pass from life to death without a cause working out under a law to its result, so certainly the soul cannot pass from life to life save by its cause and law as well, and in the fullness of its ripened time.

We are drawing near to Christmas, and we apply our truth, as our text applies it, to the birth of Christ. How was it that that great event, the greatest that our world has ever seen, followed the law of all lesser events and came only when its causes and conditions were complete? "When the fullness of the time was come, God sent forth His Son."

We cannot doubt that both the elements of preparation of which we spoke are present here as everywhere, both the internal and the external. But what the internal preparation for the Incarnation was, by the very nature of the case we cannot know. "A body hast Thou prepared Me"! How that body was prepared and the God-man made possible; how the new nature was made ready and the Word made flesh; how God approached that marvelous period in His eternity when He put on the guise of a creature and came as Christ—all this who dares to tell, who even dares to conjecture? To know that, one must uncover all the mysteries of the divine and human natures, one must know all the most secret and sacred processes of heaven and earth; nay, one must *be* God—no less than that. Between the time when the great purpose of salvation shaped itself in the divine mind, the time when the Lamb of God stood forth before the Father, saying, "Lo, I come," and the time when a Babe was born in Bethlehem who was Christ the Lord, came all the mighty work. The Deity was folded in and hidden in this perfect human nature. The divine mind and heart and soul yielded themselves to the conditions of humanity. The love for man, the sympathy with man, which first prompted the offer, somehow—slowly or instantly, who can tell?—wrought out into a visible shape the human phase of the divine Being. Only when this was done was the internal preparation perfect, was the time *full*, was it possible for Christ Jesus to be born.

And this is all we dare to say of the *internal* preparation, the preparation of the manifested life itself. But of the *external* preparation, the preparation of the circumstances which were to surround the life, it is much easier to speak. It has been a very general and no doubt a very just belief among Christians that it can be shown that when the Saviour was born into the world the world was in a certain peculiar condition which made it peculiarly fit for His reception; that it can be seen in the contemporary history of the Christian era that that, of all times, was the very time for the Saviour to come in, and so that He came, evidently, in the fullness of time.

That is too long a proof to go into now. It requires a whole survey not merely of that especial period, but of others also with which it must be compared. I only wish to point out one line of this sort of thought, and that rather for its practical suggestiveness and value.

On Christmas Day, then, when the angels sang, not to the shepherds only, but to the whole world, "Unto you is born this day a Saviour," there were in the world several different classes of men, differently related, but all bearing some relation to the promise and to Him who was promised. Let us see what some of these classes were:

1. First of all there were some very few who were distinctly expecting Him and looking for His coming. This class is entirely confined to the Jews, and among them to the more spiritually minded and scholarly and thoughtful Jews—Simeon and Anna and a few like them. To these were added later, before Jesus began to preach, the converts of the Baptist, who had learned from him that he was the forerunner of Another, and that the Messiah was just about to come. How very few these were! The gentle mother and her husband Joseph, and those of their nation who, without knowing the great privilege that was in store for the carpenter's household, knew that somewhere, in some of these dark days of Judah, the Saviour was to come—these were all; and even these, how blindly they were looking! How many of them had their own notions of

just what He must be and just where He must come from, that made it impossible for them to know Him and own Him when He came! There must, I doubt not, have been many hearts in Palestine that leaped with sudden joy when they first heard that the Messiah had been born at last, and only sank back into listless despair again when they went and searched out the particulars and found that He had come in Bethlehem and not in Nazareth. It could not be He, they said, despondently; and so they sank back into disappointment and were all the less ready to receive Him because of this short delusive hope that had turned their eager faces to Him for a moment. So that this first class is very small. Think of the crowded earth and then see how very few are in this little group that have climbed one special pinnacle of prophecy and are looking out over the waste and straining their ears into the distance to listen for the long-promised footstep, whose sound they are sure that they will know.

2. But besides these who were specially looking for the Messiah, for Christ, there was an immensely larger class in the world at that time who were looking for something—they did not know what. They reached their hands and strained their eyes in no one definite direction. Theirs were rather the wild hands of a man lost in the dark and feeling everywhere for something that will guide him, knowing nothing except just that he is lost, and that some one must come to find and save him. The character of that age is strongly marked everywhere and is summed up all in one word—dissatisfaction, expectation. This is a character that did not belong to the Jews alone. It reached everywhere.

Wherever you open the life of any of the people of that time you find this *unrest*. Eager or sullen, hopeful or hopeless, there it always is. If you were to look largely into the literature and history of that very interesting epoch you would be much impressed by it. But without going outside of the Bible I may just remind you how, wherever the life of the Gentile world breaks in a moment upon the New Testament narrative, it always seems to have this look and sound about it. Whether it be the Roman centurion coming to ask Christ to heal his child, or the other centurion by the cross, or Pontius Pilate; whether it be the Greeks of Ephesus or the Greeks of Athens, or the Roman govcruors at Cesarea—everywhere that you catch sight, through this new door opened out of Judaism, of any strong and thinking man who is not a Jew, he is always one who seems to be standing with an exhausted and worked-out religion and philosophy of life. They are idolaters who have no longer a belief in their idols. The effect was not always the same. Some of them, in their disappointment, are seen flinging their old faith away.; nay, some, in vexation and despair, are trampling *all* faith under their feet; and yet others are clinging, as men will, with all the more intense fanaticism to the delusion which they cannot any more believe, and fighting yet for their detected lie. But however you see them you recognize them all. You see the disappointment everywhere. That strange time is all reaching out after something that it has not. Never was the groaning and travailing of the whole creation so loud and strong.

3. But there was yet another class. Besides the few

who were on the lookout for the Messiah, and the much larger number who were on the lookout for something —they knew not what—there was the great mass of the men of the time who were on the lookout for nothing. They felt no need. Their lives seemed to them self-satisfying. Whatever they were, slaves or nobles, they found in the routine of daily occupation enough to keep their hands busy and to keep their hearts quiet, and so they were completely satisfied. But yet when we look back upon them we can see plainly enough that there hardly ever was an age which was so *needy* in all truly great motives and methods of life everywhere as just that age of the Christian era. It is hard to see anything that could have deeply and truly fed the earnestness of an earnest man in days like those. The first crude fervors of men's earliest religions had passed away. The calm and reasonable and conscientious devotion of later religious feeling had not come. Government everywhere had turned to tyranny. Patriotism had degenerated into local and envious pride. Philosophy had frittered itself away into threadbare sophistries. Charity and philanthropy were not yet invented. What was there that an earnest man could do? What occupation or enthusiasm could bring out the best manliness of men? What chance was there for any hearty struggle? It was the emptiest age that the whole moral and spiritual history of man had seen; and just that emptiness it was which made it the fullness of time for Christ. There never was an age which so needed to be saved—saved from itself; filled with the power of salvation, which for a race or for a man must be devoted love and hard work, enthusiasm and duty. It was out of such a deadness of millions and millions of souls that the cry for life came out, unconscious, unmeant, but no less recognized by Him who watches and answers not only the desires but the needs of men.

These were the three classes, then. Can you not picture that old world to yourself? It is the hour before the sunrise. There are a few privileged souls or a few brave climbers—call them which you will—upon the lofty peak, with eyes strained eastward, knowing where the sun must rise, waiting and longing and praying for its rising. There just below them, still in the dark, not yet touched by the anticipated daylight that has reached those highest eyes—still in the dark, but wide-awake and trembling and restless with the vague sense that somewhere new light is coming—are the great multitudes upon the mountain-sides. Then down below, filling the valley, lying in the dark fast asleep, or playing idle games, or chasing phantoms which they tried to cheat themselves were worth the catching, not even dreaming of a light to come, needing everything, but knowing nothing of their need, were the yet greater multitudes for whom all true life was a blank or a despair, who knew no high desire. Was it not time for sunrise? Was it not the very fullness of time in which "the dayspring from on high visited us, to give light to them that sat in darkness and in the shadow of death"?

.

And now I said that I had a practical purpose in this description of the age which God had shaped and made ready for the manifestation of His Saviour Son. Let me tell you what it was. As I look round upon this people here before me I cannot but think I see the

FOURTH SUNDAY IN ADVENT. 69

same three classes that were in that world of eighteen centuries ago.

1. Are there not here the *waiters?* Are there not men and women here who know well enough that if salvation from their sins and selfishness, from their fears and doubts and failures, from *their own bad selves,* comes at all it must come from Jesus the Christ alone, and they do feel a strong assurance that some day it will come from Him? There are souls that to-day I cannot find any parallel or likeness for except in Simeon and Anna waiting in the temple year after year for the Redeemer. They are not scoffers, but full of reverence. They are not false, but true. They are not light and shallow, but earnest and devout. What is it that has kept you so long waiting? Do not reject Christ just because He comes from Bethlehem when you expected Him from Nazareth. Do not refuse the Saviour because as He presents Himself you find Him something different from what you painted Him to yourself before He came. The terms of His salvation may not be just what you have supposed; but will you let Him pass you by for that? Surely there could be no more generous or easy terms than these He offers: "Behold, I stand at the door, and knock," He says: "if any man hear My voice, and open the door, I will come in to him." What answer is there for you, who have waited so long, to make but this: "Lo! this is our God. We have waited for Him; now He will save us"?

2. And then I turn to others. You tell me that you are not looking for Christ. But you are looking for something. You are not satisfied. You know you ought to be a better man. You know that you keep

sinning when you ought to be holy; that you are living a low life, doing mean things, when you ought to be full of lofty tastes and rich in noble deeds; that you are not using at all, or are misusing, the best of the great powers God has given you. When you look back the past scares you. When you look forward the future scares you too. You look around you, and the world is out of joint and things are going wrong everywhere. What will you do? To do nothing is to sink down and be lost. I beg you to cling to your dissatisfaction till it find some fit appeasing. And then I hold out to you Christ and offer Him. As if you never saw or heard of Him before, I set Him here before you, and you *must* not turn away when you hear Him say the very words you need: "Come unto Me, all ye that labor and are heavy-laden, and I will give you rest."

3. And what shall I say to you who neither want Christ nor want anything? Poor souls, you *are* satisfied; that is the worst of all for you. This worldliness, this sin, this death in life, leaves you with no compunction or misgiving. There is no tossing in the sleep your soul is sleeping. And yet it *is* sleep—sleep only—not death yet. There are powers in you to serve the Lord with, if you could only get them awake and active. Yes, powers as great as that, even in you who think that the Almighty made you just to dance and sing your life away—there are powers in you that *might serve Christ* with sweet unselfishness, with loving loyalty, with joyous gratitude, and with an energy that would amaze yourself and glorify Him. It is in you to be a Christian, I care not who you be; and so I cry, not as to one who has no powers, but as to one who has them,

but is keeping them useless—talents in napkins, unworked mines of spiritual wealth and joy: "Awake, thou that sleepest, and Christ shall give thee light."

And so with all of us is it not the fullness of time indeed? Is there one of us who can say, "It is not my time yet"? Now while the morning is at hand, the night far spent; now while we have, it may be, but a little while left us to come to Christ or to come closer to Christ, to be a Christian or to be a better Christian; now while the Bridegroom's feet are close upon us, are sounding already in the distance, oh, let our loins be girded about, and our lights burning, and we ourselves like unto men that wait for their Lord.

To-morrow morning we shall be exulting in the truth of a present Christ. Will it have a meaning for all of us? In these most solemn days, these last days of Advent, I feel most deeply—I hope we all are feeling—the richness of the gospel of our Saviour. He gives Himself so freely. He asks nothing but repentance and faith. He wants our souls. O Lord, we will not keep them back. Take them and save them. Let us see Thee now as men saw Thee of old when it is written that "in the last day, that great day of the feast, Jesus stood and cried, saying, If any man thirst, let him come unto Me, and drink."

V.

CHRISTMAS EVE.

"Because there was no room for them in the inn."—LUKE II. 7.

WE believe in the inspiration under whose guidance the evangelists wrote not least because of their great *wisdom of selection*. Every life is made up of a great mass of incidents. To single out among those incidents the ones which *really* were the making of the life; to put the finger accurately upon them so as to say, "This and this and this were important in bringing that life to its purpose; this and this and this are significant in helping men to appreciate and understand the motive under which, and the tone in which, this life was lived;" to point out just those passages that shall reveal the character and kind of man whose life is being written —this is the great difficulty of biographers. This difficulty is the reason why we have so few good and so many poor biographies among our books.

We rather *feel* than *think* how divinely the gospel writers have subdued this difficulty. We do not stop to dwell upon the fact that they have put on record just those incidents of Jesus' life which let us most directly into an understanding of Him; but as we read their story we find ourselves attaining a real knowledge of their subject such as no other writers give. The things they tell are just the very things we need to know. Even the slightest items they relate are all significant; the faintest touches bring out effects and meanings in the picture, and help us to catch the idea of Christ and of His mission which the inspiring Spirit intended to convey. Yes, when the poor carpenter of Nazareth brought his wife up to the inn at Bethlehem, and they were turned away because the house was crowded with more favored guests, and her Son found His birthplace among "the beasts of the stall" and His cradle in a manger, the crowded house and the rejected applicant take their place in the narrative as true exponents of the earthly lot of Him for whose nativity there was " no room in the inn"—nay, as a significant foreshadowing of the future of His gospel, which has with such difficulty found for itself a place in the overcrowded world.

The use that I would make, then, of this apparently trivial incident is this: Does not the reception of the new-born Christ typify with strange accuracy the reception that His gospel has met wherever it has been introduced into an unwelcoming world? Is not this His first experience the experience of all the Saviour's life both in His flesh and in His Church—that, crowded out of the hospitalities of life, out of the inns and homes and cheerful haunts of men, He has found His resting-place in the world's sheds and mangers, among the poverty and degradation of our race? What is the aspect of our busy and unbelieving world as you stand and look across it but the repeated picture of that Jewish inn in which there was *no room for Jesus?*

For I believe that if we search its character we shall see that this is just the form which opposition to the cause of Christ is now most generally taking. The gospel is not fought against or frankly met in any way. It is simply *crowded out.* The Christian religion has won for itself a certain great respectability. Men do not sneer at it as they used to. Nay, men who in their hearts are anything but Christians are jealous for the credit of the faith of Christ. I dare say there has been no age since Jesus lived when the character of Jesus, in its unsullied purity, its calm consistency, its high-toned heroism, has been more proudly lauded or more cordially acknowledged; there has been no age when the moral power of Christianity, as the great social salvation of states and communities, has been more profoundly felt; but yet we cannot find a time when the great *deadweight,* the mere brute *force,* of a sheer overcrowded life has been so immense in keeping out the personal presence of the Saviour from the intimacies of our hearts and homes. This, it seems to me, is the form that our irreligious life is more and more assuming—just a great inert *overfullness.* Religion is met, not, as it was a thousand years ago, by a man in mail upon the threshold, with a sword or an ax or a firebrand to kill it out—the brutality of that folly is obsolete; not, as it was a hundred years ago, by a cunning diplomatist in the vestibule with wiry words and smooth-tongued irony to circumvent the new-comer and make even religion herself faithless and untrue—the cowardice of that folly, too, is dying away; but nowadays, when the new stranger comes up to the doors, the opposition is just the great, impenetrable, passive fullness of the house she tries to enter. Christ comes with His truth to the intellect. What is the answer? Every chamber of the intellect, from garret to cellar, is preëngaged. Science, morals and physics, politics, history, art—all these are with us and must be royally fed and lodged. For this new applicant " there is no room in the inn." Christ comes with His work to the will. But what chance for quarters here when the very entry-ways of the human will are packed to stagnation with a thousand little ephemeral plans making their flying visits, and a hundred great absorbing schemes that have taken up their permanent abode? What answer but again that this great inn is full? Christ comes with His love to the great, roomy, hospitable human *heart*. But the hospitality—not so wise as lavish—has it not been already more than wasted on a host of beggarly and unworthy claimants, so that when the heart's Master comes there is no room to spare? Thus daily is the scene of Bethlehem repeated. He comes unto His own; His own receive Him not. The world is too full for Christ, and the heart too crowded for its Saviour.

Now if this be true, and this be the special form which ungodliness is taking in this age of ours, then we must direct what care we have for the advancement of Christ's kingdom to this special difficulty, and ask in much anxiety, How can a way be made for the Saviour to penetrate this crowded life?

And first of all men must no doubt be made to feel that it will in some way be of advantage to them to receive Christ into the plan and operation of their lives. Is not this the tone of everything to-day: " Whatever can help us, welcome! Whatever cannot help us, stand aside!"? Every branch of industry has its appropriate rules and its own useful appliances. The whole tendeney is to simplify things—to throw away what is useless, to keep all that is essential. The wheels of modern enterprise spin so fast that all that is not bound close to them by the strong necessity of usefulness is flung away and got rid of by the centrifugal power of their speed. The great design of life to-day is to make things run light and run quick. Every heavy impediment that does not help the motion must be cast off into space. But this same great principle which teaches us to tolerate nothing that is *useless* teaches us by a parallel lesson that nothing really useful must be despised. I presume there never was a class of minds that gave to every new device which laid claim to that highest merit, usefulness, such a fair test, and, if it proved its claim, such a free welcome as it gets from the best and most active minds of our own century. There never was such a fair field for a new-comer. Once prove to men that your new invention has in it the seeds of new and genuine and profitable *use*, and you need have no fear. *Men will find room for it*, no matter how crowded this great engine-room of a world appears already. What good is it? What can I do with it? That is the only question now when you offer a man something he has never seen before. *Self-interest*, that great king with his crown of gold, has fewer rebels in his realm to-day than perhaps he ever had before.

Now I believe this principle will help us in understanding this phenomenon of a world finding no place for Christ. It is full, very full—crowded even to the bursting gates—with manifold interests and hopes and plans; but yet, as we have seen, it never refuses to receive another applicant if it can once be made to feel that it needs Him, that He can be of use. And it is only because the world does not feel the need—nay, to put it blankly, does *not see the use of Jesus*—that Jesus finds to-day no resting-place except in her mangers and her stalls. If ever, close and hot about the world's great heart, that great feeling shall be brought home— the feeling that she needs a Saviour, and that the Christ whose gentle application is at her doors is the only power that can save her from sin and sorrow; if ever humanity shall deeply see what Christ can do for her, then, in spite of all her crowded fullness, the great doors shall find abundant room to be swung back, and Jesus Christ, the long-rejected, shall be welcomed in to take His place of honor and do His saving work.

So that, after all, don't you see that this plea of *over-fullness* is a false one? I come to you and urge on you to be a Christian. You tell me, "Yes, I know the importance of the matter, but I am too busy, my life is too full—too many cares, too many interests. I have not room for Christianity, but yet I know its importance and I feel its use." That is not true. You do *not* feel its use. *If you did*, no matter how full your life was you would find room for it just as you would for any other new expedient which offered you a help you really needed. The fact is, you *do not want* to be a Christian. If you did, the want would make you room, would make you time. If you saw and felt how Christianity was to help you, your own principles, which spur you on to zeal in every other helpful enterprise, would turn you into a zealous servant in the work of God. This is the true difficulty. What men need is not new offers of the gospel—the echoes of these eighteen hundred years are *tired* with their long reverberations—but they want to be made to feel that the gospel, if it could once be admitted into the homes of art and trade and politics and social life, would be a *real help* to trade and politics and art and life. They want to be made to feel that it is no useless stranger asking admission and free lodging, for which it will give nothing in return, but that it is an element which, if they admit it, will mingle itself with all their other interests and crown them all with a better and more luxuriant success.

Fill a cup with water so that it seems as if it could not hold another drop. Drop a bullet in it and it makes the cup overflow. But you can add an amount of water double the bullet's bulk and it mingles itself with the other water and clings particle to particle, and the cup will hold it all. So, if religion were a mere dead-weight to be dropped like a bit of lead into the full soul of man, then you might say, perhaps, there " was no room "; but if it be a living principle that is to pervade and leaven and infuse all the life into which it is cast, to give it all new consistency and strength, then there *is* room; and if you can make men feel this, they will *make* room to receive the gospel.

Who do you suppose were gathered in that village inn where Joseph and Mary and the new-born child were crowded out? No doubt the usual assembly of such places: stout Jewish farmers come up to Bethlehem with their money-bags to pay the taxes; a petty governor or two, great with the pride of small official business; half a dozen Roman soldiers, brutal in the insolence of their great citizenship; a few traveling priests; a rabbi, laying down dogmatic oracles to his wide-mouthed hearers; and a few inn idlers hanging round the doorway or lounging by the fire—a company dead and forgotten centuries ago, crowding the little inn and filling it with heedless merriment; while Immanuel was born into the world He came to save and "laid in a manger, because there was no room for Him in the inn." Little they cared where the poor woman met her mother's pain. But do you think if they had dreamed whose the birth was that they excluded; if they had known what the new-born might do for them; if they could have looked down the fields of prophecy and seen what He should do for the world; if they could have seen this Church of ours to-day and have known that it was the Child of the manger whom we have worshiped as the Lord of life—do you think that even their stolid indifference would not have thrown the poor inn door wide open and spread its choicest chamber in what faint fitness they could devise for the nativity of the Redeemer? =They would have found room enough if they had known it was the only Saviour of Jew or Gentile that was being born. And you would find room, dear brother, for Christ to be born in your overcrowded heart if you really felt that in His birth there lay your only chance of goodness here and joy hereafter.

Thus, then, the great cause of this misconceived idea that the world and the heart have not room for Christ lies here: we do not understand the nature or feel the need of the Christ who offers to make our hearts His birthplace, and so we do not care to make room for Him there. There is another reason. By the figure we have been using, the birth of Christ in the soul, we mean a full reception of His truth, His character, and His life-giving power among the essential plans and purposes of our existence. Now, though we do not any of us fully comprehend that truth, that character, that power, we all have enough of heaven's instinct about us to feel that it is something immeasurable, great, and glorious. You may not love Christ or care to imitate Him or to invite Him; but you do feel, when you deliberately think of Him and of the world-work that He has done, that there is in Him an immensity of grandeur and holiness before which you grow ashamed. And when this perfect ideal, this full divinity of character, comes and demands admission into your life, what wonder if the meager dimensions to which your life has been cramped *show out* in all their meagerness! What! take the pure Jesus into a dwelling so impure, take a faith so venerable into a poor abode so vile and base, take so great a religion into so small a soul? In the humility of shame we feel that Christianity, with its grand motives, its divine means, its stupendous issues, is on too large a scale for our little, trivial, frivolous lives to harbor, and so we shut our doors and cry, "No room! no room!"

Now here, it seems to me, is just one of the divinest offices of our religion. It makes us feel the littleness to which we have reduced our lives, and then proclaims, in contrast with that littleness, the great scale on which God built those lives and the great capacity God meant for them to have. "You have cramped your life," it seems to say. "You have made it small and narrow. By long unspirituality you have made its doors so low that none but short or stooping thoughts can enter. You have made its rooms so mean that great truths cannot live in them. But never dare to think that this was God's plan for your life. He drew its architecture on a lordly scale. He designed for you great, generous, capacious lives. He built you to be 'temples of the Holy Ghost.' There are chambers in your nature, walled up by long obstinacy or rubbished by long neglect, which were shaped and garnished for His own holy occupancy. Man—in the face of all his degraded humanity be it spoken—was *made* fit for a birthplace of the Christ." If the manifestation of the Saviour had done nothing else, would not this be much—this eternal reassertion of the essential dignity and capacity of human life? The gospel stands forever in the midst of little, base, degraded lives, and protests that this is not the true exhibit of the life humanity *might* live. To the sensualist who has turned his soul into a home of lust; to the poor inebriate whose life is reeking with the fumes of stale and sickly habit; to the trifler who has industriously tented himself about with glittering tinsel; to the mean man who has been deliberately cramping up his stingy heart, walling up windows, pinching in doors, studiously making his existence *small*—to each of them the gospel brings its protest: "You may make your lives foul and tawdry and meager; you may diminish them and overcrowd them till there *is* no room for a noble thought or for a pure desire; but you do it at your peril. God made them roomy; and there *is* room for His holy Son to find a nativity within them if you will only set and keep their chambers open."

This second reason, as you see, may rest on a better

base and takes a more conscientious tone than the first. I know that there are many persons who, when the offer of a purer life and free salvation by the gospel comes to them, when Christ presents Himself at their heart doors and asks admission, turning and looking at the poor hospitality to which they can receive Him, seeing how small and foul their souls have grown, how unworthy of an occupant so pure, in sheer humility are almost driven to shut to the door and say, "Thou must not enter here. There is no room for such as Thou in such a heart as mine, O Lord!" But let me warn you how you yield to such an impulse. It is humble, but it is not truly reverent and is certainly not the spirit of trustful faith. God made your heart and knows it better far than you do. Christ knows whether there be room or not. Once let Him in and He shall find Him room where you have never dreamed of. He shall throw open chambers wholly new to you, and you yourself shall be amazed when the great spiritual capacity of your nature gradually unfolds itself to entertain its spiritual Guest.

I appeal to any one who ever watched the process. Have you ever seen a man thoroughly taken possession of by Christ? Was it not wonderful to watch how what had seemed a low, contracted, insignificant nature, of meager intellect and narrow heart and feeble will, gradually, under the inspiration of the new birth that was going on within it, rose up and reached itself out on all sides, unclosed new avenues for spirit-influence, opened new chambers for accumulating spiritual knowledge, spreading with each new demand into new grandeur, till what had been so narrow and corrupt and contemptible by nature grew to a broad, sweet, open, glorious *new man* in the power and regeneration of the Lord Jesus? Have you ever seen a *little man* rise to a *great Christian;* ever seen a dull and commonplace character grow absolutely *splendid* with faith? If you have, never yield to false humility when Jesus comes and asks to unfold your life and work the same miracle on you.

These are the influences, then, under which the plea of the Bethlehem innkeepers has been perpetuated down through Christian history. Under these influences the crowded homes of comfort and content have closed their doors, and in the mangers of Christendom has been the cradle of the Christ. The knock was at the gates of palaces, and the answer came, "No room! no room! We are too full already." And to the sound of trumpets and the dance, the slighted Saviour turned away. It fell upon the study door, and the pale student turned from his books only to chide the stranger that stopped him on his way to wisdom: "No room! no room!" And the Lord of all wisdom turned away from the door of haughty and mistaken science. It rang upon the warehouse gates, and commerce tossed a beggar's fee to the meek applicant, and bade Him stand aside and not impede the crowding wealth that was flooding into the overflowing treasury.

Yes, in this great caravansary, where travelers are met midway upon their journey from eternity to eternity, there has been room for every interest except religion and for every friend but Jesus. Truths which were to His truth like a fire-spark to a star, hopes which were to His hope like the phosphorescence of death to the warm, life-giving sunlight, have found an open welcome in the crowded world. Only for Jesus there was "no room in the inn."

No room! And is your heart so full, my brother? No room for Jesus, when Jesus is your only hope? No room for Jesus, when salvation never crosses any threshold where His feet have not been set? No room for Jesus, when, except by Jesus, there is no eternal life? I warn you, if it be so, *make Him room*. Fling out your choicest treasures, if need be, as sailors with the black rocks in front of them, and the hungry sea reaching up at them its cruel mouths on every side, fling out their silks and gold to save their lives.

No room for Jesus! Let the guests that keep Him out stand up before Him, and see how full of shame their faces turn when they meet His. They know (the spirits of earth and hell to whom you give His place)— they know, if you do not, whose place it is they have usurped.

No room for Jesus! I assure you, my dear friend, my heart would thrill with joy for you—nay, what is that?—the angels on the walls of heaven, and God who sits upon the throne, would know it with the ecstasy that only spirits such as theirs can feel, if you would open your closed heart to-night and find your Saviour room.

VI.

CHRISTMAS DAY.

"And the Word was made flesh, and dwelt among us."—JOHN
I. 14.

UPON one more bright Christmas Day we have come to rejoice together in the birth of Christ. We want to catch at once the pure and fresh simplicity of the story of Bethlehem as if we were, indeed, there to-day, and all were going on just as it did so long ago. And we want also to get the advantage of living so long after and understanding the richness and meaning of the story more than those first spectators could, from having seen it worked out into countless lives and made the motive of the world's greatest changes. And both of these are offered to us in the Bible. We have at once the story of the nativity told as it seemed to those who were at Bethlehem on the first Christmas Day, and then we have St. John writing years afterward and telling us what it all meant, in those rich and wonderful verses that begin his Gospel; the story and its explanation, how it all seemed to Mary and the shepherds and the wise men from the East, and how it all seemed to the great apostle with the enlightenment and inspiration of God filling him; the history of Christ's nativity, and the philosophy of the Incarnation. I want to dwell upon the first to-day. It belongs to the great Christian festival, not to search into the deep mystery of the Incarnation of God, but to put ourselves as thoroughly as possible into the places of those who surrounded the Saviour's cradle, and see the wonderful spectacle with their eyes. But still I have made these deep words of St. John my text, because it really is impossible, as it is undesirable, for us to forget that there are deeper meanings in the event than any who were there had comprehended, but which have been made known to us. This will indicate what I want you to do with me, if you will, to-day. I want you to go with me to Bethlehem. I want you to take the three groups who are recorded in connection with our Saviour's birth, to look with their eyes and see Him as they saw Him, and at the same time, by your higher Christian privilege, to look deeper than they could see; to unfold, as it were, their simple and crude emotions and find in them all that the souls in fullest Christian light have ever felt in reference to Christ; to see if the entire richness of the best Christian experience was not germinally and representatively present there around the Saviour's birth.

1. Who are the first group, then, that are concerned in the nativity, that are gathered about the birth of Jesus? Certainly those who stood the nearest to Him. Certainly His parents, and especially His mother, who had borne already so long upon her heart the coming mystery. What was the nativity to her whom all generations have called blessed as the mother of our Lord? What should we see if we could look into her heart on Christmas Day? Painters, you know, have tried to tell the story in exquisite pictures which represent the

mother on her knees before her Child, who lies before her. She is wrapt in adoration of Him; she is lifting up her hands in homage; she is imploring His blessing and owning Him for her Lord. But while that is what art has seized upon, it is remarkable that there is not one word about that in the Bible. There we have one key to the mother's heart: we have the beautiful psalm, the Magnificat, which she sang when she went to visit Elizabeth before the Saviour's birth. And it is certainly noticeable that that psalm is mainly of her own privilege: "He hath regarded the low estate of His handmaiden: for from henceforth all generations shall call me blessed. He that is mighty hath done to me great things." It is not adoration of her Child. It is a sense of what that Child's coming has been to her. Because He has deigned to be born of her she is forever blessed. Because of this close union between His life and hers she is lifted up out of her insignificance. Because He has shared her lot, her lot has ceased to be mean and wretched. She is sacred because of the God who has come and lived in her life. The poor Jewish girl is not despicable, no one shall despise her, she never will despise herself again, now that her life has been capable of containing the very life of God.

Afterward, no doubt, there came the adoration. Afterward, as Christ grew and she knew Him more, there came forth in Him a Divinity which she could not share, before which she could only stand in loving awe. Afterward she saw how different He was from her. But at first the thought is of how they are one with each other, and of how by her oneness with Him she is lifted and glorified. At first it is not the sense of how far His Divinity is above her, but of how truly it is in her and how it makes her divine. On Christmas Day she is not on her knees before her Lord, but she is holding her Child tight to her heart to assure herself continually that His life is really hers, and so that her life is really His.

Now extend all this—make it not merely the experience of the Jewish virgin, but the consciousness of humanity at the birth of Jesus—and we have this, which I hold to be true: that the first thing which human nature feels when it comes to the knowledge of the coming of Christ is the mere fact of the Incarnation, and the illumination and exaltation of all human life by and through the Incarnation. With her it was a feeling of personal pride and privilege. Out of all the maidens of Judah she had been chosen to be the mother of the Lord. But with men to whom the same truth comes in its larger way its narrowness is lost; it becomes comprehensive; it is a sense of the exaltation and illumination of all humanity together, and of each man only as he has a part in that humanity by the coming of God into its flesh.

Carry this out into a slight detail with regard to the life of Mary. As Christ grew older this first feeling must have grown only stronger with her. In everything her life must have been elevated by seeing how her Son could share it with her. Her humble house must have seemed glorious, her simple meal a banquet, her husband's workshop sacred, the ordinary household thoughts not commonplace, because they were not hers alone, but His. That must have been the first power of the Incarnation. Only after that was fully felt could the second power of the Incarnation be experienced. Only after she had thoroughly conceived the dignity of her daily tasks when Christ took part in them could she begin to perceive how differently He did them from the way in which she did them, and so learn how her actual life fell short of the dignity with which the revelation of His birth had vested it. The Incarnation must have stirred her pride before it stirred her shame.

So it ought to be with us. So the first simple, broad, pervading sentiment of Christmas Day ought to be of how sacred and high this human life is into which the Lord was born. Not merely the body and the life of the virgin—she was like all her brethren and sisters. All attempts to separate her from them is a wrong to their common humanity. But the body and the life of man are able to take in and to utter God. Christ could be born into such flesh and such relationships, into such duties and such delights, as ours. At once a radiance streams in upon them, and they are no longer dull. Their luster shines out splendidly. Fathers, your labor for your children is not bare duty. Children, your service of your fathers is not a weary slavery. Neighbors, your daily courtesies to one another need not be empty shams. Men and women, your bodies are not base, your routines ought not to be deadening. Each is worthy of his own and of his brethren's respect; for there has been an incarnation. This humanity has held Divinity. God has been in this flesh. O my dear friends, if your lives are hampered and held down by any self-contempt, by any feeling that human life is low, that to be a man is to be something narrow, dry, and barren; if any such thought is keeping you from doing broad justice to yourself and to your brethren, cast it aside on Christmas Day. Believe that Christ was born of Mary. Let your soul magnify the Lord with the same bounding and leaping sense of privilege that exalted hers. Let the Incarnation, with all its inspirations and its shames, possess and fill your life.

2. But now turn to another group which also comes into close connection with the Lord's nativity. I mean the little company of the wise men who came traveling out of the East, under the leading of a star, to greet Him. "The Three Kings" they have been called for years in song and legend. There is no mention of any royalty belonging to them in the Bible story, but here, as very often, perhaps we may see in the legend something of that sort of secondary revelation which comes through the instincts of the human heart and has shaped itself into an addition to the story which, whether historically true or not, expresses a spiritual truth that is perfectly in harmony with the story to which it is fastened. The idea in the legend of the kings is that of the loftiest and noblest bowing down to Jesus. It is therefore merely an additional emphasis laid upon this second truth of the nativity, which is the kingliness of the newborn Christ. That is what this second group expresses. Mary taught us of the dignifying of humanity through the Incarnation. The wise men teach us of the true place of humanity in obedient subjectship to the Incarnate.

And see how their visit brings out also the character of the subjectship which they acknowledge and which they represent. The King whom they find and bow to, before whom their choicest treasures are cast down, is a child, a mere speechless baby. Sitting there upon His mother's knee, He is weakness personified. He cannot compel one prostration of all that He receives. They are bowing down not to a sword, for those feeble hands cannot hold one; not to a crown, for that tender brow could not bear one. They are bowing down to a nature which shines all the more clearly through the weakness of the flesh in which it has enshrined itself. They are like true courtiers before their infant Sovereign, giving Him a loyalty wholly different from the sulky submission which a conquered soldier renders to his conqueror. They offer Him their obedience, not because they have to in any grosser or material sense, but because their kingly souls own in Him a soul more kingly. It is all of the soul. That is its dignity, and that is what is represented by the Greek monarchs kneeling before the little Child.

And so they represent the perpetual acknowledgment of Christ as the spiritual, and so the real, King of men. This Christmas scene is the picture of the way in which the souls that know Christ always take Him for their Lord and Master. It is the only kingship that the Saviour wants—not that which awes and frightens men with the drawn sword which it holds over them, but that which bows them into a far more complete submission by the felt majesty of His character and the desire to serve a Master who is so gracious and so great. Every subtle and mysterious and sacred influence draws such servants to Him, as the soft and silent star led the wise men. And when such servants come where He is they find nothing to fear—only the divine pity and love and holiness incarnated, as gentle as a child; and they serve Him, not because they must, but because their whole soul feels the privilege and glory of such obedience. See how this comes home to our life. When a man submits to a failure which he knows that God sent him because he cannot help submitting, there is nothing of the Christmas spirit there. When a man relieves a poor beggar's need because the poor beggar will be dangerous to him if he is not helped and grows desperate, there is no Christmas spirit there. When a young man restrains his passions because his health or reputation will suffer if he lets them run their race, it is not the Christ of Christmas to whom he yields. But when you bear your disappointment because it is good to be trained, even to be disappointed, under God's education; when you help the poor man because it is a joy to minister to Christ, and the poor *are* Christ to you; when you say "No" to your lusts because it is a glory to be pure through grateful emulation of Him who is purity itself—then you are coming in the wise men's spirit to do the wise men's act: to claim Christ for your King, and dignify your life by obedience to Him.

So that on Christmas Day the human life not merely feels Christ come down to claim it, and so a man learns what his true honor is, but also it goes up to claim Christ, and by entering into His service to begin its fullest life. What a relief it is! I think of those old wise men. What worthless kings they had lived under! What unrule, what misrule, they had known in the cruel, treacherous East, where their days had been passed! Perhaps they really were kings, and then how unkingly, how unworthy of their name, they knew that their government had often been! But here was a true King at last. Men would not own Him. He was only a baby, so weak and so poor. But that was nothing to them; they had found their King in Him and were satisfied. So no matter how men find fault, no matter how they say, "Oh, it is only Jesus Christ;" when you have really found your King in Him, and the law of your life is to do His will out of love, then peace—His peace—shall descend upon you. No more distraction and rebellion, but calm, sure, happy going forward through His service into His likeness here and hereafter.

3. But there is one more group which no one who thinks of Christmas Day forgets : "There were shepherds abiding in the field, keeping watch over their flock by night." How familiar and how full of rich association these old words have grown! Try to think what their story must mean, what contribution it makes to the symphony of meaning in which all these attendants on the birth of Christ unite. Remember what is told us. They heard a song of angels, a voice from heaven telling them that a Saviour was born in Bethlehem, and that glory had come to God and peace had come to men. Then they simply stand looking at one another, as if in dumb wonder. Then they can only say to one another, "Let us go to Bethlehem and see this strange thing." Then they come and find Christ, and then they go abroad to tell other men about Him. That is all. There is a certain dumb, blind movement about all they do, yet with a certain simple, eager straightforwardness about it. They sing no psalm like Mary. They do not follow the star nor go to Herod like the wise men. They simply hear a voice from heaven telling them that there is a Saviour and where He is, and they say, "Let

us go there." And they do go there and they do find Him. I am sure that I need not tell you what an eternal element in Christian life they represent. Always there will be those who will be exalted with the thought of the Incarnation, upon all whose life and occupations it will cast a glorifying light. Always there will be those who out of much unrest and anarchy will seem to come into a rich and conscious peace as they submit themselves to Christ's kingship. But such experiences will always seem too subtle for some souls. Always there will be many whose whole experience will be merely this: that, hungry, needy, empty, wanting a Saviour, they just heard a voice from heaven telling them that the Saviour whom they needed had come, and they just went to Him and found Him all they wanted, and then, like the poor shepherds, "made known abroad" to other men all that had come to them. No doubt in their experiences, simple as they seem, the whole richness of those others will really be included. But to the multitude of human souls Christ will be simply the Satisfier revealed from heaven, and they will turn to Him almost as a creature shut up in the dark turns without thought, without plan or anticipation, to any corner of its darkness where a bright light suddenly shines.

Are there not moments in the Christian life of all of us when this alone is all our Christianity? Men tell us this and that about Jesus, this and that subtle thought about the mystery of His nature, this and that profound theory of the work by which He makes Himself our redeeming King. We do not doubt and we do not deny. It is as if, when we were turning with full heart aching for sympathy to find our dearest friend, some one should stop us and tell us deep things about the philosophy of friendship. We do not doubt and we do not deny. It may be true. No doubt it is true. But all is overswept and drowned for the time by a blind, eager, passionate longing of the heart that needs Christ to get to Him. Men tell us why we need Him. We cannot listen, but our heart is full of one consciousness: that we do need Him. Our lips can shape only one question: "Where shall we find Him?" Our wills are all absorbed in one strong resolution: "Let us go now even unto Him." It is good for us to think as richly and deeply of Christ as we can. It is good for us to analyze in patient meditation all that He is to us and all that we can be toward Him. But oh, let us beware lest any subtlety of thought or depth of meditation ever deadens or dulls in us that first great, deep longing of the soul for Him who is its only Saviour. In deepest grief, in uttermost perplexity, often in great and overwhelming joy, always in conscious sin, that yearning, that unquestioning and passionate desire, asserts itself. It is as instinctive as the movement of the hurt child to its mother, or of the parched beast to the river. Always at the bottom of such strong experience what is stirred really is the sense of sin, and that none but the Jesus sent to take away our sins really can relieve. By His forgiveness, by Himself given to us, He does forgive it, and then, while others call the wondrous Lord by partial names that utter some one side of His wondrousness, to us He has but one name —Saviour. He is that and that alone, and all besides only as it is wrapped up in that.

Who is this, then, that lies once more to-day before

the world, the Son of God and Son of man, at Bethlehem? Mary bows down and learns the Incarnation, and feels the solemnity and sublimity of the human life into which Divinity has entered. The wise men come and find their King in this weak babe. The shepherds see the hope of Israel fulfilled, the Saviour come. Oh, on this Christmas Day let us be with them all. Let us feel thrilling through this humanity which we so often scorn the glorifying fire of the Incarnation. Let us give up our lives to Him and beg that He will rule them. But, more than all, let us give our souls, hungry and sinful, a Christmas leave to go to Him who is their Saviour, whom they will know for their Saviour if we let them go to Him.

It is a day of joy and charity. May God make you very rich in both by giving you abundantly the glory of the Incarnation, the peace of Christ's kingship, and the grace of Christ's salvation.

VII.

SUNDAY AFTER CHRISTMAS.

"And because ye are sons, God hath sent forth the Spirit of His Son into your hearts, crying, Abba, Father."—GAL. IV. 6.

IT has seemed to me as if this were the very text that we needed for the morning after Christmas Day. The festival is over, and yet its spirit is still all about us, and its meanings are perhaps growing clearer to us than they were yesterday. It is somewhat as when, after the first excitement of a friend's arrival is over, we sit down and calmly think of what his coming means, and of what difference it will make in our life. The joy of his welcome is still there, but its tumult has grown still. So the birth of Christ, which we celebrated yesterday, is not simply a brilliant and beautiful point in history. It is the beginning of a new order in the human story; and to any man who makes it *his* great event, it is the opening of a new volume of existence, with new and infinitely deeper, clearer meanings.

And this is just what St. Paul says. In the verses that went before he has just been telling the story of the nativity: "When the fullness of the time was come, God sent forth His Son, made of a woman, made under the law, to redeem them that were under the law, that we might receive the adoption of sons." There is the story. The Child of the woman, who was also the Son of God, came to tell all the children of women, all humanity, that they were sons of God too, and to bring those who would receive Him so close to God that their sonship should be a reality to them, a *life;* that they should receive the adoption of sons. That is what God sent Jesus for; and now when Jesus has really come and done His work, and men by Him have become the sons of God, this is what happens: because men are God's sons, the Spirit of that Son through whom they know their sonship enters them and takes possession of them, until their whole life becomes a turning back, an appeal, a cry, a trustful, yearning *claiming* of their Father, a crying "Abba." And "Abba," you understand, is nothing but the Hebrew word for Father.

Here, then, is the whole process of redemption, and I said that it seemed to me the very text for to-day. Close to the birthday of the Redeemer what can I preach to you about but His redemption? With the songs of wondering angels and the footsteps of wondering shepherds yet in our ears, we cannot talk of anything but what He who stirred their wonder came to do. No partial thought of life, however true; no single duty, however important it may be, can draw us off to-day from the sincere attempt to comprehend in its completeness the work of Him whose life covers all life, and in obedience to whom all duty is included. Feeling this, I may ask you to reach your thought out with me while I try to tell what Christianity means by its one great, all-embracing word, *redemption.* We shall be false to the spirit of Christmas time if in speaking of our great theme we fail to be simple, clear, and direct.

In these verses of St. Paul's, then, see what persons or powers are brought together. We are impressed first of all by the great gathering of interests. Nothing that is really majestic in the universe is absent. First there is the Father of all things—He who, as the fountain and origin of life, gathers into Himself the complete richness of that word *Father*. From Him proceeds the action of this whole drama: "God sent forth His Son." Then, second, there is the Son of God, Jesus Christ, born of a woman, incarnate, coming for a great work—"to redeem them that were under the law." Then, third, there is the Spirit of this Son, whom, after the Son has done His redeeming work, the same God sends to take possession of the human heart and fill it with heavenly longings and desires: "God hath sent forth the Spirit of His Son into your hearts." And then, lastly, there is man, to whom this heart belongs, for whom this work is done, standing at the end of the whole process, claiming the Father of all things as *his* Father, and looking up to Him with confidence and love. Were there ever verses that had a sublimer occupancy? God is there, and Jesus Christ, and the Holy Spirit. And in the midst of them all, as the being for whom they all are working, there is *man*. As the windows of these verses open, this is what we see: all the prevalent influence of heaven gathered around man, and by its united power bringing him into the perfect sympathy of God. The Father sees him and loves him; the Son comes and seeks him; the Spirit spreads through his heart the sense of all this love; and then he, loved, redeemed, and quickened, reconciled to God, is seen, at the last, lifting up his hands and claiming God, crying, "Abba, Father."

What a vast chorus of sublimest life! How the soul stands amazed and awed! Here is all heaven and all that is capable of heavenliness upon earth met together, and the end of their meeting is complete accord. God is pouring His life into man. Man is sending back his tribute—rendering his life to God. It is the chorus of reconciled Divinity and humanity.

Now let us try to put into the plainest and least exalted language the truths about God and man which are involved in all this glowing picture. What does it really mean, this meeting of God and man? Let us see whether they are truths which we can understand and recognize. The first truth is that man *belongs to* God by nature. If that is not true, then there is no possibility of any religion—if it be not true that God made man in His own image, with the capacity of living a life that should be like His own. But the Bible says it is true, and however men hesitate at other things which the Bible says, their hearts bear witness in them to the truth of that, and they do believe it. Every movement of conscience when they do wrong; every leap of enthusiasm at the sight of goodness, as if they saw one fresh from the land where they themselves belonged; every indignation with themselves; all their highest memories and hopes, are their instinctive testimonies that they know they are God's children. He is their Father. That is the first truth, on which everything else depends. And as real as this truth of man's belonging with God is the truth of man's *estrangement* from God. That, too, is both in the Bible and in the heart: in the Bible in the history of the type-nation, the story of the Jewish life; and in the heart in the testimony which every man's conscience gives of how selfish his life is, of how he forgets the duty and lets go the privilege of living for God. Tell me, is there one of you who, if a voice which he *must* answer asked him, "Do you belong to God?" would not answer, proudly, "Yes"? And how many there are who, if the same voice asked them, "Do you serve God, and have you kept fast hold of the truth that He loves you?" would not have to answer, in sadness and humiliation, "No"! And the next truth is *Christ*. It stands written where we cannot doubt it that One who not merely belonged to God, but was God, came and set as a visible fact into the midst of man's life that which man had forgotten or lost out of his feeble grasp: that God loved men intensely, unsparingly, even to the mysterious extent of pain and death; and One who likewise, by the human life of devotion and obedience which He lived, reclaimed for man the right and power to serve God like a son. And then the truth of *inspiration*: that from this Saviour there goes forth a Spirit which finds out the hearts of men and touches them and melts in with them and makes itself a part of them, and spreads through every vein of all their life these two truths of the Christ whose Spirit He is: that God loves man, and that man is his true self when he is filially serving God. He is the Spirit of regeneration or a new birth, because the power of these truths thoroughly filling a man makes him a new life. And then, once more, there is the truth of *restoration*. When this Spirit really occupies a man, when he is living the new life whose essence is that he is God's child, his nature opens like the nature of a plant brought out of foreignness where it does not belong and set into its native soil, or like the nature of a child early stolen from its home, long kept in a degraded life, at last brought back and set in the old household, under his father's care, under his mother's love. Look, as he sits there, how bewildered memories come back over his perplexed face, how strange familiarity comes out in the unfamiliar furniture, how the long-smothered childship, like a frozen sap, begins to stir at his heart, and his dead life opens, new thoughts come vaguely to him, new feelings flush his cheek and fill his eyes, the colors of his whole life deepen, and every newly wakened sense is flooded with the one sufficient and supreme conviction that *he is at home.* There is his father and he is that father's child. So the man in whom the Spirit of Christ has thoroughly wrought home the message of Christ—that he is God's son—comes back into his Father's house, and as he sits there his sonship rises like a rising flood around him, till his whole life becomes the utterance of it, and he cries, not merely with his lips, but with every activity of his awakened being, "Abba, Father."

These are old truths. A long time you have heard them. I have preached them to you for these many years, and I cannot say how many years you heard them before I began to preach them to you. And yet I never can preach them without feeling a fresh, new hope that the grandeur of the circle which they embrace, the truth of the story of humanity which they tell, may come to you as it has not come before. I seem to feel it specially this morning. How majestic is the circle marked by this great opening, advancing truth of man's reconciliation to God! How it moves from the light of man's first ideal into the darkness of his actual experience, and then sweeps grandly back into the brightness of his redemption! It begins with the Fatherhood and childhood. It sees the childhood stray away into selfish, sinful independence, and then it closes with the Fatherhood and childhood once again restored. All history is comprehended in it. All the books of history, all the stories of the nations, are but single beads on the great string of this encircling truth. And then, with that strange identity which always runs between the two, it is as true of the individual life as of the world's life. Each of us also has his ideal sonship, his actual estrangement, his redeeming Christ, his inspiring Spirit, and then his real sonship, in which he rests forever. All other philosophies of life seem to me so thin and meager by the side of this. All accounts of sin are weak except that which makes it the wilful departure from God into selfishness. All accounts of goodness seem insufficient save those which see in it the effort of God's child after his lost sonship.

I want so much that you should feel and understand it all that I venture to put it in yet one more figure. It is like an island of which some great king is lord— a noble king, ready to help and lift his people; a true king, really the source and fountain of his land's prosperity. That is the first primal relationship. He belongs to them and they to him. Then comes rebellion: "We will not have this man to rule over us." The banner of revolt is set up. The castles of the sovereign are broken down. The land goes to waste. The reckless rebels tear to pieces the very works which the sovereign has built for their protection. Then comes reconquest. That sovereign sends himself under some representative, some true son of his authority. The champion enters in, and in their own behalf conquers the insurgents and crushes them. He defeats them in their rebellion that he may bring them back into obedience. He sets the banner of the king safe, strong, unassailable, once more in the reclaimed island. Then what comes? Through the streets of that reclaimed island goes a new messenger, the self of the king under some new representative; the intention, the spirit, of the king and of the conqueror, proceeding from the ruling father and the reconquering son. Through the whole land he goes, awakening everywhere the slumbering loyalty, bearing in his hands the righteous laws which show how their king loves them, planting *him* anew in every household, making men know that *he* is what their disorder needs to turn it into order, and what their misery needs to make it prosperous. And shortly, out of the farthest corners and the inmost center of the land, there rises a great stir of loyalty. The mountains blaze with bonfires and the valleys ring with songs of reconciliation. The people have come back and found their king, and all the busy hum of renewed labor, and the shouts of joy that ring through all its life, are but that island's " Abba, Father " to its new-found lord.

This is the gospel of reconciliation. Father, Son, and Holy Spirit have met in their divine omnipotence to rescue man. Remember it does not float in the mere atmosphere of theory, where it seems, perhaps, as if we had placed it all. It is brought close to the heart that will receive it by all those languages which the heart knows best. The love of the Father is interpreted by all the tokens of His love which appeal to the lower lives. All nature, with her voices of beneficence, claims the Son for his Father. All the capacities of thought and feeling which are in him assert the Father whom they echo and from whom they came. And the redeeming Son is full of pitiful and powerful appeal by the tragedy of His cross. While He is conquering man out of his rebellion, He is at the same time winning his heart by suffering for him. And the Spirit who has brought Christ to us has shed His influence out of every most familiar and appealing thing. As the sun that lightens us makes all the objects round us the reflectors and distributers of his radiance, and so brings his light to us clothed with the clearness that belongs to them, so to the Christian the Spirit of his Saviour seems to have subsidized everything to make some new and more perfect revelation of Him. The home relations and the things in nature, our books, our friends, our thoughts, have all been made interpreters of Christ. Oh, there are times when, as one sits in meditation or moves quietly about in work for Jesus—when all this seems so rich and plain. A beautiful, serene simplicity seems to come forth out of this complicated snarl. We catch the music of one great pervading purpose in all this tumult and clatter. It is all *redemption* working out its plans. God made that hillside so perfect in order that He might show me His fatherly love. Christ gave me this task to do that I might understand His self-sacrifice for me. The Spirit brought me into my friend's friendship that it might so interpret to me the friendship of my God. At such times all seems plain. The world is for the sons of God, and all that goes on in the world is reclaiming and training their sonship. The whole creation is waiting for the manifestation of the sons of God. Those are the times when the world is ideal and beautiful and sacred.

It is always needful to ask what any general theory of life has to say to the great burdens and hindrances of living, to those things which are always coming in to make men tremble or rebel at life. No matter how noble or how compact your theory may be, if it has no word for these, no help for those who are suffering under these, it cannot take possession of men and hold them.

Let us ask, then, What has this gospel of reconciliation to say to *trouble*, to those keen hours of suffering when the light seems to have gone wholly out of life under some cloud of sorrow? What had it to say to you when the light of your house was darkened and the life that had made your life worth living was snatched away from you? Whether it said anything to you depended upon whether you believed it, whether you had really caught sight of this as the purpose of all things—this plan of God to bring His children back to Himself. If you did see that, then the gospel of reconciliation had surely very much to say to you in your great grief. Of your friend—perhaps your child —who had gone it had to remind you that it certainly was not strange if God, whose one wish about all His children was that they should come to Him and know Him, had taken this, who to you seemed the most precious of all children of God, into His own more immediate presence, to teach and train his life with a directer ministry of His own. Death could not seem inexplicable or desperate to one who had caught sight of a design of life which issued from and which must return into the spiritual world, which did not begin and which could not be completed here. And for yourself, if that same plan included you, if for you too there was one supreme wish in your Father's heart that you should come perfectly to Him, then it was not strange —certainly it was not incredible—that He should have tried to draw you by taking to Himself that which was like your other life, your second self; and you could not have asked Him to spare you the pain if it was by the pain only that He could take hold of you. As well might the child complain of the tight, painful grasp with which his father seized him to drag him out of the river. Far be it from me to preach any mere cheeriness about sorrow or about death, as if it were a light and easy thing, easy to understand or easy to meet. My lips refuse to speak, and your hearts will not receive, such doctrine. Death is terrible. Its mystery grows deeper and deeper. No familiarity with it makes it anything but awful. But the gospel of reconciliation overleaps it, and on the other side shows the soul that has passed through it and been purified, we know not how, by it, received into the Father's house toward which it has so long been struggling. It cannot *explain* death—there can be no explanation till we each understand it by undergoing it; but it can, it *does*, overpass death and stretch its purposes of life into eternity.

It is not only the *suffering* in life that needs to be spoken to and helped. There is something else, I think, that is almost more exhausting than our suffering in its constant wearing pressure upon the hearts of men. It is that feeling of the *insignificance* of life that often grows so hard to bear. I am afraid that many of you know it only too well. Not merely on some moody day, but have you not felt it as the constant temper of long stretches of your life—the wonder whether it meant anything, the utter loss of any insight into what it meant, this work of living? That is what rubs deep into our strength with its dull and heavy friction. It rises up like a self-begotten mist out of ourselves. It is reflected and shed on us from other men around us. It haunts the home of poverty, and, even more bitter and disheartening, it sits down at the rich man's feast. Who can speak to and dispel this specter? Who can tell us with authority that life has a meaning, and make us see it and rejoice to live for it? Who but the gospel of reconciliation? If *that* is true, if all these heavenly forces are at work upon our life, if all this watchful interest hovers over what we are doing, if we may really go on and be the children of God, where is there any insignificant detail? Who can help feeling *purpose* run like life-blood through the half-dried veins of his discouragement? How life lifts itself up with interest and dignity when it really becomes the culture of God's redeemed children for their Father's house!

But there is something else. Deeper than suffering and insignificance lies *sin*. Ah, that is at the root of all. These are but the symptoms; this is the disease. And what has the gospel to say to sin? Ah, fancy Him who was the gospel meeting, as He walked in old Jerusalem, these woes and hindrances of human life which we have spoken of. He walks along, and first He meets a sufferer, some soul wrung with pain and bereavement. He stops and lays His hand upon the wretched head, and says, "Be comforted: thy brother shall rise again. I am the resurrection, and the life." Then He goes on and meets a poor man (poor or rich) fretted and wearied with the insignificance of life. To him He says, "Arise; be strong. He that believeth on Me, the works that I do shall he do also." But then He comes to another who is a sinner bowed down with sin, sorrowing and sighing because he is so wicked. Ah, how the Saviour's face lightens anew! This is the soul He wants. He came to seek and to save the lost. He was called Jesus, because He should save His people from their sins. And as He says to the poor soul, "Thy sins are forgiven thee," you are sure that the Saviour is speaking the words that He most loves to speak, and that the gospel of reconciliation is doing its deepest work.

Out of suffering, out of insignificance, out of sin, we come, by the love of God, by the Incarnation of Jesus, by the ministry of the Holy Spirit, into the full life of the sons of God. O my dear brethren, I claim you for that life. If you will read your own hearts you will know that you belong to God. If you will stand before Christ He will take you for God's. If you will open your heart to the Spirit He will bring you to God. And when you come there your heart will know the God whom it belongs to, and call Him Father.

Both here and hereafter it is only in being God's children that we are truly men. May God, who sent His Son into the world, send forth the Spirit of His Son into all our hearts, that we may know and love our Father.

VIII.

ASH WEDNESDAY.

"Blessed are they whose iniquities are forgiven, and whose sins are covered."—ROM. IV. 7.

ANOTHER Ash Wednesday opens for us to-day another Lent. If we have really swept aside our ordinary occupations and thoughts in any real way, it is that we may look in upon our own lives and souls, which our ordinary thoughts and occupations hide from us at other times, and see them as they really are. The abandonment of any thoughts or occupations is not something that is good in itself, unless the things which we give up are intrinsically bad, and then we ought to have nothing to do with them at any time, in Lent or out of it. It is the sight of ourselves which our simplified life in these weeks will give us that makes them valuable. It ought to be as when the clouds over a landscape part, and one who has been standing above, seeing only the clouds which the hot ground had flung up from its bosom, sees suddenly the landscape through the clouds—fields, woods, and hills lying quietly down below. So is it when a man for a few moments or a few days breaks through the cloud of crowded businesses that hide his soul from his own eyes and really sees himself.

And when a man sees himself he always sees sin. That is what gives Lent its sad and penitent color. Think what Lent, the days of self-sight, would be if it were not so. If men, pausing from their busy life and looking in upon the self that lived the life, found nothing there but perfect obedience and unbroken goodness, then with what a humble but perfect joy these weeks would be filled; and when they were over, how men would take up their active work again, with only a new thankfulness to the God who had kept them so pure, and with new trust that He would still preserve them! But now how different it is! He who would estimate himself must estimate his sin. Self-knowledge means humiliation. Not that there is only sin in us. To think that, to say that, of ourselves would be as false as if we said there was no sin at all. Men try to say that of themselves, and it makes all their effort to understand themselves unreal. No, there is much in us besides our sin which we must know in order that we may know ourselves. But there is sin, sin everywhere. It runs through every part of us—through mind and soul and body. We must understand it before we can understand ourselves, as we must understand salt before we can understand the sea; as we must know what fire is before we can comprehend the sun. And so Lent becomes the season of sadness and repentance, with the hope that is always born of thoroughness and earnestness burning underneath and keeping it from gloomy wretchedness.

On this first day of Lent, then, I must speak of *sin*. And just as soon as the word passes my lips I feel what a vague sound it has acquired. It has grown to be a word of sermons, sometimes a word of prayers, but it is not a word of men's most real thoughts very often. They think of this sin and of that sin; but of sin itself, as a persistent presence, as an element in life, but few men think. Shall we say that the trouble is in the word, and try to put some other word into its place? Oh no, the trouble is in the thing itself; it is the very thought of being wrong that is so vague to men. You never can make a half-apprehended idea clear by giving it a new word to call itself by. The new word, though it may have been so sharp-lined and concrete that you could take hold of it before, grows dim and misty the moment that you fasten it to an idea which men cannot or will not distinctly comprehend. It is not the *name* sin. It is the *thing* sin that is vague to us. I look about this morning upon earnest faces. You have not come to church—I will be sure that you have not come to church to-day at least—out of any curious idleness. Or if by chance any of you have so come, with those of you, at least, I cannot busy myself. God grant that the most trivial and unearnest of them may gather something out of the influences of the day! But my business on Ash Wednesday morning is with the earnest people—with you, dear friends, who really want to know yourselves. To know yourselves you must know sin; and so to take sin out of its vagueness and make it real, to pluck it out of abstractness and show how we can find it in our own history and hearts, will be my task this morning.

I have thought how I might do this best, and it has seemed to me that if we could perfectly understand any one sin that ever was committed—trace it completely from its beginning to its end—we could hardly help seeing what sin is. All sins are sinful. All sinfulness is one at heart. Let me really, deeply know how the mean, base, cruel thing which Simon Peter did when he denied Jesus in the hour of His bitter distress came to be done, and I shall know how Cain came to murder Abel, and how I came myself yesterday to do a deed that to-day fills me with shame. That is the sin which I have chosen for our study. We shall meet it fully, face to face, when the last week of Lent brings us to the trial of the Lord; but to-day let us quietly look at it from the beginning to the end—see where it came from, how it grew to ripeness, and by what death it died. The history of a sin—this is our subject.

I must take it for granted that you all know in general the story of St. Peter and his denial of the Lord. Assuming that, I shall have to speak about four points in the man's history which mark respectively the beginning of his chance to do his sin, the warning of his danger, the actual doing of it, and the removal of it by forgiveness. I can dwell but a few moments upon each.

1. The first scene takes us away back to the beginning of Christ's public work. It was the bright, fresh morning of the Gospel story. It was morning, too, upon the shining Lake of Gennesaret. The hills were bright around the lake; the lake within the hills was bright and leaping in the sunshine. Everything was full of life and youth. "And Jesus, walking by the Sea of Galilee, saw two brethren, Simon called Peter, and Andrew his brother, casting a net into the sea: for they were fishers. And He saith unto them, Follow Me,

and I will make you fishers of men. And they straightway left their nets, and followed Him." How ever new the sweet old story sounds! Simon called Peter left his net and followed Jesus. He went out of the old life into the untried new life,- following this Master. He went out to a friendship and a work that were to fill his days with delight and inspiration. He went to new thoughts, new hopes, new duties. But did he go to nothing else? As he turns and follows Jesus does he not go burdened with new *dangers* which he did not have before? The chance to be loyal to his new Master involves the chance to be disloyal to Him. The privilege of faithfulness carries with it the peril of unfaithfulness. If from that moment of his choice it is possible for him to acknowledge Christ, is it not possible also to deny Him? If the glory of the transfiguration mountain begins to glow before him, does not the tragedy of Pilate's judgment-hall also loom in sight? These two together, both half realized but both real, are in the face of Peter, making him sober and quiet in all his enthusiastic joy as with his brother he leaves his nets and goes where the wonderful Stranger leads.

And so it is with every call, with every privilege. To the sick man there comes back health. As he leaps from his bed and goes out into life with other men, does there not come to him a power of active wickedness as well as of active goodness that was not his when he lay languid in his weakness or tossing in his pain? To the poor man wealth is given. Is it not a new candidate for meanness as well as a new candidate for charity, who takes the unfamiliar bags of money into his trembling hands? To the childless man God sends a child. All the sins of fatherhood as well as all its noble virtues become possible with the first taking of that child into his arms. To the heathen man Christ is preached, and as he hears and believes, out of the darkness that has been crowded about his lot come flocking dangers of impiety and faithlessness shoulder to shoulder, hand in hand, with all the glorious hopes of his new life. There is where sin is born; there is the first opening of the chance of sin. No wonder that to any serious man privilege becomes a solemn thing. No wonder that the answer to a call of God is spoken out of lips that tremble with fear while they burn with love. No wonder that a man sits in his richened life, hardly knowing whether he is glad or sorry, awed and oppressed with the richness for which he has prayed, and which has been given to him in answer to his prayer.

Does not such a truth as this, when it is understood and deeply felt, make men reject the privileges which bring such dangers with them? Does it not make all conscientious and sin-fearing men seek a meager and restricted life, giving up much chance of goodness because of the chance of being bad that must come with it? Happily it is not so. It seems, indeed, as if there were two kinds of fear, one ignoble and paralyzing, the other noble and stimulating; and as if this fear of privilege were always *trying*, at least, to be of the noble sort. Sometimes it fails, and the men who see what danger privilege brings shrink from it altogether, and try to live the smallest life they can. But commonly the scale of men's construction is loftier than that. Commonly the man who is man enough to see this truth is man enough to meet it. It fills him with a soberness which is energy and not despair. And besides, men see that it is a danger which they *cannot* shirk. To avoid privilege in order to escape the chance of sin which it brings with it is essentially to commit the very sin of which we are afraid. For Peter to refuse to follow Jesus because he sees the denial looming in the distance is really only to anticipate his sin and to deny his Master *now*.

And yet another truth comes in here. We talk about the dangerous privileges that may be given men in life. But really it is *life itself* which is the dangerous privilege. The chance to sin is wrapped up in the very fact that we are men. We could not have the lofty hopes of heaven without having, too, the haunting fear of hell. Here is the only real light we get upon the problem of evil. It is not conceivable that man should have the chance of being good without the other chance of being bad. But then it follows that no man can escape from privilege till he escapes from life. You may disown this or that special call that comes to you, and so seem to have escaped the danger of the special sins that were awaiting you down these special paths; but still your human life remains. Still while you live you must be good or bad. And if you do the basest, meanest act that man is capable of, and by a cowardly suicide try to escape from life, still you have only condensed your treason to your privileges into one miserable deed. And who can say upon what strange yet familiar shore of the other world the disappointed suicide may find, to his dismay, that he has not escaped; may be appalled to meet his old humanity, which death could not kill, and have to take up for eternity the struggle from which no man can escape so long as he is man?

Here, then, is where our sins are born—deep in the bosom of our chances. How wonderful is the human nature which, in a world all filled with this truth, still, with its moral buoyancy, takes up its privileges with undying hope! Wonderful is that ineradicable heroism of humanity which makes danger a necessary element of joy. The wisest men go out to life, not with depression, but with serious joy, bearing within them their consciousness of privilege, made critical, made pathetic, made even glorious, by their possibility of wickedness.

2. I pass on to the next stage in the history of the sin of Peter. The scene is altered, yet the same; still the Lake of Gennesaret, where the disciple answered to the Master's call. Only now, not the bright morning and the solid shore, but the dark night and the howling tempest out on the middle of the lake; the shore out of sight, and through the darkness the figure of Jesus walking on the water toward the frightened boat. Then Peter, when he knows that it is Jesus, starts to go to Him across the water. "But when he saw the wind boisterous, he was afraid; and beginning to sink, he cried, saying, Lord, save me." Think of the man the moment afterward, when Jesus has taken him by the hand and held him up, and gently rebuked him for his faithlessness, and brought him into the boat again, and the wind has ceased and all is calm. See him sitting in silence and thoughtfulness. What has come to him? He has had *warning of his weakness*. He has

seen that there are possible moments when his faith in his Master may give way. The *chance* of sin, which, as we saw, was involved in the very following of Jesus, has stood up vividly before him, and is the *danger* of sin. However afterward, in eager self-assertion, he may say, "Though all men shall be offended because of Thee, yet will I never be offended," he never can say it with such perfect certainty as he could yesterday, or as he could the moment when he stepped down from the ship's side upon the water. That is what has come over him and made him thoughtful. Henceforth he never can be the perfectly buoyant Peter that he has been hitherto. He must always think differently of himself. He must always look on his Master's face with other eyes. He has caught sight of the possibility of denying Him. He has had warning of his coming sin.

Such warnings come in the lives of all of us who have any thoughtfulness. Just as before a great invention opens its full wonder on the world the brain of the inventor is haunted with visions of the coming moment in which the perplexed conditions shall all fall into their places and the destined miracle be born; just as before some great act of self-sacrifice startles and delights the eyes of men the soul that is to do it feels in itself the movement of capacities for self-surrender which it cannot really believe that it possesses, so the warning of the sin that is to tear one's life asunder, the first dim thought that possibly the dreadful thing is possible, comes long before the sin is done. No sin is sudden. The warning may be only half recognized, but when the sin of our life comes, who of us has not felt, strangely mingled with its strangeness, a certain dreadful familiarity, such as one might feel when a man whom he had never seen, but of whom he dreamed last night, and whose face he remembered from the dream, stepped in the living flesh across his threshold? Let me try to point out some few of the ways in which such warnings come to us; though, indeed, this stage of a sin's history is so occult and subtle that no enumeration of special forms that it may take can do more than suggest its character. Sometimes a man undertakes a task which he thinks is pure supererogation. He is not bound to do it. He might leave it undone and yet do all his duty. He thinks that his real life is not staked upon this venture. Out of mere excess of moral vitality he undertakes some moral feat, some piece of quixotic charity, some exercise of honesty beyond the strictest standards or most scrupulous scruples of the best men. That really was what Peter did when he offered the undemanded trust in Jesus of the walk upon the water. The man fails in his self-appointed task. The extra strain upon his moral power is too great for him. He goes back to his assigned duty, his expected work. But he has touched the point of weakness. His strength no longer seems to him infinite, and thenceforth through his safest doing of his daily tasks must run the knowledge that there is a point where conscience will be too weak and resolution will break down. The athlete who has recklessly tried to lift his five hundred pounds and failed has caught sight of the possible day when he shall fail to lift the two hundred which is so easy to him now.

Or again, a man finds himself doing just the opposite of this. He catches himself questioning duty to see how little he can get along with and yet be dutiful. The man in business, spurning the very thought of cheating, as ready as he ever was to strike down any man who dared approach him with temptation, finds himself some day questioning duty and trying to make it say that it is not duty, or seeing how close he can run under the lee of a doubtful transaction and yet sail out safe. He has not sinned, but if he is a sensitive and thoughtful man he sees, as he opens his eyes to what he is doing, how he *might* sin. He shudders as a man might who, walking in his sleep, woke up and found that what he thought was music is the roaring in his ears of the chasm on whose brink he stands. His coming sin has given him its warning.

Or yet again, a man here by my side does a sin whose very form my imagination has never pictured to itself. I expect to find myself all full of horror, but to my surprise a strange sort of sympathy takes possession of me instead. I expect to be filled with loathing for the wicked man, but instead of that I find myself forgetting him altogether, and deep unfamiliar questions about myself are stirring in my soul. Some bolt in the mysterious chambers of my self-consciousness has been pushed back. Not merely, that man is what I might have been; that man is what I *may be*. The sin of which I stand in danger has given me its warning.

Or once more, just the opposite of this may happen. A pure, bright spirit who has been by my side suddenly leaves me. Some sudden call, to which its bright ambition instantly responds, lifts it out of the round of commonplace faithfulness, and it is doing some heroic, some angelic thing. I instinctively try to follow it. It is as if a bird and a beast that had been shut up forty days together in the ark, and had grown to be friends in the sympathy of that restricted life, were let loose together upon Ararat, and as the bird soared to the open sky that it was made for, the poor beast felt for the first time what a heavy and clumsy beast it was. So the sight of the best things that the best men do, if it stirs me at all, shows me how near the limit of my power I am living, how little margin I have, and the day when my strength shall fail even *within* its limits; the warning of my coming sin grows up before me.

These and a multitude of others like them are the times when the unborn sin stirs in the womb of the chance where it is hidden. It is like the gathering of a coming bankruptcy. The merchant will not own it even to himself, but when the day of his suspension comes it is not sudden. It is like the approach of death. The man assures himself, in spite of every symptom, that he is a well man still; but when you tell him he must die he is not surprised. You never did a sin that did not give its warning so to you before you did it. Perhaps you did not hear, but it was not that the warning bell did not ring. Perhaps you called that first sign of weakness a mere accident, and tried to believe that it meant nothing; but if you gave your thought to it you knew it was not so. You knew it was the house's feeble timbers creaking before their fall. There are such warnings of coming sins that every one of us here has received—sins yet undone; sins which, it may be, are to make our whole life dark some day, whose threatening we can read, if we are only wise enough, in something that has come to us already. Once you have drawn back from duty because it looked hard. It was only for a moment. The next instant you were on your feet again, and did the duty bravely; but it gave you a glimpse of the dreadful days of self-indulgent idleness and uselessness and moral degeneration that might come. Once you have trembled under some very zephyr of an evil passion. It was the first warning of the tempest of lust which may come howling about your purity some day. Once you coveted what was not yours, trembled just for a moment on that high ground of calm content and happy honesty on which you stand. That moment you got a sight into the dark depths of a thief's life. Life is full of such warnings. No man grows to be more than a mere boy without learning on what side of his moral nature he will fall if he falls at all. Every one of us knows, who is in the least thoughtful, what sort of villain he would be if he grew villainous. Thank God, these warnings may save us from the things they warn us of. These blessed bells that ring out in the darkness may turn us resolutely off from the cruel surf that roars behind them. Peter may be all the more faithful when the great night of his Master's trial and his own shall come, because his faith once failed him on the lake. Only, such a strange, unreasonable mystery is this human nature, the bell that warns one man from his ruin may be the very fascination that drags another to his fate. There is a mysterious reversal of our whole moral machinery which sometimes takes place, by which the more we are warned of the danger of a sin, and of the misery that it will bring, the more we hurry on to complete it and see it out to its very worst. Oh, how our poor souls need to pray continually, " O Lord, not only send Thy warnings and give us ears to hear them, but give us hearts to know how dreadful is the sin they prophesy"! Not merely intelligence—that never saved a man alone; but a changed heart, which, like the heart of God, shall dread and hate a coming sin.

3. But we must hasten on. And the next step brings us to what these first two stages have been foretelling. Again the scene is changed. But Peter and Jesus are still there, the sinner and his Lord; as they have been in both the other scenes, so they are here. It is the high priest's palace. And as Peter stood there, a man " confidently affirmed, saying, Of a truth this fellow also was with Him; for he is a Galilean. And Peter said, Man, I know not what thou sayest. . . . And the Lord turned, and looked upon Peter. . . . And Peter went out, and wept bitterly." The deed is done! the sin is committed! How quick it was! how simple! Away back on that sweet morning by the lakeside it became possible. Here in the grim hall of the high priest the thing is done. How quick! how simple! The elements have met, and see! the flame is burning. I doubt not the first feeling that a man has who has done a flagrant sin must be wonder at its wonderful simplicity. Is it possible that that little blow has killed the man? Is it possible that between ten o'clock and two minutes past ten I have become a thief? The Lord turns and looks upon Peter, and he knows that it is true. The look recalls the past, and all the preparation of the sin which is back there gathers up around the present to assure him that it is

really done. The voice of the Lord had called him across the waters of the lake. The hand of the Lord had caught him when he was just going to sink. Now the eye of the Lord sends all that past into his soul and bears him witness with its piercing sorrow that the dreadful development is finished, and the sin that has been seeking birth so long is born at last.

These two influences, I think, were in the look that Jesus cast on Peter. It recalled the past, so that the man became aware how far back the roots of this sin ran; and it was full of present pain, so that he knew what a terrible critical thing it was that he had just done. These two things every sinner needs to know about the sin he has committed. All its long preparation must give it solemnity. It must seem to be not the sudden birth of one bad moment, and yet the one bad moment must lose none of its conscious badness, its manifest responsibility, by the extension of the sin's history back into the past. Its long maturing must pour its seriousness into the final moment when the man at last chose whether he would crown the process with the conclusive word or fatal deed. Indeed, all life is made up of these two elements—long, silent growths and quick, decisive actions. The sacredness, the awfulness of life lies in the two together. The soberness of life is kept by the fact that nothing in the world is sudden. The intensity of life is kept by the fact that everything is sudden. In these two elements we have the full consciousness of the man who has just done a sin and sits in his place and thinks of it. At once his past life has reached out all its myriad arms, and seems to be holding him helpless, and out from the very ground at his feet a terrible power has sprung forth and seized him. His whole habitual character and his single present will—both of them are wrong. He asks what he is to do, and he sees that it is not enough to repent of this one moment, as one might pluck a single unaccountable weed out of his garden and go his way rejoicing that now his garden is all pure. He must repent of all the past. He must renew the very soil. He must struggle not merely with the circumstances that made this special sin, but with his whole sinful self. And yet here is this one special immediate sin standing black before his eyes, crying out hoarsely in his ears. Repentance is so vast, so thorough, as one sees it then. It is the casting of this one rebellious will upon the altar. It is the casting of the rebellious heart upon the altar, too. All this grows clear to the poor sinner as he sits with the fresh misery of his sin upon him, or as he turns and goes out from the high priest's hall. In one quick moment everything is altered. The great dark walls are there, the group about the fire, the servants passing to and fro, the inner chamber with the eager accusers and their prisoner and the high priest —all that is there as it was a minute back; but everything is altered. The poor man's heart is broken. His past is all powerless. The present moment is trembling on the border of despair, for he has done his sin.

4. Only one more scene remains to complete the history, and we are taken back again from the great city to the quiet lake to find it. Jesus has been crucified, dead, and buried, and He has risen from the dead, and now once more He stands on the same bank of the lake where He stood three years ago. Peter again, just as

on that never-forgotten morning, is off on the water in his boat. Jesus calls to him again and tells him where the fish are to be caught. Peter is dazed and bewildered; but the moment that John, with his quicker insight, tells him that the stranger is their Lord he is in the water, and the next instant he is at the feet of Jesus, and Jesus by and by is telling him, in words in which, if there is any reproach, it makes the welcome only more sweet and gracious, of the work he is to do for Him. Look at them there and say where is the sin that we have seen grow up between them, and that came to its completion on that dreadful night in the high priest's palace. You say, "It is forgiven!" But was there ever set forth the simplicity, the marvelous simplicity, of forgiveness as it was set forth there? Where are the hard conditions with which men and churches have surrounded it? There is no sign of penance; nay, there is not even confession. Peter does not even say, "I have sinned." He does not even declare his resolution, "I will sin no more." There he is, simply able to look up in the face of Jesus and say, "Thou knowest that I love Thee," and waiting for the Lord to tell him what his work shall be. I think there is something nobly beautiful in Peter's perfect confidence in Jesus. He knew Him so well. He knew that Jesus wanted that dreadful sin out of the way as much as he did. He knew that Jesus would not keep the sin there one moment after it might be forgiven, waiting for any kind of expiation or atonement. And so the moment that he had repented he knew that Jesus had forgiven, and he came, not with passionate prayers, as if he had to wring forgiveness from reluctant hands,

ASH WEDNESDAY. 127

but with the overflowing joy of gratitude, and with a heart leaping with desire to manifest its love.

Ah, my friends, there is the true end of a sin. The true sign of forgiveness is not some mysterious signal waved from the sky; not some obscure emotion hunted out in your heart; not some stray text culled out of your Bible; certainly not some word of mortal priest telling you that your satisfaction is complete. The soul full of responsive love to Christ, and ready, longing, hungry to serve Him, is its own sign of forgiveness. Must there not be sorrow for sin? Can you picture this loving, waiting soul rejoicing in the memory of its wickedness, gloating upon its old unholy joy? Must there not be resolution of amendment? Surely there must; but do you want it in cold, hard words, or leaping in passionate desire of a new life from the eager eyes? Surely it is not sorrow for sin, for the sake of the sorrowfulness, that Jesus ever wants. He is no such cruel inquisitor as that. He wants sorrow for sin only that it may bring escape from sin; and when the sorrow for sin which wept in the street outside the high priest's palace turns its other side and is joy in renewed devotion such as burst out confidingly by the lakeside, I am sure no Christ that we believe in can do anything but welcome it. I think that with all we know of the divine heart of Jesus He would far rather see a soul trust Him too much, if that is possible, than trust Him too little, which we know is possible enough. When a man who has sinned, and who, like Simon Peter, has not a shadow or a ghost of an excuse to offer for his sin, has so known Christ that he never thinks of Him as one to be propitiated, never doubts for an instant that if he is forgivable he is forgiven, and so lets his hatred of his old sin break out in an utterance of his love for the Holy One, and lets his sorrow for his treason only show itself in his desire for loyal work, then that poor sinner's sin is dead and gone. When it went he may not be able to say. But here is the pure, clear air between him and his Lord. The sin is not in that. It must be dead and gone.

And yet that is not wholly true. The sins Christ has forgiven are dead, but they are not gone. If none of the dead go from us, if when death comes a new and finer life begins, and he whom we call dead is with us in sweetest, subtlest portion of his life, with everything of harshness, every disagreement, every power of harm taken out, why may it not be so with our dead sins? It is so, surely! There is a soul in them which lives on still while their body of wickedness has perished— a soul of patience, of watchfulness, of gratitude, and of never-dying love. O my dear friends, we have not done with a sin of ours, we have not finished its history, until, long, long after it has died in the kind forgiveness of the Saviour, we have traced the eternal career of the spirit which its death has liberated into life, giving steadfastness to duty, and charity to friendship, and unutterable tenderness to the love of the Saviour till eternity shall end.

That is what our sins shall be to us forever. They die as sins in forgiveness that they may live forever as the impulses of holiness and the exhaustless fountains of love. The sin that never dies that death of forgiveness lives on as sin. This is the difference of the sin of Judas and the sin of Peter. The sin of Judas sails right on to ever-growing sin, to ever-growing misery. The sin of Peter dies in pardon to live again in grateful love; and he who has sinned and been forgiven finds in his new life with his Master the old life restored, but deepened and fulfilled. We leave by the lakeside him whom we found there, and the same Jesus is with him. But his knowledge and his love have been transfigured by all that has come in between. He is richer by the history of his sin.

They say in England that as the wind blows on Ash Wednesday so it will blow the whole of Lent. Oh, if to-day our Lord would send us deep, true, simple thoughts of sin, making us see how the chance of it is bound up in our very manhood, how the warning of it sounds through all our life, how the doing of it is something on whose brink we are always walking, and how the forgiveness of it is ready in the merciful hands! Oh that all this might be with us so thoroughly to-day that these coming weeks might be filled to the brim with seriousness and thoughtfulness and fear and hope! Then, indeed, God's blessing should be upon our Lent. Oh, may He grant it, for Christ's sake!

IX.

FIRST SUNDAY IN LENT.

"Then was Jesus led up of the Spirit into the wilderness to be tempted of the devil."—MATT. IV. 1.

THE temptation of Jesus is certainly a very wonderful event. There is no incident in all His history on which the imagination may expend itself with a more lavish speculation; and, on the other hand, there is none that comes nearer to practical life with stimulus and comfort. Christ, with His baptism just accomplished, went into the desert, and after He had fasted forty days and was become very hungry, the devil came to Him and tempted Him. The story is familiar to us all. It is far too large to treat generally in a single sermon; but, assuming a knowledge of the incident, I want to make a few suggestions to-day, first upon the *fact*, then upon the *purpose*, and then upon the *method* of our Lord's temptation.

1. And first of all, how strange it seems to us sometimes that there should be such a thing as temptation in the world at all! However we explain it, whatever glimpses we get of its meaning, it must always be strange to us. God sends us into the world and hangs in the great distance before us certain lofty prizes—goodness, truth, purity—which He has made our hearts capable of

FIRST SUNDAY IN LENT. 131

desiring. He starts us out toward those prizes. There they hang attracting us. Our souls really desire them. But we have not really started toward them before the presence of another power begins to show itself. Hands pluck at us to draw us out of the straight way. Voices call to us with enticements or with threats to make us turn aside. A tempting figure lifts itself close beside our pathway. Once begun, that experience never ends. We never get rid of temptation. We give up one form of occupation and think to escape being tempted, and the same enticement to sin in some new shape intrudes itself right in the midst of our new task. No adoption of any strict rule of life, no separation of ourselves from a certain region of dangerous occupations, sets us free from the persecution of temptation. We are tempted to sin everywhere. It is pathetic, almost terrible, to think how long this has been going on. Through all those weary years which it tires us to think of, they have been so many; through all those monotonous generations that we hear flowing on endlessly through the cavernous depths of history, as one listens to a stream dropping down monotonously forever underground; through all the years and generations of human life men have been tempted—not one that ever lived that did not meet this persistent, intrusive enticement to sin. It was not strange that some men learned to doubt of a God at all. It was not strange that other men came to believe that the world had two masters, almost equal rivals in power, and was divided between God and God's enemy. It is only strange that with this endlessly reiterated experience so many men were able to keep on believing in one good almighty God.

It shows how dear and near that great belief lies to the human heart, that not even its own sharp, clear experience can slip in between and separate them.

And now what effect has this temptation of our Lord upon this strange universal experience of men? That which is strange and universal is apt to become unreal to men. They explain it away. They become deadened and deafened to it. And men in many ways have tried to get rid of this persistent, puzzling fact of a great, wide, evil influence in the world trying to allure men into sin. It is a mere form of education, they declare. It is a mere phase in man's upward growth. "It is not possible"—so runs the instinctive remonstrance of the heart—"it is not possible that every man, to come to God, must come through fire. It is not possible that every soul must walk the dizzy verge of sin and ruin before he comes to holiness and life. It would make the world too terrible." And then, with men saying and feeling that, there comes the incarnate Christ. Summing up humanity into Himself, He lives the human life, and lo! right at the very gate of it He meets temptation. There stands the fact. I do not know that the temptation of Jesus makes one whit more plain the awful mystery of the presence and origin of sin. It does not tell us why that precipice of temptation must skirt the human life. It does not tell us what the devil is. But it declares the fact of temptation. It declares that there is a devil, and that all men must go through the danger of sin. All theoretical possibilities disappear before the convincingness of that sight. It is as if we had been studying our own projection of the heavens in our library and said, "There can be no star just there, in that spot of the sky—there is no room for it there," and then stepped outside our door and looked up at the heavens, and there burned the star that we said could not be, just in the very spot where we could see no room for it. So, if a man receives the story of Christ being submitted to temptation, all his own theories that God could not let His children be tempted must give way. Here is the Son of God, and to Him the devil finds free access. The fact stands plain to Him upon the old hill of Quaritania. The man who has seen Christ tempted will not deny temptation thenceforth. He will not be found explaining it away. He will not delude himself with vain hopes of escaping it and living a smooth, untempted life. He will read in the temptation of the perfect Life that that is impossible forever for any man. When he is depressed and hungry and exhausted, he will look for the devil as his Lord did, and when he sees him coming, when he hears his words and feels the desire of sin stirring in his heart, he will not say, "Oh, this is nothing but one stage of my growth." He will recognize the old enemy of his Master coming for the old battle, and gather up his strength and pray for his Master's strength in the hour of terrible, inevitable struggle.

One other truth comes out from the very fact of our Lord's temptation. It is the truth of the real limits of sin. It makes us see where sin begins, and keeps us from thinking that to be sinful which is really innocent— an error which is hardly less dangerous sometimes than to think that innocent which is really sinful. It makes us see that temptation is not sin, nor does it necessarily involve sin. Christ was sinless and yet tempted; therefore it is possible for man to be tempted and yet sinless. Now so many of us, the moment we are strongly tempted, seem to fall into a sort of demoralized condition, as if our innocence were over, as if the charm were broken and we were already sinners; and so we too often give ourselves up easily to the sin. A man goes on through his boyhood in the sweet purity of unconsciousness. What a heaven, what a very garden of Eden, as he looks back upon it out of the hot life that comes afterward, seems that quiet, untempted region lying cool between its four rivers, fresh from the creative hand of God! But by and by the lusts awoke. The time came when the things about him, which he had found pure while he looked on them with pure eyes, sent out a wholly new character, and began to entice and threaten and allure his soul to vice. To many men the first discovery of that capacity of being tempted by something which had been pure to them before is such a shock that it seems as if the sin were done already. The very power to be tempted seems to be a degradation, and, losing our pride, our hope, our loyalty, our courage, we fall with a too terribly easy ease. It is as if a soldier, approached with a bribe and asked to be a traitor, should be so humiliated that any man should think him possibly capable of treason that he should seem to himself almost a traitor already, and so cross the line which seemed to him so narrow and become a traitor really. To any soul in such a state what could we say but this: "Look up and see the truth in Jesus; do you not see it there? To be tempted is not wicked, is not shameful, is not unworthy even of Him. It is the lot, in one view it is even the glory, of humanity.

FIRST SUNDAY IN LENT.   135

Sin does not begin and shame does not begin until the will gives way, until you yield to temptation. Stand guard over that will, resist temptation, and then to have been tempted shall be to you what it was to your Saviour —a glory and a crown, a part of your history worthy to be written with thanksgiving in the Book of Life, as His is written in His book of life." Is not this the strength and courage that many a soul needs?

If this be true, then any temptation through which a man may go without yielding is a glory and a strength. But this brings in another point. Shall men go on courting temptations, finding them out, and running into them, so that they may come out glorious and strong? Again, look at Christ's temptation. There is one phrase there which lights up the whole story. Christ was "led up *of the Spirit* to be tempted of the devil." He had a certain work to do. That work was not His own, but was His Father's. His Father's Spirit guided Him and told Him how to do it. For some reason (who but that Spirit can say wholly what?) it was necessary in the doing of His work that He should meet the devil in the wilderness. Therefore the Spirit led Him there, and, filled with the Spirit all the time that He was there, by and by He came down safe and victorious. My dear friends, we too have a work, a duty. Our Father gives it to us as His Father gave His to Jesus. In doing our duty the Spirit of our Father may often lead us into temptation, but if He really leads us there He will protect us there. If He does not lead us, if we go of our own self-will, we have no pledge of His protection. We leave at the door the Guide whose company is safety. We have no more right, then, to expect to be kept from sin than Jesus would have had to expect to be kept from death if a little later, in His own self-will, He had really cast Himself down off of the temple. Here is the true distinction. Every temptation into which God's Spirit leads you you may hope to conquer. Into every temptation which you enter of your own self-will you carry a weakness that already prophesies defeat. If your duty lies right by the gates of hell, walk there boldly, and the gates of hell shall not prevail against you. If your duty does not carry you there you cannot be too fastidiously careful for your purity, to keep it out of the way of every lightest zephyr of temptation. Such is the manifest difference of the temptations into which God leads us and those into which we run ourselves.

For God does lead us into temptation. Let us always remember that that petition of the Lord's Prayer which anxious souls have prayed for centuries, "Lead us not into temptation," is always prayed just as that other one is prayed, " Give us this day our daily bread." Both are prayed with a clear sight of the possibility that God may see it best for higher purposes to do just the opposite—to cut off our daily bread, to break up the walls about us and lead us right into temptation. Both are prayed as all prayers must be prayed—as loving, trusting, filial confidences, telling our Father what we wish that He would do, and begging Him just as much to do the opposite if He sees that we are wrong and that the opposite is better for us.

2. So much we say of the mere fact of our Lord's temptation. But there is something more than this. We are almost compelled to ask what we can know

about the *purpose* of it. Why should the Saviour coming into the world have been subjected to these attacks of sin? Can we give any answer to that question? Not the whole answer, certainly! We must know a great deal more of the mystery of the Incarnation than we know yet before we can open the heart of God and see the meaning of all the phases through which the incarnate Life was led. But something we can see. There are three suggestions as to how it came about that Christ was tempted, each of which has comfort and assurance in it for us who follow Him and are tempted too. The first thought is that the temptation was involved in the Incarnation—that it was necessary; that it could not be avoided. That is purpose enough. If you meet a man in a steamer going to Europe, and ask him why he came to sea, he tells you what his business is in Europe—why he had to go there. The purpose of his going there is his purpose in crossing the sea. He could not do one without the other. And so we can well believe that the perfect holiness could not come into this wicked world to save us without coming to struggle with the sin of which the world is full. The Incarnation was a real incarnation. Christ did not play at being made man. Into everything that really belongs to humanity He perfectly entered. Only because sin does not really belong to humanity, but is an intrusion, an excrescence, He did not enter into that. But on the human nature into which He did enter sin had seized, and when He came He found sin there and the fight was inevitable. Surely it gives us a deep idea of how thoroughly Christ was made man, of the humiliation which He undertook for us when He was made man, and of the inveteracy and universality of sin in our human life, when we think that the Incarnation was impossible without a temptation; that Jesus could not come into the world without meeting the enemy who claims the world for his own. If this is true, then the love that brought the Saviour to the world is reason enough for His temptations. But we can see other purposes which must have had something to do with it. It must have had something to do with the developing self-consciousness of Christ. It belongs to that group of events in what is the springtime of the life of Jesus, when His power and work were breaking its restraints and issuing into the summer of full activity. The springtime is always full of sweet tumult and mystery; but its great idea, manifest everywhere, is education, the bringing forth of life. Now certainly Jesus was being educated there in the wilderness. When the devil said to Him, "Do this," and He, turning it over in His perfect mind, saw that to do that would be to disown His Father, and so indignantly refused to do it, what was going on? The knowledge of His Father, the need, towering above all other needs, of honoring Him, the sense of His mission of struggle and victory, the need and glory of resting on His Father's strength—all these were growing strong in Him there. He was grasping and trying the sword of the Spirit. When He came down out of the wilderness He knew all these things by heart. He was holding the sword of the Spirit strongly in both hands. And then the other thought is this: that a part of the purpose of our Lord's temptation must be in its power of example and influence for us. He was the leader of men into the new life, and so He must go the way that they would have to go. If mankind were to be led home into the city of God, it might be by an angel flying overhead, clear above all the tops of the trees through which they had to force their way, out of sound of the roaring torrents they had got to cross; or it might be by a Man walking before them, planting His feet first in the pathless ways where the serpents might be lurking, wetting His foot first in every cold stream that His followers would have to ford. Millions of men who would have lost sight of the angel will follow the fellow-man. He bears every difficulty first, and many of the difficulties He takes away by bearing them, so that His followers do not have to bear them at all; as he who walks first through a forest breaks down many a branch, so that his followers easily tread underfoot what he has once for all cast down. This is the power of example and vicarious leadership in Christ's temptation.

What other purposes there may have been we cannot say, but we are very sure that these purposes were in that wonderful event; it was inevitable; it was part of Christ's education; it was for the example and salvation of mankind.

And now may we not take these same purposes and find them in any temptation into which God's Spirit really leads any of our struggling souls? You, my dear brother, are tempted terribly to do some wicked thing. Will it not help you if you can have some sort of answer to the question that is crowding on your heart: "Why does God let me be so tempted? How is it possible that He can let His child be so buffeted and enticed by sin?". The answer comes from the manifest purposes of your Lord's temptation. It is inevitable for you, just as it was for Him. You cannot be man and live a man's life without coming into this world where sin is and where you must be tried. He cannot save you from it without taking you out of manhood and lifting you into some superior life where all that is dear, as well as all that is dangerous, in this human life shall be left behind you. That is one reason. And the next is that you are being educated here. That great temptation that comes swaggering up and frightening you so has got the best part of your character held under his brawny arm. You cannot get it without wrestling with him and forcing it away from him. That mountain that towers up and defies you has got your spiritual health away up on its snowy summit. That is what shines there in the sun. You cannot reach it except by the terrible climb. Ask yourself what you would have been if you had never been tempted, and own what a blessed thing the educating power of temptation is. And then the third purpose comes in too. As Christ's temptation was vicarious, and when He conquered He conquered for others besides Himself, so it is with us. There are men and women all around us who have got to meet the same temptations that we are meeting. Will it help them or not to know that we have met them and conquered them? Will it help us or not to know that if we conquer the temptation we conquer not for ourselves only, but for them? Will it help the master of a great business house or not to know that if he resists the temptation to cheat on a large scale it will help every clerk at the counter to resist his petty temptation to his little fraud? Will it help a father to keep sober or not if he knows that in his victory over drink his son's victory becomes easier? The vicariousness of all life! There is not one of us who has not some one more or less remotely fastened to his acts, concerning whom he may say, as Christ said, "For their sakes I sanctify myself."

These are the purposes of temptation. Let a man feel them, and they take all whine out of him and put all manliness into him. Let a man feel them all, and then, as temptation comes, he gives it a brave and humble welcome. "Come on," he says. "I am going to be tempted. I am going to meet the inevitable necessity of my manhood. I am going to meet the chance of being a better man. I am going into a dark, rough path, which, if I walk it well, shall be smoother and brighter for other men who are to walk it afterward." Can you conceive of a man meeting temptation so manfully as that and not conquering it? And remember, it is only into the temptations where it is at least possible for these purposes to be fulfilled that the Spirit of God ever leads a man, or a man ever has a right to go. Is there not here a practical rule? What a line it draws! That man who seeks the drinking-shop of his own free will is going neither by a necessity of his manhood, nor for education, nor for example to others. He has no business there. It is not God's Spirit that is leading him. That young boy who went out of the pure atmosphere of a carefully guarded home into the corruption of the regiment and the camp went because he could not stay away and be a man; because there was the chance there to be made purer; because if he were pure there other men around him would be pure too, by his purity. It was God's Spirit that called him out to be tempted of the devil. So may we always test our temptations.

3. And now that we have spoken of the fact and purpose of our Lord's temptation, let us say a few words about its *method*. This takes us a little more into detail, and obliges us to recall the three different approaches that the evil spirit made to Christ. We can say only a word on each. I hope you remember the story well enough to follow me. The first temptation is told thus. Remember He was all worn out and hungry. "And when the tempter came to Him, he said, If Thou be the Son of God, command that these stones be made bread. But He answered and said, It is written, Man shall not live by bread alone, but by every word that proceedeth out of the mouth of God." Now see what that temptation was. It appealed to the healthy senses of man. It said, "You need food. God made food for you. God gave you the power to make it for yourself. Now use your power and fulfil God's will." And there was the hunger gnawing all the while and saying "Amen" to the devil's words. Jesus knew that bread was good. When He was made man He was made to need bread just like the humblest and most degraded being who wore a human body. There was nothing low in the desire. Man was made to live by bread; only—and here comes in Christ's noble sword of the Spirit, cutting the knot of the specious temptation right in two—only, man was not made to live by bread alone. God gives him bread to live by; but when the Giver of the bread puts out His hand upon the loaf and says, "Stop! Now there is a higher life than that which is fed by the tasting of bread, and that is fed by the not tasting it";

when He who gave the body its food takes that away in order to feed the soul, and sends hunger because only by hunger can come truth, what shall he say but this: "Man shall not live by bread alone, so I shall not wonder even when He takes the bread away, nor dare nor wish to interfere"?

So far from thinking it strange that Christ should have felt the pangs of hunger and the craving after food, I cannot but believe, believing, as I do, in His perfect humanity, that food had a healthy beauty and delight for Him just in proportion to His perfectness. I believe that there was never a man in whom every keen appetite of human life was so alert and strong. I believe that to His eyes the blue skies were bluer and the green carpet of the earth greener than any duller eyes have ever seen them. His ears heard something in the insect's chirp and the bird's song that no other ears have ever caught. No other man has known the wind so fresh, the flower so fragrant, or the sun so bright. The beauty of the world and the joy of living in it have never come so near to any senses as they poured themselves into the perfect perceptions of the Man of Nazareth. And so we can know nothing of the degree of that temptation which He conquered when He said, "Yes, they are all good and beautiful, but they must all break away to let down on Me what is worth them all—one clear utterance of the will of God: 'Man shall not live by bread alone, but by every word that proceedeth out of the mouth of God.'"

Do you not see what the temptation was and what it is forever? O my dear friend, God made these things, and made you to live by them, but not by them alone.

Go on; gather the joy out of the earth and sky, out of the bread He gives you power to win, out of the water that He makes to gush at your feet; only, when the time comes—as it is sure to come some time, as perhaps it is to come now—when, in order to speak some word out of His mouth to you, some word of duty or charity or holiness, He takes these things away, and you are tempted to shut your ear to His word in order that you may keep these pleasant things, then you are just where Jesus was—the devil is at your ear. May God help you to see what Jesus saw—what He said afterward, perhaps remembering His own temptation: "The life is more than meat." May He help you to say, "No! Nothing—not even His gifts—shall blind or deafen me to Him. Man shall not live by bread alone, but by every word out of the mouth of God"—the blessed sacrifice cf sense to spirit.

What was the next temptation? St. Matthew tells it as simply as he told the first: "Then the devil taketh Him up into the Holy City, and setteth Him on a pinnacle of the temple, and saith unto Him, If Thou be the Son of God, cast Thyself down: for it is written, He shall give His angels charge concerning Thee: and in their hands they shall bear Thee up, lest at any time Thou dash Thy foot against a stone." And Jesus answered, "It is written again, Thou shalt not tempt the Lord thy God." The exact nature of the transaction need not concern us now. History or parable, its lesson is the same. And what is it? "If Thou be the Son of God, cast Thyself down." The appeal is made to the deepest self-knowledge of Jesus. He knew that He was the Son of God. Just before He came into the wilderness, at His baptism, His Father had claimed Him from the opened sky, saying, "This is My beloved Son!" and we cannot tell what memories and sympathies, what a flood of self-witness, that voice stirred in the soul of the divine Lord, just becoming conscious of His own divinity. He knew that He was God's Son, and yet here He seemed deserted and shut out and lost. He could not recognize or find His Father. That must have been a pain to Him to which the hunger of the body was nothing, that hunger of the soul. And then the devil says, "Prove your Sonship; find your Father, force Him to own you by flinging yourself into a danger from which He must save you." It was an appeal to the spiritual nature—a more trying temptation to a more sensitive part of the being than before. And what does Jesus say? How calm His answer is! "No! I must not tempt the Lord My God. I *am* His Son. I know it even when I seem most deserted. It is not Mine to dictate how He shall show His Fatherhood. It is not Mine to create difficulties just that His fatherly care may conquer them. Let Me wait, and in His own good time and way He will show Himself to Me more clearly than if His hand caught Me half-way between the pinnacle and the pavement." Do we know anything about that temptation? Does any such enticing whisper ever creep into our ears? "I am a Christian, and so Christ must keep me, and I can go here and be safe, I can walk through that mire and not be defiled, I can walk through that fire and not be burned. I am a Christian—Christ holds me in the hands of His supernatural grace; and so the natural care and caution, the watchfulness over my actions, is less necessary to me."

Do we know anything of that spirit? If ever our religion has weakened our moral vigor instead of strengthening it, if ever we have forgotten that we are made Christians, not that we may be freed from any responsibilities, but that we may take every responsibility more steadily on shoulders made strong for it by the strength of Christ; if ever in any way the thought of spiritual privilege has tried to draw us away from the everlasting, central thought of duty, the absolute necessity of watchfulness and faithfulness; if ever, in order to realize God more completely, you have been tempted to go out of the path of simple duty where He has set you, it has been Christ's temptation over again.

I hope you see how much harder this temptation is than the other. Strange how as a man grows more spiritual he meets new dangers that he never knew when he was carnal. The higher man attains higher temptations. The climber on the Alps meets dangers up among the clouds that men and women in the valleys never know. To hunger for bread is terrible, and may drive a man to great wickedness; but to hunger for a God who seems to refuse Himself is infinitely more terrible, and may drive to wickedness far more intense the soul that cannot wait in trust till God shall claim the child whom He has not forgotten for an instant, in His own way.

Of the third temptation we can allow ourselves but a single word: "Again, the devil taketh Him up into an exceeding high mountain, and showeth Him all the kingdoms of the world, and the glory of them; and saith unto Him, All these things will I give Thee, if Thou wilt fall down and worship me." And was that a temptation? Did Jesus want those kingdoms and their glory? Surely He did. Not for themselves, not for the comforts they could furnish Him, not with the ordinary covetousness of avaricious men, but yet He wanted them intensely. He had come to win them, He had come to purchase them with His own blood. He stood with His heart full of blessings, and the world would not take them. He wanted that world that He might pour His blessings in upon it. And here stood the devil and said, "Once bow the knee to me and it is all yours. Do one wrong thing and all those great divine longings of yours shall have free course, and you shall do for this stubborn world all that you want to do!" Ah, you and I must know how Jesus longed to bless men before we can have any idea what that temptation was to Him; but if you have ever had a friend whom with the purest sympathy and love you longed to bless and help, who shut himself up against you; and if the time has come when you have seen, or thought that you have seen, just how, by one wrong act, by one concession to his standards, by one compliance, you could get the access to him that you wanted; if then all your love for him has poured in its influence to make you do that one wrong thing, then you know of what sort this last temptation of our Saviour was. And it is the most terrible temptation that any man can feel. It burns its way into the life with all the fire of our warmest love. How it touched Jesus to the quick we can see in the intensity of the indignation with which He turned against it. "Get thee hence, Satan," He cries out. This temptation had come nearer to His heart than either of the others.

Again we see how as a man becomes higher he becomes capable of higher temptations. Of these three temptations of Jesus the first appealed to His bodily appetites, the second to His need of His Father, the third to His love of His brethren. To be tempted in the first way one must merely be a man; to be tempted in the second way one must crave for himself the life with God; but to be tempted in the third way one must have passed beyond himself and long for the highest blessings of his fellow-men. None but the Christ-like man can know what it is to be tempted like Christ.

Does that seem hard? Does it open a dreary prospect to know that as you grow higher and higher, while you leave many temptations below you, you will be always meeting new ones in the upper air? But if it be so that this world is all tuned and tempered with temptation, if the life cannot live without it here any more than the lungs can breathe without oxygen in the air, then may we not be thankful that there is no mountain-top whose atmosphere is so thin as to lack this ever necessary element of life, and so there is no mountain that we may not climb? There will come a world where there will be no temptation—a garden with no serpent, a city with no sin. The harvest day will come and the wheat be gathered safe into the Master's barn. It will be very sweet and glorious. Our tired hearts rest on the promises with peaceful delight. But that time is not yet. Here are our tempted lives, and here, right in the midst of us, stands our tempted Saviour. If we are men we shall meet temptation as He met it, in the strength of the God who is the Father of whom all men are children. Every temptation that attacks us attacked

Him and was conquered. We are fighting with a defeated enemy. We are struggling for a victory which is already won. That may be our strength and assurance as we recall, whenever our struggle becomes hottest and most trying, the wonderful and blessed day when Jesus was "led up of the Spirit into the wilderness to be tempted of the devil."

X.

SECOND SUNDAY IN LENT.

"It is written, Man shall not live by bread alone, but by every word that proceedeth out of the mouth of God."—MATT. IV. 4.

A QUOTATION by Christ of the words of the Old Testament has a great value apart from the common use which is made of such passages in connection with the evidences of the Bible. The Old Testament—it is very necessary that we should always feel it—is on a far lower plane of life than the New. That was the preparatory, this is the perfect book. In that man was working under God's guidance; in this God works directly, taking His place among men in the person of His Son, teaching by His own audible words, guiding by His own visible hand. When Christ, then, quotes from the Old Testament, when He takes the words that were spoken of some of the men of old and uses them of Himself, He is really asserting the intimate connection, the identity of life, between the lower and the higher, the human and the divine, planes of being. He is declaring that what is true of one in an inferior is true of the other in a superior degree. He is extending the conditions of humanity and showing how they represent and echo the conditions of Divinity. Every one of these lines of quotation running between the Testaments—what is it but one of a multitude of golden chords which hold the life of God not merely into a connection of relationship, but into a connection of resemblance with the life of man, who is His creature and His copy? All together, what are they but a new assurance of that truth whose supreme revelation was given us by the manifestation of the Divine-human in the Incarnation of our Redeemer?

I find this truth, which makes so much of the life of my Bible, peculiarly evident in the words from which I am to speak to you to-day. Christ was in the midst of His mysterious temptation. The tempter had tried upon His weary and exhausted nature one resource of devilish cunning after another. At last came this appeal: "If Thou be the Son of God, command that these stones be made bread." It was the very magnificence of effrontery, it was part of the same superb impiety which once in heaven had counted God's authority capable of overthrow, which thus tried to derange the calmness of divine consistency by an appeal to the low necessity of hunger. We read the chapter so often that we do not realize how strange Christ's answer is; but if we had stood there and heard the Satanic demand made we should have waited, stopping our breath to hear some supreme assertion of the Godhood that repelled so low an insult. "Go to men," we should have listened for the Lord to say—"go to men with arguments like those. Their natures are built to answer such appeals. All that a man hath will he give for that life which bread must feed. But God must be tempted, O tempter, with higher trials than that. Do not bring to the Divine those inducements which entice only the human."

I love Christ all the more when I see how different His answer was from that. I love Him when I see Him declare Himself a man, and from the human standpoint fling aside the tempter's plea. I reverence and cling to the true human nature that there was in Him when I hear Him go back and take up the words that had been on human lips, that declared the resources of human nature, that asserted the higher life in Man: "It is written, Man shall not live by bread alone, but by every word that proceedeth out of the mouth of God." The danger is to us who hold so much to the divinity of Christ that His humanity will mean too little. Let us remember that in times such as this of the temptation there is a strength for us in the thought that it was a man who fought and conquered, which no simple assurance of His being God could give.

The subject that these words of Christ include, then, and of which we are now to speak, is the requirements of life in man. "Man shall not live by bread alone, but by every word that proceedeth out of the mouth of God."

What is it in the highest sense to do what all men try to do in some sense, to get a living? Those words are very lightly used, and narrowed down to very insignificant dimensions. In their largest employment they include all the maturest culture and best growth of the human body, mind, and soul.

"Man doth not live!" Before the thought of life all treatment practical, as well as speculative, stands defied and puzzled. Just as the surgeon's knife lays skin and flesh aside, dissects the mystery of every vital organ, hunts being back into its most sacred citadel, and finds it there elude him—finds everywhere the machinery of life, nowhere life itself; just as the metaphysician lays an authoritative hand on thought, emotion, will, and bids them stand before him and declare the secrets of their operation, but no profoundest searcher has yet found what mystery it is by which the being lives who thinks and loves and wills so wonderfully, so to the teacher of the proper conduct and true results of life, that life itself always abides behind his work, wrapped in an eternal mystery which is only typified by the unbroken reserve with which the great earth clothes her white fields for our eating and pours out rivers for our drinking, but lets us know nothing of the untold nature out of which the springs and the corn-fields come. Or again, the thought of life is like that untouched line we call the sky, which sweeps around us the clear circle of its horizon, from which we measure with a perfect accuracy, and builds above us a blue dome under which our life goes on protected and assured, but which, when we try to reach it, proves to be not one single line, but an infinite depth, heaven beyond heaven stored with what strange uses and benefactions we dare not say. So is it not true that the idea of life is realized thus only as it exists in degrees infinitely deep, taking sharp lines for practical uses, just as the atmosphere does in the distinct outlines of the sky?

At any rate, no one can doubt that this word "life" means very different things for different people and at different times. Life, first of all, is that about this *physical* structure by which it is kept active; it is that unfound something by which this heart beats on from the baby's first cry to the veteran's last prayer; by which the red blood runs its silent errand and all the forces of which the physiologist gives you the names are kept in operation. And again, life means something more when the purposes of beating hearts and tireless blood are taken into account. Every result to which this living man may minister is included under this great word. Intellectual life we speak of—the thinking, knowing, learning, inventive faculties in all the circle of their operations; this constitutes the second circle of the great whole of life. And outside of that, above it, larger than it, what we call moral life, the powers of choice and duty, involving the whole social or related being, the emotional existence, with the complications it involves —every part of human nature which leads to and results in an ought or an ought not; this is the third zone in the great atmosphere of being. And beyond all these, the outermost of all, highest of all, most infinite, bounding most closely on the life of God, man's spiritual life, whereby his nature is in connection, through its distinctively religious faculties, with the nature that is supernatural and divine.

Now the true thought of life includes all four of these; not any one or two or three of them, but all four. Breathing is not life, thought is not life, duty is not life. The perfect life includes them all. No man is thoroughly, that is, through and through, alive unless from end to end of his capacity that capacity is full. Complete life involves the conception of a body with every power perfect, a mind with every ability active, a conscience that never swerves from purity, a spirit that reaches to and fastens itself on God. Everything short of that is stagnated, impeded, partial life. To complete that high result is what a man ought to mean when he talks about "getting a living." Is it not one of the mortifying things, dear friends, to take now and then these words that we are using every day so lightly and see how much they really mean; to wipe through the dust and rust that are on these coin-words, which constant friction has worn so smooth and unimpressive, and look upon the royal image and superscription that is on them?

Now we are obliged to keep this thought of life complete in all its parts if we want to understand our text. We want to fill ourselves full of this idea of what it is to live, and then we are prepared to read: "Man shall not live by bread alone, but by every word that proceedeth out of the mouth of God." With a sublime figure man is represented as feeding on the words of God, and every word of God must come for nurture to the life that is made up of many parts. How splendid the figure is! God stands upon the summit of His nature and speaks His words, which in the absoluteness of His power turn themselves at once to deeds and blessings. He speaks once: "Let the earth bring forth grass, the herb yielding seed, and the fruit-tree yielding fruit." And as He spoke, those words, "proceeding out of the mouth of the Lord," were caught by the quick, obedient ground of Genesis, and became the power by which the physical life of man in all his generations has been nourished. He speaks again, in that vast voice which utters itself through all of nature and of human history: "Let man be wise, let him learn, let him know," and all that endless word of God has been the food of man's intellectual craving since the first student rejoiced in the first truth. Again, He speaks out of some Sinai mountain, or out of that Sinai of the inner life, our conscience. "Do this," He says, "and live," laying down duty after duty, which the moral nature takes to itself and feeds upon, and grows by them into rectitude and strength. And then, last of all, to the highest life of all, He utters His sublimest voice. What shall we say that last word is by which He utters Himself to, on which He feeds, man's deep religious nature? What can it be but that eternal "Word" which was in the beginning with God, which was God, which was made flesh, and dwelt among us; that bread of life which came down from heaven, of which a man may eat and never die; the fullness of divine utterance in the world's Saviour, Jesus Christ?

This is the impressive figure of human nature feeding on the words of God. Its truth is simply an announcement of the vast and various demands of human life; of the needs of man, and of the special provisions —by providence, by wisdom, by duty, and by grace— which God has made that no one of those needs should go unmet.

What have we reached, then? We have seen that human life exists by God's decree in various departments or degrees, and that He has made specific provision for the support of each one of these kinds of human being. If this be so, then it is evident that each life needs and must have its own peculiar nourishment; that the life of one of the lower natures that belong to man can never supply the lack of life in a higher. No man grows wiser by simply growing physically stronger. Any magnificent ruffian out of a street mob, with his splendid strength of body and his wretched emptiness of brain, will prove you that. And no man grows good by mere increase of intellectual development. Look at the melancholy record of the private lives of many of the most brilliant thinkers and scholars. Look at the dissoluteness of the bad, bright times of Greek or Roman culture. And just exactly so no man reaches any high progress in the highest life, no man grows holy, except by the one single means which God has provided for bringing a world of sinners back to Himself and lifting them up out of their unspirituality into the holiness in which He Himself resides. As powerless as is the mere training of the body to educate the mind, or the culture of the mind to reform the morals, so utterly hopeless is it that any man living under God's inevitable laws should grow by the mere struggle of moral rectitude into that condition of resemblance and spiritual nearness to God which we mean when we speak of a man's being holy. That high estate, the abiding of the divine life in the human soul—you must set it down as the first truth of your religion—can be ever reached only by the personal acceptance of that means by which it was first and forever typified—the indwelling of the Divine in the human in the great representative miracle of spiritual history, the Incarnation of Jesus Christ. That Incarnation is to be the image of every man's highest life. As there in Bethlehem so constantly in us the higher life can take possession of the lower only by a miracle, only by the direct operation of the Holy Spirit of the Lord: "Not of blood, nor of the will of the flesh, nor of the will of man, but of God." As in the Christ so constantly in us the higher life, once present, takes the lower utterly under its control, wields it with a supreme despotism for its own uses. As in the Christ so constantly in us the lower life has to meet all dangers and all agonies—the hunger, the thirst, the weariness, aye, even the scourging and the cross—when the purposes of the higher call for it; for this new life into which he enters who is "born again," though just as intimately and wonderfully connected with the old physical and intellectual life which the man lived before he was converted, is just as distinct from it, just as distinctly superior to it, as was the divine nature to the human nature in our Lord.

I do not forget, when I thus speak of the spiritual life, wherever a man attains it, as surpassing and subjecting all inferior lives within him, that nevertheless those inferior lives are necessary to make him a perfect man. I believe most fully that a man will be a better Christian if his body is healthy and his mind is wise and his morals are correct. It certainly is true about the body. Take two spirits equally pure and holy, and lodge one in the frame of a strong man whose full blood is only waiting for some high impulse to do heroic acts, and house the other in some poor, broken-down body that vexes and restrains its high inhabitant with useless limbs and the weariness of everlasting aches, and there is no doubt that the development of the former will be into a more robust and hearty piety than the sickly growth of the other ever can attain. I believe in muscular Christianity as far as that. And I believe we ought to know more about and think more about the necessity of a perfect body to a perfect man. If by any means a man can help it he has religiously no right to be dyspeptic or deformed. Here the physician becomes an evangelist with a most specific and responsible work to do. And just so about the mind; the time is gone by when men talked as if ignorance and want of culture were necessary prerequisites to piety. As Christianity advances all that false idea must and will be more and more utterly abandoned, and the larger doctrine take its place that all truth is God's truth, and that every truth a man can learn, no matter how far off it seems, down to the natural history of insects and the rule of three, may by some divine connection minister to his growth in spiritual grace. And another day has gone by, too—the day in which men used to defame morality for the sake of building up religion. As the distinctive character of true religion rises we see it builds itself infinitely past our ken without degrading any other culture. I will not say, as you often hear it said so paradoxically, that an immoral man is easier to convert than a moral man. Conversion is so hard and so easy a thing at once—so infinitely hard for us, so infinitely easy for the Spirit of God—that I do not believe we can tell much about which are the hardest and which are the easiest conversions. But I cannot feel a doubt that of two men, one moral and one immoral, the man who takes Christ into a life in any degree correct grows more rapidly in the spirit of his Master than another who takes him into a house which is not merely foul within, but broken down and running over with its foulness at every loathsome chink.

No! I accept all this. I cannot help it. When I see religion every day hampered by weak bodies, narrow minds, and wicked habits, all of them defects originating before the man became religious, I am perfectly sure that man's religion would be truer in its expressions, and so freer for its growth, if all those lower lives were perfect. They minister to this the highest life of all. But again we must insist that they do not, they never can, create it. By none of them does the man live. There is a higher life above them, which they can help, but into which they cannot grow, into which whosoever entereth must be "born again." Always I long to see those lives perfecting, each feeding on its own appropriated "word of God." I rejoice in every body strengthened, every mind enlightened, every fault reformed; but always above them I hear a higher word, the Word of God Himself, the Christ, the Saviour, and I do not know how to count any man truly living till he has come and found the life that is in Him.

I speak to you to-day who have not learned how grand and precious is this truth of the superior nature of the spiritual life. Why can ye not learn that religion is a distinct attainment and demands a distinct method of its own? To be religious, to be a Christian, means something accurate and specific. It is not to be a little stronger than the strongest, a little wiser than the wisest, a little truer than the truest. It is something more. It is something different from all. It is to have taken up a new quality of being, which God only gives through Jesus Christ; to have learned ambitions which the best wisdom or morality never dreamed of; to have become the subject of forces deeper, dealing with profounder regions of the nature, than were ever stirred before—all this accomplished by the act and habit of complete personal dedication, under the impulse of gratitude and love, to the service and education of a personal Master and Saviour, Jesus Christ our Lord. Let a plant try to be a bird forever and it will forever fail. It may grow to be a very superior plant, unfold a lordly beauty to the wondering sun, but between it and the song and the flight and the nest lies forever the gulf that separates flower-life from bird-life and never can be crossed. Let a man try to be a Christian forever. The struggle may make him, I believe it will make him, a better man; but between him and the strength and the peace and the love yawns forever the gulf that separates man-life from God-life, and which no man ever yet crossed save as he stretched out both his helpless hands to God and felt a Hand too powerful not to trust clasp them and lift him, whither he knew not, till lo! the gulf was crossed and he had entered on the new life that they live who live in God.

Do I need to tell you the uses to which this truth of the subordination of the lower lives to the higher may be and has again and again been put? What a strength there is in it for every tempted man who has to put some low good aside that he may go on to the better! It is the law of self-sacrifice, and so must be the law of every worthy life. By it the martyrs stood while the flames burned away their outer life and purified and made manifest at once the inner truth which was more dear to them. By it reformers since the world began have given up the hope of popular favor and worked for thankless generations that did them but a grudged honor years after they were dead, over their moldering bones. By it the nation that God blesses has to learn in God's good time how to rise up from her careless ease and put her easy prosperity away, that by toilsomeness and blood she may mount to the higher mercies of completer freedom and a profounder loyalty. "Man shall not live by bread alone, but by every word that proceedeth out of the mouth of God"—by every word, from the gentlest to the severest, that the eternal lips know how to speak; from the tenderness of the God that spoke to Hagar: "What aileth thee, Hagar? fear not," to the sternness of the pitiless God who spoke to Abraham: "Take now thy son, thine only son Isaac, whom thou lovest, and offer him upon one of the mountains which I will tell thee of." Blessed is the state, the church, or the heroic man that is strong enough to put the bread away without a murmur, no matter how sweet it be to his hungry lips, if by tasting it he robs himself of any nourishment for the higher life that feeds, not upon bread alone, but upon every word of God.

And remember this is not a doctrine for the world's heroes and martyrs only; it is for every living soul when it is called on to give up the lower that it may attain the higher life. It is for the man who has to give up his dollar that he may keep his honesty, to give up a doubt that he may win a truth. It is for the young man who has to give up a fascinating acquaintance that he may keep his purity, to let go a tempting chance of business because there is something about its associations that is going to degrade his life. It is for the old man who has to give up the friendship of a lifetime because his loyalty to truth and principle is worth more to him than his dearest friend; for the woman who abandons worldliness to serve her God, who turns her back on fashion and its wretched littleness that she may go up into eternal life. It is for the minister who is tempted to say smooth things instead of true things to the people whose favor he desires; for the people who are readier to have a church that is popular and always full than one where, full or empty, no truth shall go unspoken, no righteousness unpraised, and no sin unrebuked. Wherever truth and interest conflict (and where is the life so narrow and obscure that it has not furnished many a battle-field for that eternal struggle?); wherever the desire to be popular, to be rich, to be wise, to be anything else has to be cut away and cast behind a man that he may go on unhindered to be good and true and holy, there the law of the martyrs and the heroes, there the law of the Christ, whose meat was to finish His Father's work, and who for the eating that eternal meat fasted from the bread that perisheth, comes down and proves itself the law of all true life.

I know perfectly well that there is not a man or woman here that does not need this truth to-day. There is not one of you that some way or other is not trying to feed your higher lives on that nourishment which is fit only for the lower. How much there is to learn! You rich men have got to learn that character is not built up of gold. "How hard is it for them that trust in riches to enter into the kingdom of God!" You have got to sweep the dry crusts of avarice off of your tables and heap them with the sweet luxury of charity before you can feed your souls with the strength of holiness. God give you grace to do it! You amiable triflers in society, making your life one long aspiration after the applause and good will of triflers like yourselves, you are frittering your days and nights away, and you dare not stand up in God's sight and even pretend to have grown in high principle or any godly grace, feeding on this straw that tastes so sweet! Where should I stop if I began? There is not one who does not need the strength of God to refuse some bread the devil is holding out to him, that in the hunger of his lower nature he may feed his soul on some eternal word of God. May our Lord give you power each in his own secret struggle to be victor.

And again, what a truth this is, not merely for the weak man who needs strength, but for the afflicted man who wants comfort and faith! I go to some poor creature and find him utterly desolate in his forlorn and emptied life. His money is gone, his house is burned, his health is broken, his friend is faithless, his child is dead. I hear him cry out in his bitterness, "Yesterday my table was heaped up; now where shall my hungry mouth find its crumb to feed on?" What shall I say to him? What can I say but in some form or other just this truth: "Man shall not live by bread alone, but by every word that proceedeth out of the mouth of God"? You say God promised to supply your needs, and where is His provision? Yes, but He loves best to supply your highest, not your lowest needs, and it is the law of all His universe that it is better for the lower life to hunger, if thereby the higher can be fed and made to grow.

Here again this is no doctrine for great sorrows and bereavements only. Every time that God applies His law and we shrink under it, every time that He deprives the body that He may feed the soul, this is His call for us to find a consolation in the certainty that on some word of God, if not on the bread that my ignorance is craving, I may, if I will just be obedient, be fed into an unexpected strength. This is the way the saints were made; this is the way that everywhere, where faithful souls are suffering, the gradual glory of new sainthoods is gathering now. The world falls off from them, is torn away from them, it may be, but its very desertion leaves them clearer in the light, more utterly within the influence of God. New aspirations take the heart made empty of the old, and the soul that once clung to man flies in the hopefulness of hopelessness to God, and finds no path too hard that leads its new ambition up to Him. It learns a new prayer that grows to be its only prayer:

> "Nearer, my God, to Thee,
> Nearer to Thee!
> E'en though it be a cross
> That raiseth me,
> Still all my song shall be,
> Nearer, my God, to Thee,
> Nearer to Thee!"

All that we have said to-day starts from and results in the truth of the distinctive and separate character of the Christian life above all others. Let us come back to that and make it our closing lesson.— To be a Christian is to be in a definite and specific state; to become a Christian is to undergo a definite and specific change. No previous state by any possibility develops into this state, no previous process by any possibility accomplishes of itself this change. By one distinct new act the man who never has been Christ's servant gives himself to Christ, and then he is a "new creature," for he has been "born again."

If this be so, then it follows that the Christian Church

must have one very definite and special work to do. The object of the Church is, first and last and all the time, this one single object: just to save men's souls—nothing else; not to improve their bodies, not to inform their minds, nothing but just to tell them of the new life of holiness, and to invite them to enter it through the new and living way which the crucified Christ has opened.

I am sure there must be some among you who feel the attractiveness of such a truth, there must be some who are longing for just this same new way—not an old way that you have been trying and failing in till you are weary of it and have no heart left to try it any longer, but some experiment by which you can start fresh, throw the dead past away, and be a "new man" in the fullness of your strength. What shall I say? It seems to me as if your wish were just the Bible offer. Here is a new life to live—not the old one in a higher progress, but a new life, whereon men enter by a wholly new admission. What you want is just what Christ provides. And there is no other way for your want to be satisfied unless you can see Him standing by the side of His cross, pointing you to its foot, saying, "Leave your past there; let the dead bury their dead; follow thou Me. It may be into the fellowship of My sufferings, but what of that? It certainly shall be into the fellowship of My glory and My holiness forevermore."

XI.

THIRD SUNDAY IN LENT.

"Again, the devil taketh Him up into an exceeding high mountain, and showeth Him all the kingdoms of the world, and the glory of them."—MATT. IV. 8.

WHEN one travels in the Holy Land it is interesting for him to watch himself and see which are the places which take most hold upon him. Very often, I think, such a one has found that it is not the places which have been the scenes of the most picturesque events in our Lord's life so much as those which witnessed the inward struggles and the development of His nature into full consciousness of itself that have most fastened the spirit of the Christian traveler. The hills above Nazareth, where Jesus must have constantly wandered when He was a boy; the side of the Mount of Olives, where He fought out the inner battle of Gethsemane—both of these scenes are full of power of the most subtle and imperious sort. And among all such scenes none can have stronger power than the scene of Christ's temptation, out of the story of which the words are taken from which I want to speak to you to-day.

Those words describe a notable moment in the Saviour's life. Up to this time He had been hardly more than a boy. He had lived in the small town of Nazareth. His mother's household and the labors of His father's shop had been His scenery. He had at last come up to Jerusalem and been baptized by John. But now in some mysterious way, in this scene in the desert, His vision opened and His world enlarged. It does not matter to us just what it was that outwardly occurred. Before the soul of Christ the whole wide world lay open. He saw how large, how rich, how beautiful, how manifold it was. Judea and Nazareth were still the center of His outlook, but the world stretched away around them as the ocean stretches out away around the sailor in his little boat. Surely it was a great day when the Saviour of the world saw for the first time all the kingdoms and the glory of the world which He had come to save.

Do you not see what the subject is of which I wish to speak? In every vivid young life as it grows up there comes a time which is to it what this moment was in the life of Jesus. It is the time when it catches sight of the world; sometimes all of a sudden, as if a traveler among woods and country roads turned a corner and in an instant there lay before him the great city, flashing in the sun; sometimes very gradually, as if the man walked on and on, hour after hour, along a long straight road, with what seemed at first a distant flash of gold opening hour after hour into the splendor of the vast metropolis. So does the young man in some moment or some period of his life come in sight of the great world. He comes out of the guarded seclusion of his home; he presses against some narrow standard of his boyhood until it bursts and shows broader standards lying out beyond it. Ordinarily such vision of the world is involved with some change of circumstances, but the real essential thing is in the heart of the young man himself. Shut a boy up in an island by himself, let him grow up in solitude, and the time will surely come when his human heart will tell him stories of the unseen world of men, and he will sit upon the lonely rocks and seem to see that crowded human world far away across the unbroken waste of waters. You remember how the weary spirit, recalling that experience, sings in front of Locksley Hall:

"Make me feel the wild pulsation which I felt before the strife,
When I heard my days before me and the tumult of my life
Yearning for the large excitement that the coming years would
  yield—
Eager-hearted, as a boy when first he leaves his father's field,
And at night, along the dusky highway near and nearer drawn,
Sees in heaven the light of London flaming like a dreary dawn,
And his spirit leaps within him to be gone before him then,
Underneath the light he looks at, in among the throngs of
  men."

Do not these words somehow recall to us the young man taken up into the high mountain and shown all the kingdoms of the world, and the glory of them? It is all very vague—it must be. That traveler upon the road to London, all aglow with its vision, does not trace how every street and alley runs in the great city, nor see how the bricks are laid in every man's back yard. It is the "light of London," not the lamp in this or that shop-window, that he sees. And so it is the world, all vague, mysterious, and wonderful, which the spirit of the young man sees from his mountain, not this or that which is happening in the world. It is the world all together, the world of tumultuous, roaring, awful, fascinating human life, the kingdoms of the world, and the glory of them—this is what he sees. There is a special value, a special contribution to the total experience and character of a man, in the years which hold that vision—the years when the narrowness of childhood is broken, but the absorption in the details of life has not yet begun; the years wherein the young man is catching sight of the world. Blessed is he who keeps those years pure and lofty.

In spite of the vagueness which necessarily belongs to this first sight of the great world it is still possible to discriminate so far as to see in what different ways this enlargement of life will come to different men. Let me point out a few. To one man it will come simply as a sight of the possible greatness of experience, the mere surprised realization of how much there is which may happen to a man. The boy's life has been all safe and guarded. Little has come to him in any way. He has drifted about, as it were, in a little pond, striking forever the same shores, repeating over and over again the same experiences. By and by the time of larger vision comes. Some new thing happens; a great sorrow, a great task, starts up like a mountain in his way. If he climbs the mountain, instead of being crushed under it, he looks abroad from it on the great world beyond. The pond, as it were, breaks open and becomes a stream, flowing he knows not to what end. Something almost terrible, yet something which tests a man and brings out all the latent largeness which is in him, lies in such a moment. The heart beats high. The breath comes fast. How long and broad and deep life is! What wondrous things may happen before the end is reached, and the man, tired but enriched, passes out through the gate of death into the yet larger life beyond!

All this specializes and so intensifies itself as the young man chooses some particular occupation or study. Perhaps he goes into business. Think of him as he stands there upon the borders of the business world, just far enough into it to feel himself a part of it; not so wrapped yet in its details that he cannot feel the great general magnificence of its entire mass and movement. He must be dull indeed if he does not feel something of the inspiration which so many ardent young merchants in every age, in every land, have felt. The sight of the thousands of enthusiastic, toiling men, the sound of clashing wills and roaring passions, the sudden spring or slow upheaval of enormous fortunes, the ring of powers happy in their energetic and successful use, the constant suggestion of danger, the constant need of courage, and, over all, like a great light in the sky from a city blazing with a million lamps, the sense of the growing happiness and the growing goodness of humanity as the result, in spite of a thousand drawbacks, of this great world of commerce—this is the vision which ought to greet the young business man at the beginning of his business life; this is the way in which he sees all the kingdoms of this new world which he is entering, and the glory of them!

And the young student has his visions, too—great outlooks into mysterious sciences: the heavens above, and the earth beneath, and the waters under the earth, all teeming with possible knowledge; the wisdom of the wise men and the wisdom which no man has yet been wise enough to know. Alas for him who sits down to his higher school and college life with no such new sense of the greatness of the world of knowledge, solemnly, beautifully, opening in his soul!

Or public life! You step into some trifling public office and try to do its work. You perform the first duty of the fundamental office and cast your vote. You are within sight, as you do that, of all the grandeur of government the wide world over: of the tidal rise and fall of dynasties, of the great shepherds of men, of the despotisms, of the struggles of the people, of the slow birth of liberty, of all the thrones and parliaments and battle-fields.

Or religious life! You say your prayer of consecration, and lo! as you pray, the curtain lifts. All that prayer means, all that God might do, all that God ever has done, for man, all the struggles of man's nature after God, all the faiths, all the speculations, all the superstitions, lie before you. The imperfect religions, the temples, the synagogues, the cathedrals, the altars to the unknown gods, the deep thoughts and hopes and suspicions, and then Jerusalem and Jesus Christ and all the Christian history—all these stand round the young disciple praying his first prayer.

You see, then, what I mean. The larger aspects of his general human life and of his special work in life open to a man at times as they opened to Jesus. To all earnest souls, as to His soul, come times when to them are shown all the kingdoms of the world and the glory of them.

And then we turn back to our text again, for there is

something else there which we have not looked at yet. In St. Matthew's story of the temptation, from which our text is taken, it is said that it was "the devil" who took Jesus up into a high mountain and showed Him the greatness of the world. Does that part of the story also find its correspondence in our lives? Is it the devil, the spirit of earthliness, the spirit of evil, which holds up before men's eyes these larger visions of life of which I have been speaking? I think we cannot really answer that question until we go back and take in the whole of the story of our Lord's temptation. This visit to the lofty mountain was only a part of Christ's experience in the wilderness. And at the beginning of the whole you remember how it is written, "Then was Jesus led up of the Spirit into the wilderness to be tempted of the devil." I think that that verse makes the matter plain and suggests the deepest truth concerning our own life. The larger government of our life is not in the devil's hands, but in the hands of the Spirit of God. All that the devil can do to us he can do only within the great fact that we are God's children and that God holds us in His unforgetting hands. We need not go into the devil's wilderness at all unless God's Spirit takes us there. If God's Spirit does take us there He will not turn round and go away and leave us. He will stay with us and have the final power over our lives —a power which, if we do not hinder it, may not save us always from pain, but will certainly always save us from sin.

I would fain hope that as I so state what seems to me to be the doctrine of life and of the influences which are at work upon it which this verse involves, your own hearts might recognize it from your own experiences. Have you not known, many a time, that there were two powers at work upon your life—one larger and one smaller, one superior and one inferior? I seem to live within two spheres—one close upon my actions and my thoughts, the other wider, vaster, outside this inner sphere, and the real master of it. My pains and pleasures, the actual circumstances and incidents of my life, the world, kindly or hostile, as it may please to be, can govern. But the real thing I am—let me determine that that shall be God's, and there is no power in the universe that can pluck it away from Him. To the man who, as he goes on living, becomes more and more aware that he is in the power of the world, but also becomes more and more aware that he is in the power of the world only within the power of God; that God put him where he is, and is always ready to sustain him there—to such a man do not these words deeply describe his own daily life: "Led up of the Spirit into the wilderness to be tempted of the devil"?

Apply this to the vision of the greatness of life on which we have been dwelling. It is the devil who shows it to us, and therefore it is full of temptation—temptation to dismay, to flippancy, to cowardice, to pride. But it is God who carries us where the devil can show it to us. Therefore it is full of glorious opportunity—opportunity of aspiration, of enlargement, of humility, of trust. The times of bursting visions are the devil's hour, and they are the hour of the Spirit, too. Then, when the world grew big around them, men have given themselves up to Satan or have given themselves up to God. Then, when the greatness of life confronts the soul, then (oh, how the thresholds of our stores and colleges and churches are strewn with the corpses of those who were ruined, and are marked with the shining footprints of those who passed on to highest things!) —then, when the greatness of life confronts the soul, then is the time when the soul is lost or saved.

And what decides whether it shall be ruin or salvation? We may not answer wholly, for the individual will which lies behind every fortune and decision of our lives is too important for us to leave out, and too subtle for us to trace in all its workings. But one thing, clearly, we may say: the power which the larger vision of the world will have over a man will depend primarily upon the kind of religion which is in him when that vision breaks upon him. And that is only another way of saying that it will depend upon what sort of man he is. For a man's religion, if it be real, is not what a man holds, but what he is. See, then, whether I am not right. A boy or man comes to one of these enlargement places. All that I described takes place for him. The world grows great around him. Suppose, then, that what he calls his religion has been of the sort of which so many men's religion is; suppose that it has been selfish and that it has been formal; suppose this man or boy has always thought of the service of God as something which was to be done in order that he might be saved from suffering—something which God would punish him if he did not do, and also something which consisted in a set of habits, in certain special outward actions which he must not omit to do. There is a thing called a religion which never gets further than those two ideas. And then suppose that the great world enlarges itself in vision round a man with a religion such as that. What power has his religion to make him equal to the enlarged, enlightened world? His little idea of personal safety goes all to pieces in the midst of this vast view of how great the world is, and of what great things God is doing in it. Who is he, that there should be a compact of insurance between his soul and God? And the set of habits, whether of thought or action, within which he has intrenched himself has not such flexibility as to take in this larger life. So they fail him and he has no protection. The little boat breaks and is sunk on this great ocean. It was fit only for the quiet river where the life has been peacefully lived thus far. Oh, of how many shipwrecks this is the whole story! How the shore where youth and manhood, childhood and manhood, meet is strewn with the ruins of what once seemed to be religious convictions and religious resolutions, which all broke up into fragments the moment that they came in sight of the immensity of life! Sometimes, when I see the good children trained in some selfish and formal religiousness hurrying on to the time when the devil must certainly show them the kingdoms of the world, and the glory of them, it seems to me as if I saw a great company of bright-faced boys and girls hurrying down with their toy boats in their hands to the ocean's edge, expecting to get into them and sail over the Atlantic to Europe. They will never get through the fringe of surf on the sea-shore. The sight of their hopeless life is infinitely sad and pathetic.

There is a religion which is wholly different from this. It is entirely unselfish and it is profoundly real.

THIRD SUNDAY IN LENT. 177

Down at its base there is the most earnest love for God and the most complete conviction of His love for us. His service is a joy and delight. And joy and delight are never formal, but are of the very essence and substance of the man himself. Let this religion stand face to face with the enlarged vision of life. This man is all wrapped up in God. His young heart beats and throbs to see God glorified and to do something for His glory. The little world where he has lived thus far has seemed too small for all that he wanted to do for his Father. Now let the world enlarge. Let science open all her shining fields. Let commerce turn the key of locked-up lands. Let the winds come laden with the sound of hymns which faithful souls are singing in the dark of blind religions. You cannot make the world too large and manifold for this man's God. His religion really is for God, not for himself; therefore the largeness of life does not bewilder and dismay, but satisfies it. The soul takes that which the devil shows it, and reads divine meanings in it and makes divine uses of it, and waves aside the dark guide, while it passes forward into the light on which that guide has opened for it the door.

Oh, how good it is when sometimes one sees that! O my dear friends, it is a terrible thing when one's religion is too small for the world, and is always leaving great parts of the world's life unaccounted for, unilluminated, and is always dreading to have the world made any larger, lest this religion shall seem even more meager and insufficient. But it is a great thing when the world is too small for one's religion, and the soul's sense of the glory and dearness of God is always craving larger and larger regions in which to range. Then welcome all discoveries, all illuminations, all visions of the greatness of the world of God.

Here, surely, one may plead with parents, even with those who are very conscientious in the religious training of their children. You have taught your boys and girls that they must not do wrong or God will punish them. You have taught them to say their morning and night prayers. You have brought them to church, and perhaps you rejoice to see how well they follow the service, how reverently they kneel, how the charm of the liturgy seems to have caught their ear. I have no fault to find with any of that. God forbid! But oh, there must be something more than that, there must be something deeper. The time will surely come when, unless there be something else behind them, the fear of future punishment will fade before the tremendous fascination of the world, and conformity with religious habits will seem trivial or slavish beside the vivid activity of a life which summons the children with its voice of thunder. Are you leading your children to know God; to know God the Father of all life, the fountain of all energetic action; to know Him so loftily that to exist for Him, to work with Him, shall seem to them to be the glory of existence? If so, then you are preparing them for life. No matter how little and limited their lives may seem to-day, when they come forth and behold the kingdoms of the earth, and all their glory, it will not disturb their faith, but establish it by seeming to display a worthy kingdom for their King. The young lawyer comes in sight of the vast complexity of human interests; the young doctor comes in sight of the mystery of the operations of the force of life; the young politician comes in sight of the vast complexity of government. Do they know God—know Him as their Father and their Friend? If they do, their knowledge must rejoice in this enlarged enlightenment. It is as if the sun had shone in a little box, its glory beaten back and restrained against the narrow walls; but now the walls are broken down, and all the wide-spread landscape, river and field and hill and lake, lies waiting for his beams. Now it seems worth while for the sun to shine. So let me know God, and then every enlargement of the world shall make it seem more worth while for God to be, and so more sure that God is.

I speak thus very earnestly about the training of children for life, and yet I would not make it seem as if I thought that any preparation for the meeting of a soul with the enlarged vision of the world could insure the results of that meeting. The coming of a nature to its full vision is like the coming of an heir to his inheritance. Those who have trained the heir from childhood ought to have made him ready for the life which he has got some day to live. And yet no imperfection of their training can excuse the heir if, coming into his inheritance, he is unfit for its demands and turns out either a profligate or a sluggard. And so I speak to parents and bid them do all they can, by a profound and lofty and spiritual training, to make their children ready for the larger life which some day they will have to live. But then I turn to the children, to those who have now ceased or are ceasing to be children, and say to them directly, "Be ye ready!" Seek in your Nazareth homes such Christ-like knowledge of the Heavenly Father that when the windows open and the whole world lies blazing in your sight your eager faith shall claim it all for God, as Christ upon the mountain claimed the whole world for Him whom He had learned to know was King of all of it. So deeply realize the power of God in your own soul that all the world shall seem to you to be only too narrow a theater for that power's operation and display. The devil holds up the last newly discovered truth. Let your soul pluck it out of the devil's hand and make it God's. The devil shows you a new realm of living and says, "Behold a new temptation." Let your soul answer, "Nay, a new witness of my Father and a new chance to grow what He would have me be." Do you not see, if this is what the great vision may accomplish for you, how the very Spirit Himself may do His best work for you by leading you up into the wilderness to be tempted of the devil?

I do not want to draw so near the end without saying a few words upon another aspect of our subject which interests me deeply. I have spoken thus far only of the individual life and of the visions which come sometimes to it. But is not all that I have said true also, sometimes, of the world at large? Is it not true of the world at large that it, too, comes to its great times of visions? There do come times in history—and it would seem as if we were living in one of those times now—when the whole outlook of the world becomes enlarged. If you had asked a thinking man in the middle of the eighteenth century what he supposed would be the condition of the world a hundred years from then, would not his answer probably have been, " Not very different from what it is now. Some changes there will be, no doubt, but mainly things are settled, and the world will go on very much the same"? Here in the nineteenth century ask the same question, and can you imagine yourself receiving the same answer? "I cannot tell," the person whom you question must reply, "but certainly some broader, deeper things are coming. Mankind is greater than it has known itself to be. I see in a mist and haze—but still I do see—the pinnacles of a more glorious city, the outline of a larger world." So the world vaguely feels about itself. It has gone up—the Spirit of God surely sending it, and yet often the devil surely meeting it there—it has gone up into the mountain, and is seeing all its own future kingdoms, and the glory of them.

Of the causes which have brought this change we must not stop to speak. We know what many of them are: popular liberty, rapid communication, the increase of wealth, the wonderful work of science, the enthusiasm of humanity—all these have opened the world's eyes and enlarged its vision.

But this larger-visioned time in the world's life demands exactly what we saw that the time of larger vision in the life of the individual demanded—an unselfish and a spiritual faith, I said, a religion which is neither selfish nor formal. This is what must make the world fit to go forward into its mysterious and mighty future. On every side I hear the breaking of the selfish and the formal creeds. That man should just save himself out of the ruin and get to safety through some private bargain with Omnipotence; that man should try to do by ceremonies and organizations those things which of their very nature only can be done by living hearts and wills—these conceptions of religion, once the rules of religious thought, have lost their power and can rule religious thought no longer. But the faith which forgets its own salvation as it labors for the salvation of the world and the glory of God; the faith which looks for the salvation of the world and the glory of God, not to the setting up of hierarchies and the magic of ceremonies, but to the power of God in the souls of men, to the new manhood in Jesus Christ—that faith has the key of the present, and no conceivable future can grow so mighty or rich as to outgrow the power of that faith.

Because the Christian faith is intrinsically unselfish and spiritual, not selfish and formal, we know that it will prove itself, not less, but more, the faith for all humanity, as humanity enters more and more into its great future. The baser and meaner parts of her present life the Christian faith must cast away. In doing so she will become, not less, but more, herself; more purely, simply Christ. Christ, the revelation of the unspeakable love of God, the utterance of the yet undisplayed capacity of man—this, which is the Christian faith, no human progress can outgo, but every larger and richer development of human life must demand it with a more and more earnest hunger.

Such is the Christian's assurance of the future of his faith in the great world. But draw the circle in once more and let me say one closing word of your own life. You cannot make that life so large that it will not need Christ or that Christ will not satisfy and fill it. Oh, if you stand to-day where any new vision is bursting into sight, if any hope is dawning, if any work is calling you, if any new study is rolling back its silver doors, if manhood is glowing in the near sky of your dreams, if as you look out from any mountain you are seeing the kingdoms of the world, and the glory of them, may He whose those kingdoms are, because He redeemed them with His blood, be with you as you look upon them. By His strength and power may you be very consecrated and very holy, and so be master of your vision. Then may you go on into the world which you discern, and both make it, and be yourself made by it, absolutely Christ's.

XII.

FOURTH SUNDAY IN LENT.

"And David said unto Nathan, I have sinned against the Lord. And Nathan said unto David, The Lord also hath put away thy sin; thou shalt not die."—2 SAM. XII. 13.

HERE is the story of a confession and a forgiveness, told with a compactness that almost startles us, the two are crowded so closely together. King David, after his great sin against Uriah, had hardly been brought to own his guilt, had hardly got the words of confession off his lips, before the prophet, who represented before him the justice and authority of God, gave back the answer as if he had it all ready upon his lips and had been waiting for the chance to give it. "I have sinned against the Lord." "The Lord also hath put away thy sin."

We talk so much about confession and forgiveness; we elaborate their theory so much; we see such intricate relations of the divine and human natures involved in the transaction, that we almost unconsciously transfer the long train of thought into a long period of time. We feel as if that result which implies so much spiritual action must be reached only by a process of correspondingly prolonged duration. "To confess and be forgiven—that is the work of months and years, of a whole lifetime," we declare. And then comes in this simple story of how the whole was but the transaction of a moment with David—of how one minute he was standing obstinate and rebellious, stout in his sin, and the next minute the whole change had come and the hard heart was softened and the proud will had bent and the sin was gone. All this comes in to remind us that the most intricate moral processes take but a moment to result. The volcano that the chemistry of years has been preparing breaks into eruption in an hour. The blossom that the patient plant has been designing for a century bursts into flower in a single night. And so the reconciliation of a soul to God, which it has been the labor of the ages to make possible, which dates for its conception back to the dateless time when the Lamb was slain from the foundation of the world, comes to its completion in a period too short to measure, in the sudden meeting of a soul filled with penitence and a God filled with mercy.

To-day I wish to speak to you of the true nature of the confession and forgiveness of sin. But since we must find on unfolding it that the whole process is made up of many parts, and so may get this wrong idea about the time it requires, I would guard myself at the outset by this story. The whole is but a moment's work. Men, making their systems, cast out the notion of an instantaneous conversion. If conversion means turning from bad to good, from self to God, lo, here is certainly an instantaneous conversion. Because the quick chemistries of grace take our slow study a lifetime—nay, an eternity—to understand, let us not forget that it takes God but a moment to work their beautiful combinations and create the strange new life whose power is folded up within them. I say it boldly and fully: you may be converted now and here, as you sit in church. Here and now you may confess your sins and be forgiven and start a better life. Oh, if God would only grant that you might! It did not take David any longer. At least keep in mind that it is possible while I try to explain to you in full what the true nature of confession is.

What is it to confess one's sin? I think that the complete act includes four parts, all of which are necessary, the absence of any one of which makes the act incomplete. In order to make the matter plainer let us talk, not about sin in general, but about some special sin— say the sin of selfishness. I select this sin for several reasons: first, because it is the commonest sin in lives not openly vicious; second, because it is the one least easily detected and confessed; and third, because in its large scope it includes and embraces every other sin. What is necessary, then, for a selfish man really and truly to confess his selfishness?

1. To own that he has done selfish things. That is the first step to be taken. That is the first struggle. To get at the plain facts; to set out in their array the long line of acts that have not been done from any higher motive than the mere desire for one's own personal comfort or advantage. Even this is not easy. The acts know their own guiltiness and flee behind all kinds of shelter to escape scrutiny; and the man who is really bent upon discovering and confessing them has to seize hold of their reluctance with a strong hand and force them out. Are you bent on finding your own selfishness? First of all, you must not let the occasional

unselfish things that you have done, the few brilliant days when you can recall some generous deed of self-sacrifice—you must not let the luster of such rare exceptions, all the more lustrous from their very rareness, hide from your view the constant tenor of your living, which has been made up of things in which your neighbor's good has had no share of influence. And then you must not let yourself be blinded by the specious sophistry which tells you that these selfish acts of yours were not entirely selfish, because in some remote effect of them they have brought some good to some fellowman. Very possibly they have. Hardly any deed that is not essentially and necessarily bad can help resulting in some indirect and distant good. Your self-indulgences may have in some way benefited others; but if you had not this in view, if you did not purpose and intend it, as you know you did not, then the ultimate effects of the deeds do not affect their character. They were selfish-and only selfish. You must begin by sweeping aside everything that hides them, and letting them stand fairly out. Be honest first, and when the great procession of a life lived only for your own indulgence —not dissolute, not malignant, not violent or outrageous in any way, only selfish through and through; just exactly such a life as you would have lived if you had come into the world forbidden to do anything for God or fellow-man, and only by an occasional irresistible impulse breaking over the law to serve either—when such a procession of life marches round and round before the inexorable honesty of your self-examination, confession will begin and reach its first stage in the assured conviction of the fact, "I am a selfish creature."

FOURTH SUNDAY IN LENT.

2. Another struggle will come as a man passes on to the second stage, which is the full acknowledgment of the true moral character of such a life. Once convinced that he is selfish, a soul, with more or less consciousness of the sophistry that it is using, almost always sets to work to feel that selfishness is not wrong, but right. "Very well," it says, "I am selfish, I do live for myself; but what then? Whom should I live for? Is not my own interest and good my first care? Who will take care of me if I do not take care of myself? Must not charity begin at home? Is not this the way the world is meant to work, that every man should nurse his own interests, and so, by the development of each, they all should grow? Is not mankind meant to rise to its perfection as a flock of birds rises, each pair of hurrying wings moved by its own fear of danger or hope of gain, without consideration of the others, the result being that the whole solid flock rises together and moves like one great cloud of the sky? Is it not best that each should care for himself? And so, selfish as I am, is not my selfishness a virtue, instead of a sin?" Unstated, vaguely felt, this is the acted theory of thousands. No man can possibly confess till first he casts this fallacy entirely away. "It is wrong to live to myself; it is not the design of life." Around him he must hear a great long wail of human suffering, rising and falling, now wilder and now weaker, but never dying utterly away —the ceaseless claim of needy humanity to be helped by the humanity that has abundance. More quiet, but not less pathetic, he must also hear the longing appeal of what seem the happiest and fullest hearts for sympathy in their joy as others seek it in their sorrow. Let

his ears open to the appeals, and his conscience must open too. He will see that no man has a right to shut himself away from those whose life is one with his; nay, that no man has a right to do any act unless he sees that some one else will be the better or the happier for it as well as he. He will see that selfishness is wicked, and begin to be disgusted at his life, so full of it. He will add to the acknowledgment of the act the acknowledgment of the act's moral character, and his confession will be, not merely, "I have been selfish," but "I have sinned."

3. Then the selfish man passes on to the third step of his confession, which is the acknowledgment that the sin he has committed is an offense against God. Here is the first place where religion necessarily begins. All up to this point may be wholly unreligious. But the confession must be made to some one. What is the authority which has been violated by these acts of yours, which you have decided against as being selfish? Is it just the natural authority of the rights of your fellowmen—some human claim which they have upon your sympathy and help? I think not. I do not see that it is possible to show that, besides the right that every man has not to be injured by his neighbors, there is another claim by which he can complain if his neighbors do not go out of their way to help him. Is it, then, some abstract law or principle of the mutual harmonies of universal life against which the selfish man sins, to which he must confess? Surely no obedience to such an abstraction—which, after all, is only a generalization, an induction of the man's own mind—can bind a man's hot passions from their self-indulgence, or bend

his proud head in penitent confession of wrong-doing. What then? The law must come from God. We must be deeply, keenly conscious that every time we have done a selfish act we have broken His distinct commandment. We must have so entire a sense of how utterly He is love that we shall see every unloving thing that we have ever done to be a direct insult to His nature. We must keep our hearts before the spectacle of the Eternal Unselfishness, "the Lamb slain from the foundation of the world," till its great argument grows to be the source of our responsibility and the ground of our condemnation. "If He so loved us, we ought also to love one another." The new commandment must convict us. We must teach our eye to trace up the threads of accountability from all our selfish deeds and see them meeting and held fast in the one great hand of the great Judge who sits upon the throne, and we must bow under the shadow of His hand and confess our sin to Him.

No one knows till he has really thus confessed how great the relief is of a recognition of this sole responsibility to God. We mount above our fellow-men and their judgment-seats. We leave their puny criticisms far below us. They may be right in blaming us—no doubt they are. But past their blame the very magnitude of our guilt exalts us to a higher judgment-seat. The soul, full of God's power and love at once, is not satisfied to utter itself to less than Him. It must cry as David did in that Fifty-first Psalm, which he wrote about this same crime touching Uriah: "Against Thee, Thee only, have I sinned, and done this evil in Thy sight." In one word, it must be able to complete the

FOURTH SUNDAY IN LENT. 191

whole confession of our text, and say, not merely, "I have sinned," but "I have sinned against the Lord."

4. And what more is there in the true confession of selfishness? Only one thing, I think, and that is the acknowledgment that the selfish acts which we confess are representations and expressions of a selfish character and heart in which our true guilt abides. If you could make out an absolutely complete list of all the selfish acts that you have ever done, all the selfish words that you have ever spoken, all the selfish thoughts that you have ever thought, and bringing it up, should unroll it in the sight of God, and, pointing with shame down the long catalogue, should say, "Look, Lord, and read. They are all there. I have not left out one. The black tale is complete"—when that is over, have you confessed your selfishness? You have not touched it. As fertile and as foul as ever, it lies deep in your heart, ready to breed new selfish acts when these are cleared away. Not till you trace these things down to their roots; not till you say, "I did wrong things because I was a wrong thing. I lived for myself, not for my neighbors, because I loved myself a great deal better than my neighbors, and so broke God's law in my heart before I broke it with my hands. I was, I am, a living violation of it every day I live"; not till a spiritual logic traces back thus corrupt deeds to their source in a corrupt nature; not till "I have sinned" means "I am sinful," is the confession finally complete.

How feebly we talk and think about the judgment-day! We tremble when we picture God upon His great white throne, hurling at our dismayed terror the long succession of our sins. We shudder at the thought of this deed and of that deed which we must meet again. The true horror of the judgment-day will be the making manifest of hearts. What I have done will fade before the preëminent shame at what I have been. Then, if not before, deeds will take their true places as mere fruits and types of characters. Just as we grow into the solemnity of the judgment-day we attain its point of view already, and learn to enlarge David's "I have sinned" into Simon Peter's "I am a sinful man, O Lord." Then, as we said, the confession is complete.

Taking a single sin, then—selfishness—I have tried to show you how, in the heart of a man who is really trying to confess his wickedness, the confession gradually grows to fullness. First there is the seeing of the fact, then the acknowledgment of the moral character of the fact, then the owning of responsibility to God for the wrong-doing, and last the consciousness that the wrong-doing is a wrong-being, that the sins are sinfulness. It may come upon a man all in a flash, as it did on David; or it may grow hardly, fought against stoutly, conquering step by step for itself, taking years, perhaps, to get entire possession of the nature. But it must come, and it must all come, or the man's sins are not genuinely confessed. When it has all come, a man need not question how it came—slowly or swiftly, calmly or violently; however it came, the confession is perfect, and in the utterness of his humiliation there is nothing more that he can do.

And what comes then? Ah, here we come to the better news, the glad tidings, the "Gospel" of our sermon. "I have sinned against the Lord." And Nathan answered, "The Lord also hath put away thy sin." Quickly as all God's laws fulfil themselves, quick as the rain-drops catch the sunlight and the rainbow springs to sight, quick as the hillside hears the thunder and answers with its echo, so quick—immediately—the whole forgiveness follows on the whole confession. We need to know how absolute this is. I want to state it in its fullness and invariableness. There is a law in our natures that makes it necessarily certain that if you touch a particular muscle the arm will quiver; if you appeal to a particular feeling the anger will rise and flush the face. Now just so it is a law of God's nature—invariable with a godlike uniformity, more certain than the succession of the seasons or the comings and the goings of the stars—that if a human being touches Him with a true confession He must answer with an unreserved forgiveness.

Notice, my friends, who think to try, this Lent, perhaps to-day, this great experiment: it must be the complete confession that we have been describing. No element of all the four must be left out. It must have all the honesty and profoundness of the total act. No flippant temporary sorrow, no moment's gust of wild regret, will answer. But to the patient, steady, wholesouled faith of the entire confession the attempt is no experiment. It must succeed. It has succeeded as soon as it is made. "The sin is put away" the very moment that the heart has dropped its burden by the cross: "I have sinned against the Lord."

"Are you not stating this too blankly?" some cautious guardian of the Gospel asks. "Is there not something more needed before the perfect forgiveness, the entire reconciliation, can be thus assumed? Will not your words make men presumptuous unless you add something else?" What shall it be, then? I confess I do not know. Jesus says," Ask, and ye shall receive; seek, and ye shall find." Shall we say that a man must be sorry for his sin and leave it before he can be forgiven? Certainly he must; but that act of converted resolution is included, I hold, in the confession that I have described. If David meant just to go on in sinning —killing new Uriahs and taking their wives—Nathan surely would never have accepted his confession. The prophet evidently felt that it included the determination of a better life. But shall we say that this better life must be begun, that some good steps in it must be taken to prove its reality, before a man ought to count himself forgiven? That is not so, for the true ground whereon I trust I am forgiven is not the symptoms that I see in myself. That would make very poor business of my faith and peace. It is the simple belief in the promises of God. And then, besides, since one of the great incentives—nay, the great incentive—to a holy life is the delighted gratitude of known forgiveness, it surely is not right to tell me I can know I am forgiven only by seeing in myself those fruits which can of their very nature spring only from a pardon which I have already recognized and given thanks for. Or shall we say that a man's reconciliation with God is not perfect till he has made some set profession of his new intentions and entered into the outward covenant of a sacramental church? Again I say, Not so! How can that be necessary to an act's doing which has no meaning except as a token that the act is already done? A man is forgiven before he is baptized; so surely neither baptism nor confirmation is necessary to his forgiveness. Their holy place comes afterward.

Yes, there is danger lest we guard the Gospel overmuch. There is danger lest the walls we build to keep the truth in keep the souls of men out. Let us not be afraid to be as free as Christ. A whole confession must bring a true forgiveness. If we confess our sins, He is faithful and just to forgive us. The moment you cry, "God be merciful to me a sinner," the reply is ready: "Thy faith hath saved thee; go in peace."

My friends, our Lent is here. There is no magic in its days. It is only that we have resolved till Easter to give more time and thought to our religious life. All that may come to much or it may come to nothing. I beg you, let it come to much. And the way to do that is to bring your soul up to the point of whole and gennine confession. By any discontent you have now with your life, by any longing for a better heart, by the solemn responsibility you owe to God, by the great unutterable love of Christ, I beg you, as if I went from ear to ear and pleaded with each of you, not to let this Lent pass without confessing your sinfulness and being forgiven and becoming a grateful servant of Jesus Christ. May God grant it for all.

XIII.

FIFTH SUNDAY IN LENT.

" Ye are they which have continued with Me in My temptations. And I appoint unto you a kingdom, as My Father hath appointed unto Me."—LUKE XXII. 28, 29.

THERE are many texts in the Bible from which I might easily start in saying what I especially want to say to you to-day. I take this one because it will connect our study with the history of Christ. It was near the end of His ministry. He was rejoicing in its great success. Behold, He and His disciples were to have a kingdom where they were to reign like kings. But as He thinks of this successful close of His great work His mind runs back over the days when it had seemed as if it never would succeed. They who are to share His kingdom are also they who have been with Him "in His temptations." The end could not be reached without recalling the memory of all the dark stages of the journey. He could not stand in the glory of success without remembering how He had passed through clouds of failure. The days when the Pharisees had insulted Him, when the people had turned deaf ears to His teachings, when even His own disciples had staggered in their faith and hesitated whether they would not leave Him—all these days came back to His remembrance, as to the recollection of many a man the days of his failure have seemed to start into life and reality again just as he was stretching out his hand to lay it on the prize. This is what gives the profound pathos, the mysterious and solemn mingling of sadness and joy, which comes in every finally achieved success.

It is this subject which I wish to speak about to-day —the relation between success and the failures which precede it. What have the failures to do with the success? Evidently there are two possible ideas regarding their relationship. One idea would make the failures and the success to be quite separate from each other. It would suppose that a man went on failing and failing and failing for a long time, until at last his circumstances changed and everything was altered. Some lucky accident sent the wind round the other way, and then the ship, which had been struggling in the face of the gale and losing ground all the time, was caught by the new breeze and carried on triumphantly into its port. The other idea believes that the success which shows itself at last cannot possibly be the sudden thing which it appears to be. It must have been present, gradually working itself out underneath the failures, all the time. The failures must have been borne upon its bosom, and even in some degree created by the local and temporary reactions of the same force which made the great success. There is a verse of one of the subtlest and truest of the English poets of our time which expresses so perfectly this second idea of the relation between final success and the failures which precede it that I quote it to you at once. He draws his figure from the ocean, with its waves and its tide:

FIFTH SUNDAY IN LENT.

> "For while the tired waves, vainly breaking,
> Seem here no painful inch to gain,
> Far back, through creeks and inlets making,
> Comes silent, flooding in, the main."

You see the picture which is in those words—a stretch of sea-shore beach, with the waves breaking in upon it, but every wave a failure; every wave bursting with a little petulant hiss upon the shore, and falling back disappointed into the great body of the sea behind it; every wave a failure, but all the while the great sea itself, far out behind the sea-shore waves, lifted with a mighty movement and rolling itself irresistibly in upon the shore.

> "Through creeks and inlets making,
> Comes silent, flooding in, the main."

The noisy waves are failures, but the great silent tide is a success. The waves are borne upon the bosom of the tide; they share its motion; nay, the failure of each of them in some degree is a reaction of the tide's motion as it is cast back from the beach. But all the time the tide is succeeding while the waves are failing. The failures are carried on the bosom of a success which is present underneath them all the time. This is the idea of the relation of failures and success to each other which is in the verse of Clough. If we drew a sea-picture of the other idea it would not be, like this, a picture of the tide behind and under the waves. It would be a picture of the turning tide, of the flow following upon the ebb, of a tide which had fallen into failure followed by another tide which brought success. This would be the fitting picture of success and failure separate from each other, and one only coming into life after the other had died and passed away.

I hope that I do not obscure with metaphors what I want to make very plain indeed. Let us turn back and see exactly what our metaphors mean when we apply them to the life of Jesus, of which I began to speak. There had been a day, two years before, when Jesus was preaching at Capernaum; and when His sermon was finished it is written that "many of His disciples went back, and walked no more with Him." It was the darkest period of His ministry. It was the time when it most seemed as if His Gospel was going to be left on one side, and He was going to do no mighty work. And now what shall we say about that time in its relation to the other time, recorded in the chapter from which I take my text, when He sat with His disciples at the table of the Passover and calmly shared with them the kingdom which His Father had bestowed on Him? Was it simply that between these two times something had happened which had made a change in the fortunes of the Gospel, so that what once was failing afterward began to succeed? Was it not, far more truly, that the Gospel was always succeeding from the first, and that what seemed its temporary failures had always been backed by and borne upon a great movement which started at the birth of Jesus; nay—why should we stop there?—which started with the first conception of the birth of Jesus in the mind of God, and never can stop till His work of salvation shall be completely done? Do you not see the difference of these two ideas? Do you not see, also, the great difference which it must have made to Jesus which of these two ideas He Himself had about what seemed to be the failing moments of His life? Suppose He had the first—the idea that the coldness and indifference and hostility about Him meant an ebbing tide, a great swinging back away from Him of the whole soul and substance of human faith, and that there must be a total change, a whole new different movement, before He could again get hold of men and make them believe in Him. Must He not have been paralyzed? Must He not have just sat down listlessly upon the shore, or paced restlessly up and down the sand, waiting for the turning of the tide? But if He was full of the other idea—if He knew that a great success in the whole was perfectly possible even with the failure of many—aye, perhaps all—of the single manifest efforts which He put forth; if He knew that each word which He spoke to each single hearer might fall back with only the slightest effect produced upon his soul, and yet that His word as one great total power of God might be all the time conquering the soul of the world, then what patience, what calmness, and what zeal to work there must have come to Him! How He must have been conscious that He was succeeding, even though every effort fell so far short of its endeavor that it seemed to be a failure! The special wave that touched Chorazin or Bethsaida dropped defeated, and "He could do no mighty work there, because of their unbelief"; but the great ocean of His truth was pressing on and occupying the world all the time.

Now it does seem to me to be of very great importance that you and I, my friends, men and women who are sure to fail in hundreds and hundreds of the best struggles of our lives—nay, who are sure to fail in some large degree in all the special struggles which we ever make—and yet who know that life would be intolerable unless we kept the hope of some success which we should ultimately win, should have and always keep this higher view of the relations of success and failure which we have said must have been in Jesus. Here are you, for instance, wrestling with your special sin, with that old enemy whom you carry about with you, bound up in the selfsame heart with all your best aspirations and desires. Every special effort that you make to conquer that sin fails. Every time you try to be true you are half false. Every time you try to be spiritual the carnality about you beats you back. Every time you set up the white banner of purity the dark clouds of lust gather around it and it is well-nigh lost. Do you not know the picture?—the weary sense of being beaten; the old familiar disappointment that comes back at the close of the day, when you let your hands drop and say, "Well, once more my sin has been too strong for me!" What can be done? We know how to some men it seems as if nothing were to be done here; as if a total change of all conditions must occur before a man could have any chance against his sins. Some men seem to dream of heaven as if there only the soul of man could come to any great success; as if until it came there it must always be a losing fight. But the best and most faithful men have always had a truer thought. Out of God's revelation and their own experience it has been shown to them that a life might be succeeding in the struggle after goodness even while every effort of the man who lived that life to be good fell so far short of what he wanted it to be that he could call it nothing but a failure. The purpose, the consecration, of the life to God and goodness is its tide. The special struggles to do good things are the waves. The deep, persistent, and unchanging hate of the peculiar sin, which is determined never to be reconciled to it and to fight against it till it dies—that is the soul's success, which does not falter or stop, and which carries along upon it all the partial failures of which the life is full.

I am sure that I speak to the consciousness of some of you, my friends, when I speak thus. Do you not know what it is to be failing every day, and yet to be sure—humbly but deeply sure—that your life is, as a whole, in its great movement and meaning, not failing, but succeeding? You want to do that best work that a man can do—to make life brighter and nobler for your fellow-men. Not a day passes in which you do not somehow try to do that blessed work; but every time you turn away after one of those attempts to give sympathy or inspiration to your brethren, how your heart sinks, so cold and so ignoble are the words which you meant to be so generous and warm! And yet all the while you know that the whole life does not fail. Still there is the purpose! It does not die. It is not given up. It presses forward, wounded and bleeding, but more and more determined every day. Every day it grows clearer and clearer to you that without that wish and hope and resolution life would not be worth living. You want to be absolutely true. But see! the account which you gave of yourself yesterday told only half the truth. The day before you could not bring yourself squarely to face the fact. Last week you let a lie pass unchallenged and entered into silent partnership with it. Nevertheless you know that you are growing truthful, and the blessed day draws nearer when deceit shall be completely trodden underfoot. So it is true of you that in a deeper life which underlies your actions, in the life of resolution and of consecration on which the life of action moves as the waves run backward often on the bosom of the still advancing tide— in that you are succeeding, even while again and again in special acts you fail.

I hear men say, "Oh, it is not so bad for me to drink, to steal, to lie, for I am not a Christian, I make no profession, I have never pledged myself nor undertaken to live a holy life." They are all wrong. They are failing from top to bottom—failing all the way down. They are succeeding neither in the special acts nor in the general purpose of their lives. The poor stumbling saint who through a thousand fal's and defeats keeps still the consecration of his life, and will be God's through everything, melancholy enough his broken and unworthy life may be; but it is better, even so, than if he cast his consecration off; better, even so, than his brother's life beside him, who makes no consecration of his life, and sins in wanton freedom and feels no self-rebuke.

I know that I am treading here on dangerous ground. I know that I am dealing with ideas which men have terribly perverted and misused. But the ground is not to be abandoned because it is dangerous; the ideas are not to be denied because of their misuse. This truth which I am preaching is no conceited antinomianism making believe that a man's sins are no sins for him if only his heart is pious and his general intentions good. Nor is it any silly and mischievous doctrine about evil being only "good in the making"—a necessary stage in every man's progression to the purer life. No! Both of these ideas are bad. Sin is sin whoever does it. Sin is sin however out of its poisonous heart may come some blessed medicine of penitence and watchfulness for the soul that does it. Both of these doctrines are destructive. Sin is always bad—always a loss. The wave that seems to fail does fail. Only he who makes that truth the only truth of life and sees no other truth is leaving out the deepest truth, the truth in which redemption lies. Not in the leaves, but in the root, lives the tree's life. Not in the act, but in the heart, are the issues of life and death; and failure never is total and complete till the heart turns away in obstinacy and sets its face toward evil. If you know that you have not done that, then, O my friend, however you have sinned, you have not finally and fully failed, and the door of success and hope stands open to you.

It would be interesting, if we had time, to see at length how the principle of which we are speaking applies to faith as well as conduct. Many and many an attempt of yours to believe in divine things seems a failure. Perhaps all evidence that you can find for their existence seems inconclusive and unsatisfactory. Perhaps, allowing fully their existence, every effort to get hold of them, to fix them close to your life with any such grasp as could properly be called faith, appears a failure. How many such discouragements there are! How many special efforts to believe are just exactly like the reaching up of waves on to the shore, a struggle upward, a wild, convulsive, desperate reach forward, and then a falling back again into the bosom of the great ocean out of which the ambitious and enterprising wave ventured to spring! But yet we know that is not all the story. That great bosom of the sea itself is moving shoreward, and the next ambitious, enterprising wave which tries its strength upon the shore will start from a sea-line more advanced, and will make a little higher record of itself upon the sand, before it too falls away —will fail a little farther on. Is there not something like that, also, in our experience? We try to lay hold of a certain truth and we fail; but all the time there is in our soul a deep, simple, earnest craving after truth in general; behind each special struggle after faith there is a constant faithfulness, and below our craving for God's special revelations there is a perpetual hungering and thirsting after God Himself. And that is always moving on, and every new attempt to know about Him starts from a higher level of the spiritual knowledge of Him, and so attains a little more satisfaction, before it too, in its turn, falls back into that inevitable failure which awaits every attempt of man to grasp and understand the things of God. This is the history of many a faithful life. Upon the bosom of a true faith in God, ever becoming more and more successful, ever pressing forward into greater clearness, are born and live the special efforts to attain the truths of God which never can succeed. They share the movement of the deeper faith on which they rest. They are lost and come totally to nothing if they try to live apart from that movement. But, living upon it, they are healthy and vital, and every time they fail they bring back their store of earnestness and zeal to add to the body of the larger and deeper faith out of which they sprang. It is in this constant consciousness at once of succeeding and of failing that the souls most rich in faith live on year after year. "Lord, I believe; help Thou mine unbelief," is their perpetual prayer. Humility and hope grow stronger together in them every day. And life becomes at once more patient and more enthusiastic, more expectant of temporary failure and more certain of ultimate success, the longer that they live.

I am sure that it must help many of us if we can see how our truth is true, also, with regard to the matter of happiness and sorrow. There is a happiness so deep, a furnishing of the nature so profoundly with the conditions of joy, that it may bear upon its breast a hundred sorrows and yet be happy still. Alas if it were not so! Alas if the perpetual presence of disappointed hopes and broken plans and severed ties were all; if underneath them all it were not possible for a soul to carry in itself so true and rich a peace and contentment in the divinest things that it should know not merely that it was going to be happy some day or other, when the great change should come, but that it was happy now with a happiness that nothing could disturb!

And yet once more, I find in our truth of the double fact of life, the fact of deeper condition and the superficial phenomena, the fact of the tide and the wave in all existence—I find in this the real key to the state and the prospects of the world at large. The world is growing better—I know it. A great unceasing movement toward truth and goodness is carrying slowly forward ever the character of this great, mighty, mysterious humanity. How slow it is, but oh, how real it is, the study of the ages tells. And yet behold how the good causes fail. Behold how selfishness comes in to paralyze each great endeavor for the good of man. Alas for him who only sees this surface fact; who does not feel beneath it all the heave and movement of the whole race forward toward goodness, toward God! To him who hears at once the tumult of moral failures all around him and the steady progress of the great moral success beneath him—to him the world becomes solemn and beautiful, pathetic and full of hope. For him despairing pessimism and silly optimism both become impossible. A divine optimism, which, while it dares not say, "Whatever is is best," devoutly says, "The best is strongest and shall ultimately conquer and use even the worst," becomes the habit of his life. Such was the optimism of Jesus. Such is the optimism of His disciples if they catch His spirit.

"Ye must be born again," said Jesus. I ponder these divine words of His, and ever more and more they seem to me immeasurably deep. There is no end to them. To think of them is like gazing into endless space. But one great truth which they assuredly contain is this: that life for any man is not complete until a deeper and a higher life is put beneath and over the mere life of action, into which the soul can perpetually retreat, and on whose breast the life of action can be buoyantly upborne. There are men who the world thinks are always failing who are themselves conscious of a success which is a truer truth to them than all their failures. They are the men who have been born again, and who carry the new life underneath the old life all the while. The Master of that new life is Christ. The soul worried and torn with disappointments, haunted by the taunts of fellow-souls which tell it it has failed, suspicious of itself, yet keeping still its faithfulness and consecration, goes to Him, to Christ, and lo! it finds a new fact there. Below its failures He has for it success. Through all its deaths He brings out for it, as He brought out for Himself, life! "I too," He says, "seemed to fail, but in My Father I succeeded." "You shall share with Me. Ye are they which have continued with Me in My temptations. And I appoint unto you a kingdom, as My Father hath appointed unto Me."

Whatever failures He may have for us to pass through first, may He bring us all at last to that success in Him.

XIV.

THE SUNDAY NEXT BEFORE EASTER.

"And they that went before, and they that followed, cried, saying, Hosanna; Blessed is He that cometh in the name of the Lord."—MARK XI. 9.

IT was the first Palm Sunday and Jesus was coming to Jerusalem—that old picture which so many generations have looked upon and studied. As He came the whole city was full of stir and tumult. Every element in it responded to Him who was approaching according to its nature. The simple-minded people came streaming out to meet Him. The thoughtful, puzzled students, not hostile, with some degree of sympathy, sat at home listening to the tumult and wondering whether it could possibly be that this was "He of whom Moses in the law, and the prophets, did write"; whether this uproar that they heard streaming down the Mount of Olives and pouring into the city's eastern gate really could have anything to do with the old prophecy about "the Lord coming suddenly to His temple." Those whom He had cured of sicknesses blessed Him anew as they heard of His approach. Those who had believed in Him felt their faith deepen at the sound of His triumph. Those who despised Him sneered anew at the people's Idol. "Have any of the Pharisees believed on Him?"

they said over and over to one another. The priests hugged their traditions closer and said, "There is nothing about Him here." The lordly Romans stalked by superciliously, hardly deigning to glance at the passing procession, only wondering what these absurd, fantastic Hebrews would do next. Each man according to His nature answered to the coming Christ. It was like the judgment-day.

It would be easy to see in Jerusalem upon that day a picture of the way in which the world at large, with all its different classes of mankind, has always been judged by the approach of Jesus. It would be easy, and perhaps it would be interesting, to discover in the world full of men all of those different groups or classes which were in that city. But such a study would be too general. What I want to do rather than that is to see how our own souls, the soul of each of us, is represented by Jerusalem, and how His Palm Sunday offer of Himself to His own city is repeated in the offer which Christ makes of Himself to every heart. Let us set our own soul on that rocky hill and see Christ come to it. Long heard of, not a stranger, having often passed before our sight, at last He comes finally and formally to claim us for His own, to solemnly assert that we belong to Him, to bid us make our choice whether we will take Him for our King or not. Such days do come to all of us— days when we feel as if the Saviour, who had been long tempting us, had gathered up all His power of appeal and expected to be then either accepted or rejected; days when the chance of the new spiritual life seems to stand with peculiar solemnity before our heart. Such days are to us what Palm Sunday was to Jerusalem.

Our whole nature, like one great city, answers in response with many voices which yet make in the end one great decision.

There is much in a human nature, in a human soul, that is like—at least, that may be fitly represented by—the marvelously interesting life of a great city. There is the same mixture of many elements which yet make a true unity. In a soul, as in a city, there may be internal conflict and dissension, while yet at any moment the distracted soul, like the distracted city, will turn as one being to resist an invader from without. A man, like a city, has a corporate will, and does actions from which, nevertheless, much that is in him may dissent. The same sort of bewildered but yet true and effective personality which is in a city is what thoughtful and earnest men are always recognizing in themselves—a personality which, while it finds it very hard to give a satisfactory account of itself, yet accepts its duties, its responsibilities, its privileges, is proud of itself and ashamed of itself as only a genuine person can be.

Thus it is, then, that without too great fancifulness we may picture the approach of Jesus to our souls under the figure of His entrance into Jerusalem. He comes to one of us as He came to that city of His and of His Father's. Think how sacred it was to Him. Think how He loved it. Think what vast precious possibilities he could see sleeping behind its brilliant walls. There was His Father's temple. There was the whole machinery for making the complete manhood. And yet there was defiance, selfishness, unspirituality, and cruelty—the house of prayer turned into the den of thieves. O my dear friends, if Christ, as He comes to any one of us to offer us His salvation, never forgets for a moment what we might be in the sight of what we are, and never forgets for a moment what we are in the vision of what we might be; if He always sees our sins in the light of our chances, and our chances against the shadow of our sins, then what Jerusalems we must be to Him! He loves us as He loved that city, with a love full of reproach and accusation. He stops as He comes in sight of us, and "beholds the city, and weeps over it." I can think of no picture which so lets me into the very depths of the soul of Christ as He approaches a soul of man which He longs to save as that which depicts Him stopping on the Mount of Olives, where Jerusalem first comes in sight, and beholding the city, and weeping over it.

But I want to speak not so much of what is in His soul as of what is in the soul to which He comes. It cannot be indifferent to Him. And there does not come out one clear, simple utterance of reception or rejection, any more than Jerusalem was unanimous and prompt to receive or to reject the Saviour when He came to her. From the soul, as from the city, come various answers, uttering the various portions of its complex life. See what some of them are:

1. And first there is in every soul something that spontaneously welcomes Christ. It has been always so. It makes the basis to which the power of the Saviour always immediately appeals. There is a childlike element in every heart, a deep and underlying freshness of perception, to which when He, that bright, strong, divine Presence, is presented, it immediately knows Him and goes out to meet Him, as the children and the common

people streamed out on Palm Sunday to meet the coming Christ. There is something of the child, something of the common humanity, in every man. And there is something, too, of discontent, something of a sense of unfulfilment. There is a Simeon and Anna part always in the temple of our souls. There is a readiness to hear any voice that promises release and the lifting of horizons and the dawning of a larger day. And, deeper still, there is an aching consciousness of wickedness that is a mixture of despair and hope, but always has more of hope in it than despair; there is a sense of sin wanting forgiveness. All this part of our nature, the child part, the needy part, not yet drilled into submission and content, this part which either by loftiness or lowness is ready for new things (for I suppose that the company which brought Jesus down the Mount of Olives had in it the noblest and purest and also the most sinful and wretched souls in all Jerusalem)—all this part of us it is that spontaneously welcomes Jesus, crying, " Hosanna ; Blessed is He that cometh in the name of the Lord."

I think that we are always somewhat puzzled and surprised when we set ourselves to realize how Jesus appeared among His generation in Jerusalem, and what sort of people it was that He primarily attracted to Him. In the best sense of the word He was a radical. He went Himself, and carried all who would go with Him, to the roots of things; and when reform was needed He always would begin it there. His religion has been so long identified with conservatism—often with conservatism of the obstinate and unyielding sort—that it is almost startling for us sometimes to remember that all the conservatism of His own times was against Him, that it was the young, free, restless, sanguine, progressive part of the people who flocked to Him. The Church of our day has to be on her guard against those who seek her for the mere shadow of her established respectability. Jesus, in His day, had to send away more than one who came to Him as if He were the mere prophet of discontent, the captain of a company of revolutionists. Such a change in the whole attitude of men toward Christ every thoughtful observer sees. But still, changed as may be the aspect of the Church at large, in personal experience the old condition of the time of Jesus reappears. Out of the city of each man's heart it is the bright, young, free, hopeful element that starts up at His coming to bid Him welcome. Every man who truly becomes a Christian is an idealist then. Then, at that moment when he takes Christ in, he believes in the perfectibility of human life. The dry man of books, the dusty man of business, the old man crusted with the dreary years—they all grow young again; the everlastingly young part in each of them asserts itself when they take Christ. The old, dry, dusty part of them has to stand aside. The everlastingly young part of them goes streaming out at the gates, up on the road that climbs the mountain, shouting, exulting, flinging down branches, spreading clothes for the pathway where the Christ is coming. This is one of the many meanings of the word of Jesus about the necessity of being born again, and of that other word of His about receiving the kingdom of God as a little child.

2. This is the part in us that welcomes Christ. But now turn to some other parts in us and see how they receive Him, see how they correspond to other elements

which were there in the streets of Jerusalem on that Palm Sunday. There were skeptics there—groups of Sadducees who looked with a sort of superior pity upon the whole transaction. They turned aside to let the host sweep by, and then looked after it and shook their heads, with that sort of pity which is at the soul of the intensest pride. The pride that hates is never so intensely supercilious and proud as the pride that pities. And in our hearts who of us has not realized the presence of that sort of pride; who of us has not found the skeptical part of himself pitying the faithful part of himself for what it counted the childish folly of being inclined to accept a supernatural Redeemer? If I could open the history of your closets I could find there what I mean. When have you prayed to God so completely, with such perfect sense of His nearness and His love, that right alongside your faith, mixed with it in the same heart as part of the same nature, there has not been something of self-pity—a superior, indulgent sort of toleration of your own weakness in needing to pray and in venturing to pray? Surely there are many souls here who know that experience. Many and many a time the child in us prays while the man in us stands by and pities. The bright, simple, spontaneous impulses go out toward God, fly up to heaven, while the dull, earthbound habits cling to the ground and look after the aspiring desires with a kindly and supercilious admiration, as the man standing firm upon the earth looks after the birds flying up into the sky. And so if it is not prayer, but obedience. There is a part of us that tries to obey our Master, Christ; tries to do right because it is His will. But when we are called upon in any way to give an account of our efforts after righteousness, how quickly another part of us springs forward and hastily flings a veil of lower motive over this devotion and personal obedience, as if it were ashamed of it! You do some good deed simply because you really want to honor and obey your Saviour, and then you say, "Oh yes, I did it; I thought it was a wise, politic thing to do." It is the skeptical part of you disowning the faithful part of you. And so when one lives in God's communion, enjoys, delights in, day by day, the blessed society of a divine Master, and then says to himself, "Nay, but this peace, this hourly delight, who can say how much of it comes of a fortunate disposition, good health, and a successful business?" Once more it is the skeptic in us poisoning the faith of the believer in us. And how close they lie to each other, crowded in together in this mysterious selfhood, that can be measured only by One who has realized what units these complex lives of ours really are!

Thus ever in the streets of our inner Jerusalem stands the Sadducee and watches and disbelieves and pities while our ready and simple faith welcomes Christ. Blessed is he in whom the simple faith presses on, undismayed even by his own self-doubt and self-scorn, until it has brought the Lord into the central temple of the heart and made Him Master there.

3. But in Jerusalem on that Palm Sunday there were not only those who doubted Christ, there were some people, also, who hated Christ; some people whom He interfered with; some people who felt that they could not live in the same city with Him—that either He or they must give way and go out. There were the Pharisees,

who saw in Jesus the contradiction of all their most treasured traditions and favorite ideas; and there were the sinners, whom He had rebuked for all their different kinds of sin—the cheats, the liars, the blasphemers, the haters, the impure, the wicked men of every sort. The Pharisee said, "If what this Teacher says is true, all that I say is false." The sinner said, "If what this Master commands is right, my life is horrible." Between each of these men and Jesus there was war to the death. One or other of them must yield or die. What shall we say? Is there any analogy here? If there is in your heart at this moment any hard, proud, selfish, narrow notion of religion which you would have to see cast down and trodden underfoot before the breadth and the humility of the Gospel faith could take entire possession of your soul, then, tell me, have you not within you an element which corresponds exactly to what the Pharisees were in Jerusalem? And if you are living in sins of any sort which are deliberate and obstinate, which you do not mean to give up, and which Christ hates, with which He cannot live, then there is that in you which hates Christ. For hate is not merely an excited emotion; hate is a moral antagonism. Sin and goodness always must hate each other, like darkness and light. Still you may love Christ, too, at the same time; for, with all your unity, you are this mixed Jerusalem. Still you may love Christ, even while you hate Him. You have had little of the deepest experience of life if you have not learned long before this that all the strongest powers are capable of holding us with a double grasp, making us hate and love them at the same moment. The noblest man, until you unreservedly yield yourself to his nobleness, is a provocation to your wrath and to your love together. It is both the anger and the joy with which he fills you that blend in the fascination of his presence. And so Christ may be hated by the part of our nature with which He interferes and which will not yield to Him, with a hate all the deeper for the ardent affection with which at the same moment another part of our nature is rejoicing in His love. The conflict, the struggle, of such a divided nature no one can describe. Some of you remember it; nay, some of you are in the midst of it. It is raging underneath the quiet faces that you wear before your brethren. It breaks out when you are alone. Your midnight watches have seen its tumult. Oh, how anxiously the Christ whom a heart's love is carrying to His temple must watch the love that carries Him, and give it His strength, that it may not be frightened or dismayed when it has to carry Him right through the shadow of a hate which is part with it of the same human nature!

4. There is one other element in the population of Jerusalem whom I want to make you see. I never can think of that strange city in the time of Jesus without seeming to see stalking about among the native Jewish people who were perfectly at home there the figures of the Roman soldiers who constituted the garrison with which the conquerors held the now subject city. Tall, strong, coarse, rugged frames they wore, and as they walked the streets a brutal insolence mingled with a superb contempt in the cold curiosity with which they scrutinized the strange people whom they had been sent to guard. They were foreigners, but here they held the natives in subjection. They had no sympathy with

the mysterious spiritual associations by which they found themselves surrounded. They were wholly of the earth. All they wanted was to keep the peace, to prevent an outbreak. Truth, spirituality, eternal life— all these meant nothing to them. They were mere power and mere system, earthly order embodied, as they stood watching Christ's procession through the streets on Sunday, or as they dragged the same Christ to His cross on Friday. What better picture could you have of that which so many men know only too well as a true element in their internal life? Hard earthly prudence; a coarse terrestrial corner of our nature, to which all spiritual truths seem to make their appeal in vain; an iron unsusceptibility to all enthusiasm; a disposition to organize life upon its lower plane, and to think of religious impulses and aspirations only as the disturbers of the peace; materialism; selfishness; reason boasting itself of its confinement to its most terrestrial activities; the tyranny of sense—oh, what an element that is in all of us! How terrible it is in some of us! With what cold eyes it gazes on this grand, sweet, mystic Christ, who comes to claim the nature for His servant! With what ruthless, pitiless cruelty it leads him to His suffering, and sits down at the foot of the cross where it has hung Him, gambling for His clothes!

I think we grow to dread this element in ourselves and in our brethren more than almost any of the others; more than the doubt that pities, and the selfishness that hates the Christ—this hardness on which it seems as if He could make no impression; this Roman part of us which seems to have nothing to do with the Christ whom the better and softer part of our nature serves.

Often we forget the sneer of the Sadducee and the hate of the Pharisee when our eye is caught and fastened by that stony stare of the Roman soldier, too utterly cold and far away from all that we hold dear to feel either anger or scorn. And it is terrible when we find him even in ourselves.

These are the elements, then. Understand that I have been trying to describe, not the way in which many different men receive Christ, but how in one same man all these receptions are united. So Jesus came into Jerusalem. He came at once as an Intruder and a King. There were men along the streets who owed to Him the straightness of their limbs, the sight of their eyes, the clear, sane reason of their brains. They made the old streets ring with shouts of welcome. There were other men whom He had disappointed and defeated. He had trampled on their traditions, contradicted their doctrines, spoiled their trade. With muttered curses they saw Him go by in His triumph. What a confusion! The city was divided against itself. But through it all Jesus held on His way, claiming the town for His town because it was His Father's. Whether it owned His claim or spurned it, whether it welcomed Him or cursed Him, through the mixed tumult of its welcome and its curses He went on His way, claiming it all for His own. And so He claims our hearts. An Intruder and a King at once He seems to those hearts as He stands there on their threshold. There is something in every one of them that says to Him, "Come in, come in!" There is something, too, in every one of them that rises up at His coming and says, "Begone, begone! We will not have this Man to rule over us." But through their

THE SUNDAY NEXT BEFORE EASTER. 221

tumult, their struggle, Christ, whether He be King or Intruder, whether He be welcomed or rejected, goes on His way, pressing on into each heart's most secret places, claiming always that He and He alone is the heart's King.

And the struggle in any heart cannot keep on evenly balanced forever. Every heart has to decide. Jerusalem had to decide. Before the week was over she had decided. On Friday she crucified Christ. Still even round the cross there was love and faith and lamentation. But they were crushed and only heard in sobs. The hatred had triumphed, and Jerusalem had crucified her King. And so must every Jerusalem decide. So must your heart say finally to Jesus, "Come" or "Go." He never will go until you obstinately bid Him. He cannot come into the inmost temple until you welcome Him.

Do I talk parables? Let me speak plainly as I can. The moment that you trust Christ's forgiveness, and in profound gratitude give yourself to His service, casting every reluctance and doubt aside, that moment He begins the purification and salvation of your life which shall go on throughout eternity. May some one, may many of you, do that to-day.

XV.

PASSION WEEK.

"Now is My soul troubled; and what shall I say? Father, save Me from this hour. But for this cause came I unto this hour. Father, glorify Thy name."—JOHN XII. 27, 28.

THESE words belong to this week. They were spoken on that first Palm Sunday when, in the meekness of His majesty, riding over the garments of the people and the fragrant branches which they flung upon His pathway, the Saviour came up to Jerusalem to die the death which we have commemorated to-day. We have a right to-day to all the lessons they can teach us. And their lessons are most valuable if we can only find them.

For these words are full of the humanity of Jesus. "Here is a man like me, fearing death just as I fear it," says the plain man who reads them. You would be surprised to see how the men who write the commentaries have labored to make it out that it was something else, and not the death just before Him, which Jesus shrank from; to take away, that is, the very sense of Christ's perfect human nature which is the precious boon these verses have to give. No doubt there were other things to make the Saviour sad even as He rode through the hosannas which welcomed Him to His own city; but what this verse tells me is that He dreaded to die, and that human dread I claim and treasure as a proof of His humanity. Death was not yet conquered by His death, and He, the true man, shrank from man's tyrant.

Our text is the history of a conflict. We can see in it the struggle that goes on in Jesus' nature. Here He was at the very foot of the mountain on which He was to die. But He was completely, intensely alive. I think we must all feel what a strange truth there is in the old traditions of art, which make our Lord to have been physically the most perfect and beautiful of the sons of men. He was the Son of Man, the Lord of life. We feel instinctively that life must have been in Him the most complete thing possible. And if life were preëminent in Him, then the love of life, too, must have asserted itself preëminently, and even in the midst of all His sufferings and sorrows the Lord must have clung to life and dreaded death with all the power of that great unreasoning instinct which has always made the most miserable of living things wail as if at a new misery when you threatened it with death. This was Christ's position here. He stood in the present. He was part of, ruled by, the present. Death, with its untold agony, the one unknown which the Omniscient Immortal could not know, stood up before Him. He trembled at it. "Father, save Me from this hour," He cried out. Then, as if that cry to His Father lifted Him up to the divinity which He shared with Him, He looks back over His eternal history and rebukes Himself: "But for this cause came I unto this hour. What am I doing? What am I saying? Shrinking from death when I was born to die! Refusing agony when toward this agony all My joy has pointed!" He looked back, and lo! all His endless life had been busy setting up this cross. He had been traveling to this result for ages. Should He shrink from it now that He had reached it? And then the whole tone changes, and He who had cried, "Father, save Me from this hour," cries instead, "Father, glorify Thy name."

It is the genuine history of a genuine struggle. It is a memory of the temptation, and an anticipation of Gethsemane. I love it for its genuineness; for if Christ's human life be the type of the life of all humanity, then this struggle of His must be the perfect struggle, representing ours. It must include the way in which all men, from the assertion of a human repugnance, pass by degrees into an anxiety that God should glorify His name. It teaches us in general the method of all duty, or the process by which any man is led from an unwillingness to a willingness to do or bear God's will. Let us give it our study to-day from this point of view. We are standing to-day, as it were, waiting by the cross where Jesus died. If His death is to be indeed the inspiration of all the duty of our lives, we may not forget that both in Him and in us duty comes out of struggle.

This struggle of Christ, then, tells us first of all the truth that all duty must be its own revealer. No man comprehends any work that God has for him to do till the coming task brings its own light with it. How strange it was! After looking it in the face for years on earth, for ages in His eternal purposes, the death, when it came, seemed to take the Saviour by surprise, to cower and scare Him with its suddenness. But as with Him, so it must always be. No man can know a duty till it lights itself up with an immediate necessity, and then it will almost always surprise and awe him with its unexpected presence. We have all seen men led of God up to something which they have got to do. No matter what it be—the giving up of some bad habit, we will say, the adoption of some new self-sacrificing mode of life, the lifting of one of those heavy bundles of outward disesteem or inward sorrow which God lays sometimes in the middle of a man's path for him to take up and carry on his bent back thenceforth until he dies —no matter what it be, a man never meets a great duty of the active or the passive sort that it does not take him by surprise. He shrinks from it—tries by an instinct not to see the sword that God holds down to him with its handle toward his grasp; tries to get round the burden in his pathway that he dare not lift. " These things are not for me," he says. " My life is not strung to great achievement or great patience. My heart is not heroic. I am well enough for little work; I shall fail here. O Duty, go and find some other soul to dare thee. I would, but I cannot. O God, I am too weak! Let me go free; I cannot lift Thy burden. Father, save me from this hour." It is the history of all great action. There never yet was a reform but the reformer halted first before his work. The world heard afterward his bold and resolute words falling like hammers on the sins that he rebuked, and never guessed how he had pleaded with God across the pages of His inexorable Bible to send another to set Europe in a tumult, and not him. There never yet was a battle for humanity but the great captain God had chosen walked his tent all the long night before, and prayed to be released, and trembled when he saw the sunrise. Never a Moses came up yet singing his triumph at the head of his hosts, through the piled waters of the conquered sea, but that same voice that sings the Jubilate has begged beside the burning bush of his election that another and not he might speak to Pharaoh and bring the people out. So it is always. All great duty is a great surprise to the soul that must do it, and blinds him first of all with its bewildering light. He stands in the new glory with his hand before his eyes and cries, "Father, savè me from this hour." But afterward this light becomes a revelation. To the Moses or the Luther on whom the task is laid the splendor of the task becomes at last familiar, and he is able to look back and see how the past is all lighted up by it, and in its light he can see that it has been the centering point toward which the currents of his unconscious experience have all been flowing. Moses still trembles at the river he must cross; but he can see now that he was made to cross the river. The bulrushes and the king's palace and the bush on the hillside were all for that. Luther still dreads to speak the first word that is going to defy the Church; but he is overcome with a conviction that the Lord wants His false Church defied, and has made him, Luther, and none else, to defy it. Each hushes the remonstrance as he looks back on the past. The danger seems no less. The Red Sea is just as deep, the pope is just as intolerant, as ever; but now each says, "The Lord who brought me here, if I am to perish, must have purposes in my perishing too vast for me to know. I am here with the pressure of my preparatory experience pushing me on. I must do this duty, if I die; for I see now that there are ends higher than my life. My soul is troubled; and what shall I say? Father, save me from this hour. But for this cause came I unto this hour. Not that—some higher prayer!" And then the soul that duty has enlightened looks up to God, the new, strange work, be it for life or death, is seized most resolutely, and the soul passes into a new petition: "Father, glorify Thy name."

Such is the method of all duty. The great sun rises on the world and finds it dark. It stands upon the horizon and shrinks from its vast task. It hesitates and trembles. "Father, save me from this hour." But then its past grows luminous behind it. It has climbed these toilsome steps and reached this margin-line just "for this cause"—just that it might light this great dark world. That purpose brought it where it is. It must not shrink now; and so into the heart of the darkness, rolling the flood of conquering splendor before it as it goes, vanquishing the night with the victorious day, the great sun goes its way, honoring its Maker, daring all things at His word, writing its new prayer up and down the gorgeous sky: "Father, glorify Thy name."

Such is the method of all duty, not only for Moses and for Luther, but for you and me. For duty is terrible, of course, as it relates itself to the measure of personal strength—terrible for Daniel to dare the whole court of Darius and pray three times a day to his own true God; just as terrible for a school-boy to dare a little school-boy like himself and say his prayers under the terror of an unseen sneer. But each in our own degree we have all come up to some great duty of our life which took us by surprise and cowed us. We looked up to God appealingly. "Father, save me from this hour." Then very wondrously the revelation came; our past, our education, became clear. Lo! it is right up to this duty God has been leading me. Lo! for this cause came I to this hour. What then? It seems a terrible thing. It seems as if I could not survive it. But God must have had some purpose somewhere—if not for me, then for Himself; if not in my surviving, then in my perishing. Let me be satisfied. Let me learn the better prayer, "O Father, glorify Thy name." Blessed is the life that thus completes the method of all duty.

It is even more evident with the passive than with the active duties. No duty of doing frightens and dismays the human soul like the duty of mere suffering. I know nothing that will so cow and crush a strong, well man, with the red blood riotous in his full veins, as a certain conviction coming suddenly upon him that his strength is to be taken from him; that he is to be a poor, miserable, dependent invalid all the rest of his days until he dies. Nothing makes a man cry out to die like that. It is the most terrible sight one ever sees. A man is the strongest among men one day, doing every duty in his rampant strength; the next day the accident has come or the disease has smitten him, and he lies down on his bed which is to be his home, never to rise and walk among men on earth henceforth forever. We in our health cannot begin to guess the blank of his poor soul. Nothing is left—no hope, no strength, no energy; nothing but misery to wail out his forlorn and frightened cry: "Father, save me from this hour." And then it is the most beautiful sight one ever sees. As the man lies there in his misery, out of the darkness comes his past and reads itself to him. Each bright old year of health comes with its message of God's unforgetting love. Each strong deed of his vigorous youth turns to an angel, bringing him and laying at his bedside the trust which it accumulated. He slowly sees that all the past of active duty was stocking his life with the graces that should fit him for these slow years of suffering duty. This bed of wretchedness was the result to which every path of education led. Slowly his soul accepts the lesson. "Father, save me from this hour. Nay, for this purpose came I unto this hour. Father, glorify Thy name." Then the hands drop patiently from their resistance. The meek lips are put up to taste the bitter cup. The life grows happy in its new enlightenment of pain.

"'Glory to God, to God!' he saith;
'Knowledge by suffering entereth,
And life is perfected by death.'"

So of bereavement and poverty. So of every cross the life is called to bear. Every cross, since Christ the Light hung upon His, is a light-giver. O sufferer with any nameless agony, rejoice if thy cross lightens thy life as thy Saviour's did His. If it lets you see the higher end of life—that men and women were not born to live daintily and sail smooth waters kissed by sunny winds, but to bring praise to God, to let their Father glorify His name in them; that the life in which this is attained is the successful life—if this has been revealed to thee by suffering, rejoice and glory in thy every pain as Elijah must have gloried in the fiery horses that bore him up to God.

But what shall we say then? Is this the creed we come to—that God's glory being the final cause of all things, He, the Maker, just sits forever in His glory and arranges the world's scenic play for some vast selfish exhibition of Himself, putting the precious lives of men into the fire to light up with their death-flames the splendor of His life, making ready for eternal burning a vast hell where souls should blaze forever, that their agony might glorify the everlasting throne on which He sits? Is human happiness nothing? Are we the puppets and the pawns of some design outside ourselves with which we have no sympathy, which we dimly call God's glory? That were a heathen thought. That is the brutal religion of all heathenism—the religion of the Ganges and the old Druid woods.

There was a heathen old theology once, in Christian times and lands, which used to test its converts with this strange demand: "Would you be willing to be damned if it were necessary for the glory of God?" Think of some earnest soul just won by the loveliness of Christ, and glorying in its new hope of service here and heaven hereafter, vexed, and thrown back, and made desperate and miserable by the brutal blasphemy of such a question. Hundreds and hundreds were. Surely Christ's own desire for His Father's glory in His suffering clears all such foggy questions away for us. We accept in Him, as seen in our text, a genuine struggle. There is a distinct advance from the first repugnance of the flesh to the final submission of the spirit. And we see, too, how that advance was accomplished. He looked back and saw the procession of His destiny, the whole design of His nature tending to just this one result.

He remembered the unspeakable solemnity of the day when, over the ruin of the fallen world, He, the pitying Saviour, when no redeemer could be found, stood and said, "Lo, I come to do Thy will, O God!" He entered back into His union with the Father. He identified their lives again. His soul mounted up and stood by God's soul and looked over the eternal purposes with Him. And only then in this identification, seeing that the Father's glory must be His advantage too, must fulfil His most treasured plan—only then did His new submission utter itself: "Father, glorify Thy name."

And as with Jesus so with every sufferer; so with all self-sacrifice. Self-sacrifice which stops as such is a poor thing, good for nothing. Man is made to be happy and to seek happiness. The only difference of men is that some seek low happinesses and some seek higher. He seeks the highest who mounts up to God's standpoint and says sublimely, "God made me for some duty. To do that duty, to fulfil that end, must be my nature's highest perfectness, and so my nature's highest joy. But to fulfil that end must be a glory to the God who made me. What then? If I can stand where He stands, seek the same purposes, own the same laws, then we must love together, hate together, hope together, work together with one same ambition. Then His glory must be my good; my good His glory. The two no more conflict than the tree's good and the sun's glory on its leaves. The more the good tree grows, the more the glorious sun extends his glory over a wider world of leaves. God and my soul are one; and when you ask me if I would sacrifice my best good to His best glory I smile at the ignorance of your poor question. Why vex your brain conjecturing impossibilities? The two are one. I know I could not sacrifice my good unless I sacrifice His glory too."

Whatever other error our theology contains, let it keep clear of this. Let it understand Christ and His mercy better. Self-sacrifice in itself, for itself, is nothing. God does not want it. It does Him no good, gives Him no praise, for you to starve yourself, unless it does your soul some good. Then it does Him good, for His one earthly glory is in growing souls. Christ never asks me wantonly to lie down in the mire just that His chariot wheels may mount over me up to His throne. Oh no! As it concerns me, there is no glory that my Saviour wins which I must not share. If He lives I shall live also. My life He bought He has bound fast to His, and in the confidence of my humility I know He will not enter on His kingdom without looking round as He goes in for the poor sinner to whom He spoke the promise, speaking from cross to cross, from His to mine. Whatever else we let go, let us cling to this—the necessary connection of our triumph with our Redeemer's.

> "This one thing I know:
> We two are so joined,
> He'll not be in glory
> And leave me behind."

Does not this explain to us the whole theory of submissive prayer, making it very clear? There are two conceivable states of things in each of which prayer would be superfluous. In the first it would be needless, in the second it would be useless. Prayer would be needless if man were entire master of his own good, sole and sufficient doer of what was best for him; if human good, that is, were the one end of being, and man had within himself the wisdom and the power to attain it. On the other hand, prayer would be useless if man's best good were not considered in the government of things; if God were just some great Oriental despot, absorbing in His own selfish splendor all the purposes of His vast tributary realm. Pure humanitarianism and pure fatalism can neither of them pray. But let us have a world where these two purposes work on harmoniously, the Creator's glory and the creature's good being like sound and echo, like sunlight and reflection to each other; where every advance in one chronicles and repeats itself in the other. Let man by sovereign mercy be admitted into such an intimacy with his God, and then prayer—what is it? What but the answer of the echo to the sound, the uttered sympathy of the one common life, man responding to God's "Be happy, O my child!" with an ever grateful and reverent "Be glorious, O my Father!" As we go up higher in the new life prayer becomes less servile and so becomes more true. When the new life is finished, the sympathy complete in heaven, who can say what prayer will be? It will be what Christ's was, in His perfect humanity talking with the perfect Divinity to which it stood so near. There will be no wandering eyes, no listless thoughts, no formal words, no hearts that pray because they must; but souls alight with a new likeness shall leap into a new nearness to their God, and prayer be heaven to the perfected human life. God's glory and man's good— who will divide them there? The struggle will be over when our blindness clears away; and when we want to ask the best boon for ourselves, what shall it be but that which we used to pray with groans and tears of hard submission: "Father, glorify Thy name"?

Two other suggestions or illustrations of our text remain, of which I will very briefly speak. The lesson of Palm Sunday, Christ in view of His death accepting His Father's glory as His own best good, will always be a spectacle full of instruction and help to dying men. The struggle which our Lord passed through will always be the struggle of every life before it is reconciled to the necessity of death. Man loves to live and hates to die. It is not wrong. It is a part of his humanity. It is one development of his instinct of self-preservation. I believe that with every well, healthy man, with work to do in the world, an intense desire to live and do it, an intense dislike at the thought of giving it up and going away, is the healthiest and most Christian state; that any other condition is for him unhealthy and unchristian, however pious and devotional it may appear. When death rises up suddenly, full in the path of a live, vigorous man, and puts its cold hand out to draw him to itself, I believe the natural cry of the true human heart is, "Father, save me from this hour." And even when sickness comes, and the work has to be laid aside, and the road is evidently inevitably sloping downward to the grave, still the life fears to die. The last enemy has still his terrors. Heaven is beautiful, but death lies between. Oh, if there were but some escape, some way to pass dry-shod over the river and be saints, otherwise than by the pain of dying! And then to the human soul, as to Christ's soul, comes the revelation. Death, as the Christian comes up near to it, shows what it really is—the gathering up of the issues of life, the sublime grouping and grasping together in God's great hand of all the results of one period of being, that they may be handed over into another. It is the concentration or bringing to a focus of all the forces of the first life, that they may thence be reëxpanded and spread out into the second. It is the point to which all earth has been struggling, that it might thence embark for heaven. Let a man see this and all is plain. "Lo! for this cause came I unto this hour," the soul cries out in the new revelation it receives; "this is what I have been living for." As the scholar studies for his graduation, as the twilight hurries to the dawn, so truly "life is perfected by death"; and in his new intelligence the man, not simply resigned to a necessity, but rejoicing in a privilege, lies and awaits his change, praying always, "Father, glorify Thy name."

Paul tells of Christians who "through fear of death are all their lifetime subject to bondage." There are some men and women who haunt their lives and make them cheerless, for fear they will not be able to meet the king of terrors when he comes. I presume there are some such here to-day. Dear friends, learn from your Saviour that no duty reveals itself till we approach it. The duty of death, when you approach it, will light itself up, you may be sure, and seem very easy to your soul. Till then do not trouble yourself about it. To live, and not to die, is your work now. When your time comes the Christ who conquered death will prove Himself its Lord, and pave the narrow river to a sea of glass for you to cross. The work of life is living, and not, as we are so often told, preparing to die, except by living well.

And again, this general truth of the method of duty touches not merely the method of death, but even more directly the method of conversion. No man grown mature in sin comes easily from the darkness into the blinding and bewildering light of the higher life. Every soul cries out when it first sees the Saviour. Even when it owns Him it begs Him to depart, like the devils among the tombs. "What have we to do with Thee, O Christ? Art Thou come to torment us before the time? Father, save us from this hour." There are some such in this church. They ought to be Christians; they know they ought to be, but they do not want to be. Jesus holds them only by the sheer spell of duty. They would like to be away, but they cannot. His supreme, essential Lordship holds them where His love has failed. What shall they do? I tell you, my dear friend, all you need is a little clearer light. "Father, save me from this hour; let me go unsaved." Is that your prayer? Why, for this cause—just that you might be saved— for this cause came you unto this hour! If you would only look back you would see that it is no sudden emergency in which Christ has set you, but that in all your past life He has been evidently, though most unconsciously, leading you to Himself, and now only asks you to complete the process. He has been leading you in the dark, gently, tenderly, because your eyes were blind. Now His daylight dawns and you see whither He has led you; you see where He has set you—right at a duty's door, right before some great unmistakable obligation: of giving up the world, of setting about Christ's service, of becoming an open member of His Church. No one can wonder—He does not wonder—that you shrink from the newness of the task. "Father, save me from this hour." But you cannot escape it so. "For this cause came I unto this hour." And what then? The willing submission, soon or late, must come. "Father, glorify Thy name. Make of me, do with me, what Thou wilt." And then the weak hands are put out to push the heavy doors of duty back, and through the light that lies upon the other side of them your submissive soul passes into the gradual heaven of obedience. That is the struggle and the triumph of God's best conversions. God grant it may be yours.

This, then, is the lesson of our Master's struggle. The same Saviour who came in the morning over the Mount of Olives, heralded by hosannas, treading the palm-branches and the people's garments under His ass's feet—here He is in the evening struggling with His destiny, and leaving us an eternal pattern of steadfastness: "Now is My soul troubled; and what shall I say? Father, save Me from this hour. But for this cause came I unto this hour. Father, glorify Thy name."

It teaches us that struggle is not wrong. It is inevitable. To be weak and tempted is not wicked. It is human—that is all. Jesus was tempted too.

It is so hard to do right, you say. Yes, of course it is; and the soul that tries to do right does wrong so constantly. But then it is so glorious—glorious to do right through struggle; glorious to mount from the lower to the higher life, and seeing how God has bound our perfection to His own, have but one confident prayer for both: not, " Father, save me from this hour"—from any hour, however hard it be—but "Father, glorify Thy name."

And as to Christ when He prayed, so often to us, sharers not only of His struggle, but of His triumph, there shall come a voice from heaven, saying, "I have both glorified it, and will glorify it now again in thee." Who cannot dare all things and bear all things in the celestial courage of that promise?

XVI.

THURSDAY BEFORE EASTER.

"And He cometh, and findeth them sleeping, and saith unto Peter, Simon, sleepest thou? couldest not thou watch one hour?"
—MARK XIV. 37.

THE disciples of Jesus failed Him just when He needed them the most. The end was drawing very near, and on this night before His crucifixion their Lord had taken Peter, James, and John into the garden of Gethsemane, and while He was wrestling with His agony they had fallen asleep. Once and again Jesus comes back to them and finds them sleeping. There is something very touching in the tone of disappointment and surprise with which He speaks to them. He knew them thoroughly. He knew man in general, and He had known specially these three men, with their special characters and weaknesses, through all these last years of their life together. When He led them into the garden He must have seen the dimness gathering in their eyes, and known that they would go to sleep. But by and by, when He comes to them and finds them sleeping, He is full of surprise. He seems to be as much surprised as if He had expected to find them wide awake. Is there not here a suggestion or reminder of how different are different kinds of knowledge? There is a kind of knowledge, a certain final sort of conviction, which in the very nature of the case cannot come except by personal experience. However Jesus may know that His disciples will fail Him and sleep while He is struggling, there is a perfect conviction of their weakness which can come to Him only when He actually sees them lying helpless on the ground; and when that perfect conviction comes, however sure His knowledge may have already seemed to be, it is a shock and a surprise. This is something that we can understand. There is a fullest knowledge of all the things which touch us closest which can come to us only with their actual touch. You know that something which you are going to do will certainly estrange from you one who has been your closest friend. You are perfectly sure that he will misunderstand you and cast you off as his enemy when he hears what you have done. But when you actually see his angry face and feel his angry words like blows poured out upon you, then it seems as if you had not known at all before what now comes overwhelming you with such surprise. You know, as it seems, with perfect certainty, that the discontent which fills the land will make rebellion; but when at last the rebellion comes, the signal-gun is fired, and all the land is in consternation, your horror is as great as if the lightning had fallen from a cloudless sky. Your friend is very sick. For days and days you know that he must die. You stand by his bedside listening for his last gasp. At last he dies; and oh, you all know how suddenly death comes even to all those who think they are expecting it most surely. Of all these closest things there is a closest knowledge which cannot come until the touch is actually laid upon the quivering nerve. This truth seems to me to throw light upon some things in the experience of Jesus which sometimes puzzle us. Did He know beforehand what was to happen to Him, or not? If He did, there is a look of flatness and unreality about His human life. It loses all the freshness and interest and spontaneousness which give our human lives their meaning and their charm. But if He did not know what was to come to Him, did not know that John was going to follow Him, and that Judas was going to betray Him, and that Herod was going to mock Him, and that the Jews were going to crucify Him, then where is His wisdom and divinity? Does not the truth, in part at least, lie here?—that there is a kind of knowledge of Judas's treason which not even Jesus can have till He feels the cold kiss of the traitor on His cheek; there is a kind of knowledge of John's love which cannot come until He feels the disciple's head upon His bosom; there is a knowledge of Herod's scorn and of the Jews' hatred which the divine heart cannot gather except out of the sneering lips and flashing eyes of His persecutors in the hour of their triumph. All the divine foresight with which through the ages Christ looked forward to His life on earth, and all the human surprise and thrill of pain and joy with which at last He met the events of that life when it arrived—both of these become plain, and not in any way contradictory of each other, as soon as we let ourselves discriminate between the knowledge which is and the knowledge which is not possible without experience.

And this helps us to understand perhaps another puzzle. We are taught to think—we cannot well help thinking—of Christ our Master as standing over us and watching our lives, pleased when we are good, and disappointed, with a disappointment that seems to have some necessary mixture of surprise in it, when we do wrong. And yet how can this be, we sometimes think, if He knows all beforehand, if He sees perfectly and unmistakably just how we are to yield to or resist every temptation of our lives? Must we not lose that whole dear and affecting picture of the Saviour waiting and watching anxiously to see what we will do with our lives, expecting and looking to see of the travail of His soul, glad when we do right, and sorry, with a true contemporaneous grief, when we are wicked? I dare not think that I can solve all that mystery—nobody can. But if what I have said is true, there certainly must be a certain kind of knowledge of your goodness or your sin which cannot come to Jesus until the goodness or the wickedness is actually done, no matter how surely He may have known before that you were going to be good or to be wicked. No prophetic foresight can steal the freshness from that moment when at last the actual fact becomes genuinely present in the world. Do right to-day, and, long as God has known and prepared for your victory over this particular temptation, it is still your privilege to know that God is glad. Do wrong to-day, and in some true sense, some sense in which the capacity of sorrow must be present in the perfect nature, God is sorry. For to God, as to us, all things of realest, closest interest must come at last with a surprise and freshness, however long beforehand their coming has been known.

I have dwelt longer than I meant upon this opening

thought of the surprise of Jesus at His disciples' failure. But it is that failure itself that I really want to study. Here, at the very crisis of His need, He found them wanting. It was not simply that they fell asleep—that might be only physical exhaustion. Their sleeping was only a part of the experience of the whole night of their Master's trial. By and by, after a moment's outburst of Peter's fruitless anger, when he cut off the high priest's servant's ear, they all forsook their Lord and fled. Drawn to Him still, even although he would not own Him, Peter still lingers around the place where Christ is being tried, and there at last denies Him. Not one of them is ready to stand by his Master bravely and help Him carry His heavy cross from Gabatha to Golgotha. Only one of them—His best beloved, and the least unfaithful of them all—creeps to the cross's side and lingers there until the last. That utter failure of the disciples on the night of Christ's great trial is one of the strangest and most significant events in all the Gospel story. When He needed them most He looked for them in vain. When all the love and devotion and courage which He had been training in them were wanted for the instant's work they seemed to scatter into air. "Lord, I will follow Thee to death," the brave disciple had said with perfect sincerity immediately before. And when death loomed up in the distance and seemed to be coming down upon him he dropped his trembling hands and cried, "I do not know Him."

Is it a story which we can understand anything about from our own experience? Certainly we can. Sometimes a crisis, a great demand, seems to concentrate and intensify a resolution or a faith. What was vague and half formed before sometimes becomes, as it were in an instant, under the pressure of a sudden need, solid, compact, and strong. The man who did not know how he could possibly meet the enemy to-morrow, when to-morrow comes, and the enemy stands clear before him, is often amazed at himself as he feels the courage, strong as a lion's, filling his heart. But everybody knows that there is another power in a critical moment which is just the opposite of this. Sometimes we have all felt how the moment of supreme need paralyzes instead of inspiring, and we are weak as water just when the moment comes when all the strength which we thought was crystallizing into iron in us is wanted for its work. It is easy and common enough to say, with this strange difference in mind, that the hour of need is the hour of test; that all the strength which has been gathering in quiet hours comes to its trial in these hours of demand and shows what it is really worth. And no doubt there is truth in this; but it is not the whole truth, for we know very well, from what we have seen in others, from what we have felt in ourselves, that the giving way of strength in the time of critical need does not by any means prove either that what seemed to be real strength was unreal and a delusion, or that the shock of the crisis has destroyed it so that it will not be seen any more. On the contrary, many of us have known that men who seemed to break down most completely under some strain upon their resolution or their faith have come out by and by all the more faithful and courageous for their failure. Alas if it were not so! Alas if every time that the strength of any of us yielded under any task it were a certain sign either that what we had been calling strength was weakness, or that our feeble strength had died of the overstrain! It would fill our lives with hours of terrible despair if we had to believe either of these things. No, we have to feel that a time of critical demand for any power, a time of emergency which calls for the fullest exercise of any power, has a double function as regards the present possession of that. power by the man to whom the crisis comes. It is both a test and an education. And the failure of the man to respond with the power to the need may mean, not necessarily that the man has not the power, though it must mean that his possession of it is imperfect, but it may mean, also, that the power in him is just exactly in that state where it needs the self-revelation and the rebuke which will come by this failure; that it is in passage, as it were, from one condition into a higher condition; and that in this very failure there may be the force which will produce its new birth and its higher life.

There might be countless illustrations of this. Illustrations will abound in every region where strains that are too strong for them to bear fall upon the courage or the principle of men or states or churches. An attack is made upon a nation's central principle—on the idea by which she lives—in some great outbreak of rebellion. When the nation reels under the shock, and trembles to her base, what does it mean? Certainly that she is not perfectly mistress of and perfectly mastered by her great idea; but often, also, as we know full well, that she has just so far attained to her idea that she is ready to go on to a new degree of attainment, and that that new degree of attainment can be reached only through this apparent failure and the illumination and exposure which it brings.

There are illustrations which will come more closely home to your own life. Some of you who are here to-day have known what it is to have your Christian faith so shaken that it seemed to be overthrown. Just when you needed that it should stand firm as a column set into the rock, so that you might cling to it with your smitten and trembling life, just then, to your complete dismay, you felt it begin to reel and totter, so that you had to struggle to hold it up at the very time when it ought to be strongly holding you. Some of you, I know, have come to understand the meaning of that experience. Certainly it meant that your hold upon your faith was not complete, but certainly it did not mean that you had no hold on faith. Rather it may have meant—it may be that you can see now that it meant—that your faith had grown just to that point where it was only by questionings which went to its very roots and seemed to leave nothing for it to stand upon, only by deep probings which exposed its weaknesses and seemed to leave it no life at all, that it could pass up and on into a higher region of assurance and completeness. I know that there are some among you who look back now and clearly see that it was in some terrible time when they appeared to have no faith that God was really rebuilding the foundations of faith within them for a new structure which now it is their daily joy to feel growing and growing.

Now it is this second power of the failure which comes at the critical times of life which seems to me to be the real key to the story of the apostles sleeping in the garden of Gethsemane just when their Master needed them the most. No doubt their failure showed the weakness of their loyalty; but in a still more real sense it was the education of their loyalty to Jesus. It seems to me that their devotion to Him had reached just the point where it was ready to become something a great deal higher and finer and more spiritual than it had been thus far, and that the only way in which it could really mount up and attain that higher life was by just some such failure and exposure as it went through upon that night of crisis. Certainly their failure to be true to Him had nothing wanton or deliberate about it. They were asleep. They did not plot against Him. Here is just the difference between Peter and Judas. Indeed, all through that night the disciples seem to me to be dazed and bewildered. They are like men stunned. They move about almost as in a dream. And if they fail of the duty for which brave men ought to be ready—as certainly they do—it is rather by their powers being, as it were, out of connection with their wills, as a man's are when he is dazed or dreaming, than because they deliberately consider and choose with their wills not to use them.

Now notice how common a condition this is between two periods in life, or in the development of any of a man's powers. How often in transition periods there seems to be a kind of temporary pause and inaction in the faculties which are just about passing over into a higher state and a completer use! You have seen how a stream which has been flowing between sunny banks, lapsing along in peaceful, quiet current, and which is just going to enter on a new experience and be hurled headlong over the dam to fall white and tumultuous into the depths below—you have seen how, between the two, after its smooth journey through the sunny woods is over, and before its larger, more excited life begins, it pauses and lies motionless in a black, brooding pool, and seems in stillness to be making itself ready for the plunge. There are many such times as that in human life. Perhaps the time that seems most like it comes in a young man's life when, his boyhood over and his active manhood not begun, he seems to pause and brood upon the brink of life, and something almost like paralysis seems to fall down upon his faculties of faith and action. I am sure that many of you will recognize the phenomenon which I describe. A human creature who, as a boy, has been full of activity, and who is going to be fuller still of a yet higher activity in a few years as a man, comes to a stage between these two activities when for a longer or a shorter time he can do nothing. Before he easily made up his mind in an instant; now, when the most important decisions are waiting to be made, he can make no decision. Before his convictions were as clear as sunlight; now he is sure of nothing, least of all of his own doubts. Before he cared quickly about everything that touched him, was sympathetic and responsive; now his interests are hard to waken and he is contemptuous about a great many things. Before he was easily hopeful; now he finds it very easy to despair. It is not universal, but it is common enough to make one try to understand its meaning. It is the pause of life before it starts on its full career. It is the perplexity and confusion before the opening of the higher certainty. It is the uncertain dusk between the starlight and the sunlight. It is the pool before the plunge.

Now in a good many respects the disciples of Jesus seem to me to have been young men, just coming of age in their discipleship upon that night of confusion and distress, when they seemed to be so paralyzed and helpless. They had been children before, wide awake, observant of everything their Master did, ready to stand up for Him to any one who chose to question them. They were to be men by and by, alert to seek for truth or duty, compelling themselves with a man's conscientiousness to watch for their Lord's interests, and quick to answer out of a long experience and study all the taunts of scoffers and the earnest questions of inquiring spirits. But now, between the two, upon this night of terror, they were dazed and sleepy with the surprising change that was upon them; and when men asked them questions about Jesus they had nothing to say, or answered in confused and clumsy falsehoods. One hour Peter wants to fight for Jesus. A few hours later he is saying that he never knew Him. And almost instantly after that he is prostrate in the darkness, weeping tears which are neither a child's tears nor a man's tears, but belong to that period of dismay and confusion, of terror at one's self and one's own possibilities, of tender-heartedness and wounded pride, of misery, despair, and hope, all mixed together, which belong exactly to that strange period which comes between the childhood and the manhood and makes the most interesting and bewildering episode of many of the best human lives. I think that very many of the best young men, of those who by and by make the best success of life, pass through a time when they and their lives seem to be wretched failures. And in their time of failure, they often find afterward, has lain the seed of their success. It was in this night of failure that the seed lay of the spiritual success which these disciples gained when they had come to be completely men in Christ.

To us who know the later history of these disciples it is quite evident what was the character of the change and progress which was taking place in them in those critical days of confusion and distress. In one word, they were passing on to a completer knowledge of Christ. Christ is so natural to the soul of man, so intrinsically its true Master, that when a man once knows Him and has to do with Him, the changes and progress of that man's life may afterward be all noted and measured by his relationship to Jesus. And these disciples were attaining a growth, coming to a maturity, of which the sign and measure for us is the new and enlarged and deepened thought and understanding of their Lord which they attained. Perhaps that growth was not complete until the special gift of the Spirit of Christ had come to them at Pentecost. Perhaps, since all of Christendom is one long Pentecost, it is not complete yet, nor ever will be; but it began and came to a fullness which we can distinctly recognize in the experiences of that terrible night of which the sleep in the garden seems to be the representative event. They went into the cloud of that night with one knowledge of their Master. They came out of its darkness on the other side with another knowledge of their Master, which was larger and deeper. That new knowledge of Christ was, in one word, a more spiritual knowledge. It was a knowledge of the soul of Christ; and the sign of its possession by the disciples was that thenceforth Christ was not localized for them as He had been. They were no longer dependent upon the actual seeing of Him for the assurance of His presence, and they were able to understand His relationship to all men—even those who were far removed from the special circumstances in which they had known Him. Henceforward they were able to trust Christ even when they could not see Him, and to trust Him not merely for their own little group who stood the closest to Him, but also for all the world of men in every land, of every kind.

How vast a change was there! The promise and potency of all the profound spiritual life of souls communing with an unseen Christ, and of all the splendid faith and hope and work of man for the most hopeless of his fellow-men, lay in that change. And it was in the bewilderment out of which that change was to be born that the disciples lay oppressed with sleep while their Lord wrestled with His agony.

And notice, also, this: that the bewilderment and the enlightenment which followed it came distinctly from the disciples' contact with the sufferings of Christ. It was under the shadow of His cross that they learned the deepest truth concerning Him, and found possible a faith in Him as the Saviour of their souls in a perfect sense which must have made all their previous intercourse with Him seem but preliminary to this great experience—all this through the amazement of sorrow and distress with which they first learned that He whom they had loved as the best of men was to be the most tortured and persecuted. I do not see how any one can well read those last chapters of the Gospels and not feel something of what is to me more and more their solemnity and charm—the gradual opening up in the suffering of Jesus of a revelation of His nature and a promise of His work, which at first overwhelms His disciples with perplexity, and then, when they have once entered into it, becomes the substance of their faith and the inspiration of their work.

And what took place then was only the anticipation of what has taken place all through the Christian history, of what is taking place to-day. It is in contact with the cross of Christ, with the fact of His being a sufferer, with the spectacle of His self-sacrificing agony, that there has always come to the souls of men, first bewilderment which seemed to paralyze their faith, and then, by and by, a light which made their faith the glory of their lives. It may well be that some of you have passed through this experience. For years, perhaps, you knew Christ as a sweet, pure nature, as a noble and lofty Teacher. You listened to His words; you loved to be with Him; you even prayed to Him and asked for His advice, and felt sure that He heard you and gave you what you asked for; He was your Teacher, your Master, and your Friend. Can you remember any time when you began to realize that this Teacher, Master, and Friend was the supreme sufferer of the world, and that somehow in His suffering, in His willing self-sacrifice for you, lay the real value of His life for your salvation? Can you remember with what confusion and dismay that idea first filled you, how you tried to throw it off, how you clung to the old pleasant picture of Christ the Teacher sharing with you His wisdom, and how you shrank from the awful mystery of God uttering a love for you which was unutterable in any other way than by the giving of His Son to stand in the midst of all our human sin and bear its consequences beating on His innocent life, and at last die that you might live? Can you remember how in the first pressure of that deeper truth of Christ, in its first importunate appeal to be accepted as your faith, it seemed as if all faith in Christ died out of you? And then can you remember how at last that, the trust in, the love for, the suffering Saviour, the Christ of the cross, has come to be the faith in which is all your joy and hope? Ah, my dear friends, that is the story of thousands of human hearts. The passage from the love for Christ as a wise Teacher into the adoration of Christ as a powerful Saviour—thousands of times that has been made through mists and darkness where all faith seemed to grow blind and perish. But by and by the soul has come out in the light and found, as those disciples found, that the Christ on whom its eyes have opened was a more perfect Christ, while He was still the same Christ as He whom it seemed to lose in its eclipse of faith. If God, perchance, is leading any of us now through an eclipse like that, may He watch over us while we are in it, and waken us in His own good time to that more perfect faith in Him which He intends for us.

The whole great suggestion which has come to us out of the verse is the education which God wants to give us even by our failures. Failures enough we have—failures of faith, failures of love, failures of duty—failures enough of every kind. If in our failures there were no material of growth and holiness, how large a part of our life would have gone to waste, even if that were all the harm!

But it is good to know that as Christ by and by waked His sleeping apostles, and called them through their very faithlessness and disloyalty into a deeper faith and a truer service, so, if in all our weakness we can still be docile and repentant and submissive, He can and surely will bring in the end strength out of our weakness and brighter light out of the very darkness where our souls seemed lost. That may He do for all of us. Amen.

XVII.

GOOD FRIDAY.

"And I, if I be lifted up, . . . will draw all men unto Me."—
JOHN XII. 32.

WE commemorate to-day the "lifting up" of Him who spoke these words. All the religious history of mankind since that event has been bearing witness to some truth that was in them. For not even the most bewildered doubter about the life of Jesus can doubt this—that "all men" who have been brought into sight of the crucifixion have been "drawn unto" the Crucified with some kind of interest. There has grown out of the event of Good Friday a new life of thought and action for the world. The brain and heart and hand of Christendom—of all that portion of the world, that is, which has preserved any real activity of hand or heart or brain—have been busy ever since in some way developing its results. No man looks, I think, at the modern world compared with the condition of degeneracy into which the ancient world had fallen when the Christian religion touched it, or at the condition of Christian life compared with that of heathen life in all times, without feeling ready to say, in some vague and large and general way, that the death of Christ has saved the world.

The death of Christ! not merely His character and teaching; for historically, from the very first, the violent death of Jesus has had a prominence in religious influence which will not allow us, even as faithful students of history, to leave it out of view when we speak of the great formative power of modern human life. Always and everywhere the Christ whom Christianity has followed has been a Christ who died. The picture it has always held up has been the picture of a cross. The creed it has always held, however it might vary as to the precise effect of the death, has always made the fact of death vital and cardinal. The Jesus who has drawn all men unto Him has been one who based His power upon this condition, " if I be lifted up."

But what was that lifting up? What was it that was really done on Calvary out of which such an influence has flowed, so wide, so deep? We may say, I know, that it is a great deal better not to ask. Let it all rest, we may say, in that mystery and darkness which has proved itself so powerful. But yet our minds misgive us that it is not right to leave it so—that we are bound to know all that we can know of such a great event. Let us look into it this Good Friday morning. While we stand by the cross, let us try to know what it means. While we look out and see all men drawn toward it—see, with the eye of faith, all men at last gathered about its foot—let us understand wherein the power lies. I hope we may gather some clearness, and so some devoutness, into our views.

A man is dying—that is all that the external circumstances of the picture show us. But then death, we know, is infinitely various. The deaths of men crowd into focus their natures and the meanings of their lives. Between the death of the saint and the death of the suicide, between the death of the martyr and the death of the pirate, lies all the great gulf that lies between their several characters. We must go behind this death, then, to find the nature of the Being that is dying, and the object of His death. His own view of it we find summed up in the statement He has made that it is to draw the attention and shape the destinies of all the world. "If I be lifted up, I will draw all men unto Me." We surely cannot overestimate the great importance and clearness of the fact that Jesus looked Himself for the most mighty results to issue from His dying. The great importance which the Christian Church has given to that event has only echoed the infinite estimate He set upon it. He was always pointing forward to it before it came. He met it with the most awful reverence when it arrived. And with the last gasp of His closing agony He announced the completion as if it were the work of the world that had been finished.

Now what relation this death of Jesus may have borne to the nature and the plans of God, I hold it the most futile and irreverent of all investigations to inquire. I do not know, and I do not believe that any theology is so much wiser than my ignorance as to know, the sacred mysteries that passed in the courts of the Divine Existence when the miracle of Calvary was perfect. Now the death of every man affects in some way the sensitive nature of the great Father, who "is love." A wicked and presumptuous death must anger Him as no other insult to His majesty could. A patient, trustful death must touch His deepest tenderness. "Right dear in the sight of the Lord is the death of His saints." How this death, then, must affect Him—this unique and solitary death, standing alone amid the dying ages, unmatched by any other; what feeling it might waken, what changes it might work, in the mind of God, I do not know; I do not think we can know. You say that it appeased His wrath. I am not sure there may not be some meaning of those words which does include the truth which they try to express; but in the natural sense which men gather from them out of their ordinary human uses, I do not believe that they are true. Nay, I believe that they are dreadfully untrue. I think all such words try to tell what no man knows.

If this be so, then it seems clear that all we have to do with in the death of Jesus is its aspect toward, its influence upon, humanity. We are concerned with that which Jesus spoke of, its powerful effect to work upon the lives of men. And this could evidently come only by its revealing and making practically clear to men some new truth which they had not known and believed before. This follows from the profoundness of Jesus' nature and intentions. A temporary and very violent change may be brought about in men by the striking exhibition of some old familiar truth, the sudden waking up to action of some well-known but sluggish and neglected law of life. But a great, permanent, progressive influence, a steady, constant setting of the power of human life, a new way toward a new point— that is attained only by bringing, and settling firmly in, a new great truth, only by establishing a new law under which a new life must be organized. Now Jesus Christ, whom without irreverence we call the greatest of reformers, the great Renewer, whom all true reformers do but faintly echo—Jesus Christ must of necessity have based His prophecy of permanent power in the world upon the introduction by His death of some such new truth, some such new law. He did not propose to regenerate the world by sentiment—to set up a spectacle of suffering and so stimulate the human heart to action by mere pity. He was no spiritual demagogue attempting vast results by the excitement of mere transitory feeling. He did not merely set forth old truths in a striking and picturesque way. That was what Socrates did, and he did well. But Jesus' work was deeper, and so more central and effective. He set forth a new truth, which men might have guessed at and longed for, but which they never could have known, and so which never could have genuinely ruled their lives, before.

What was that new truth, then? In one word, it was the truth of the forgiveness of sins. It may seem as if that truth was not so very new. But as a revealed truth it was new entirely. The one truth that had been clearly revealed about God before was that He made laws. God the Lawmaker was the utterance of every voice that had thus far distinctly spoken to the finite from the Infinite. That utterance, gracious and inspiring so long as the laws that it announced were kept, had become fatal and dispiriting as soon as law was violated. For the quick human conscience, burdened with the certainty of sin, had reached the necessary certainty that sin must have its penalty. I believe it needs no supernatural declaration of the fact, I believe the highest human thought of God itself discerns, that when God makes a law it is not, like the laws of men, an accidental thing, the mere creation of a choice, and so capable of being taken back and the penalties that belonged to its violation abrogated. But a divine law we feel must have something necessary and essential in it. It is the result and expression of a nature that is divine. The absolute character of the Lawgiver incorporates itself in an absolute character of the law. So that when God says, "You must not lie," and you or I do lie, it is not possible for Deity to sweep His law aside and say, "No matter." He enacted truth because He was truth and could not help it. And when His enactment is despised, the nature that is in Him compels Him to make the despiser suffer for his wrongdoing. There is a moral limit even to Omnipotence, and the conscience of man decrees that He who can do all besides cannot do wrong, and so cannot treat wrongdoing in others just as if it were right. There is no strain in such a thought. It is merely an application in the moral world of that divine necessity which we are always owning and bowing to in the world of nature. You touch the fire and you must be burned. You cut an artery and you must bleed to death. The laws that issue from the very nature of the great first Source of law cannot be trifled with in their requirements without a change in that nature itself which would make it less divine and perfect.

This I hold to be the highest thought that man reaches of God with any certainty outside of the New

Testament. It describes, I think, the true state of the thoughtful, conscientious nature outside of Christian influence. We hear that such a nature, finding itself in sin, hates God. I do not think that that is so. The man does not hate God. He does not blame God. He simply holds God bound by His perfect nature to execute unpityingly His perfect laws. He sees that there is no escape. He recognizes that to forgive man would be to weaken and vitiate Himself. He says, "Yes, God is right. The blow must come. Not even Omnipotence can find an escape." His religion turns to submission, and gathering up his patience, he just bows his head and waits his punishment.

This, it seems to me, is the true description of the thoughtful man who knows his sin and thinks of God out of Christ. All that he knows of in God compels punishment and precludes forgiveness. It is what a man must be driven to who knows no quality in God except the quality of law. But now suppose that in this same divine nature there were another feature, just as essentially and originally a part of it as the other— a faculty or quality which made the forgiveness of transgression a possible thing. Man surely cannot know what that quality is, because he can really know nothing of the nature of the laws which issue from the First Cause of all law with which it has to deal. The quality will not be identical with that by which man pardons the wrongs that are done against him, for man is no source of law, and so the injuries that he forgives are really not done against him, but against God, who stands behind him. Forgiveness of man by man I take to be only the handing up of crimes past any spite or rancor of our own to the one only final judgment-seat. No! forgiveness in God must be an unknown quality. It must not be a sudden thought, a mere expedient to meet an unforeseen emergency. It must not be a mere extemporized afterthought. It is a part of the eternal Deity. It has been with God, in God, from the beginning. It is from everlasting, as He is. It has lain waiting on the power of law till law transgressed should call it into action. On what previous races, in what previous worlds, it has been exercised we cannot know. We only know that as soon as its necessity arose with reference to our world, as soon as the necessity of punishment came forth at the first sin, this gracious power of forgiveness showed itself, and Mercy met Justice in the conflict, where it was sure to conquer.

Now these two faculties or powers of Deity are manifested to the world under two personal characters. The Deity of law demanding punishment is God the Father, the Deity of forgiveness is Jesus Christ. The perfect harmony of the two powers, their coexistence in the one complete Divinity, must be made apparent; not explained, not reconciled, only made clearly known. Before a world of sinners, who know nothing of their God save that He has made laws whose dignity He has no power to infringe, there must come forth this other fact: that there is also a mysterious power which can meet those laws, absolve the penalty, and with the one condition of repentance let the condemned go free. As the law was in a person, so this forgiveness must be in a person too. As the lawgiving Person was eternal and supreme, so the forgiving Person must be eternal and supreme as well. It must not be the conflict of two contending Deities, for the two are harmonious parts of one and the same nature; therefore the condemning Father and the atoning Son must be not two Gods, but one God, at unity in every will and action. And yet the fact of self-restraint, of self-control, of the yielding of one requirement to another, of a conflict resulting in the victory of one over the other, cannot be set before the eyes and minds of men save by the outward picture of a trial and a triumph, of suffering and effort, of harmony and reconciliation coming out of pain.

Now here is our idea of Christ. He was forever in the Deity, the forgiving God, the element of pardon. Uncreated, eternal as the Deity itself, the power of pardon has rested there in Him forever. Before Adam was made, before the oldest star or earliest sun, the certain fact was there that if ever a moral race of men was made, and those men sinned, the necessity of punishment that would result must be met by a power of forgiveness which should cope with it and restrain it and offer a new life to the recreant and sinful nature. The ages rolled away. The creation of man arrived. The sin of man succeeded, and then, quick as all divine causes bring divine results, this element of forgiveness, this Christ, stood forward in the Deity and claimed His long-expected work. Adam and millions of his children, as they repented of their sins, attained forgiveness. The pardoning Saviour became the great administrator of the world.

What, then, is this which we behold to-day? What but the great announcement, the assurance, of this everlasting truth? It could not have its full effect until men knew of it. It could not tempt the sinful and degraded souls into that repentance which was the absolute condition of its action, till first it had been shown to them. And so the mystery of Incarnation came. This Christ, who had been forgiveness an eternity before man was made, who had bestowed forgiveness ever since man had sinned, came now to preach forgiveness, and by His willing suffering to show how the divine nature may sacrifice itself to reach the great end it desires of the replacement of a race into its lost holiness and hope.

"If I be lifted up, I will draw all men unto Me." If this be so, is it not evident, then, where Jesus saw the power in His death that was to rule the world? If it were really, that Good Friday cross, the holding up of a new faculty in God that men had guessed of and hoped for and dreamed about and even trusted in, but never known before, then was it a wild or reasonless prophecy that wherever that cross should be seen this new great truth, forgiveness—forgiveness by the manifest reconciliation of a yet unknown power in God's nature; forgiveness wrought by sacrifice, by pain, but wrought at any cost out of the great love God had for man—this new great truth, forgiveness, should strike the closed hearts of men everywhere and make them open, and call them up in wondering gratitude to gather round and worship with responsive love this love, so marvelous, manifested to them?

How shall we hold otherwise than this? We degrade the whole nature of the suffering Divinity if we picture Jesus just appealing to men's pity and lowering His mercy to be an applicant before their sentimental sympathy with pain. And we dishonor the divine completeness if we talk of the Atonement as if it were the late device to remedy an unprovided break in the administration of the universe. No! Christ was the truth; the new truth, yet the everlasting truth—new in its certain exhibition to mankind, everlasting in its existence in the nature of God. This was the "Lamb slain from the foundation of the world." Then—then alone—this spectacle assumes its truest majesty. From all eternity, upon whose very limit my sense aches in the attempt to measure it, this Jesus has been waiting to show this truth to me. He has come at last and shown it. He has written it out in blood. He has hung it up where I must see it. He has laboriously translated it into a human life, that I may not mistake it. And then, when He can do no more, when the truth that has been true forever has been thus fearfully announced, the work is over, and crying, "It is finished," the Saviour closes His eyes and drops His head and dies.

Oh, what a finishing that was! It is as if eternity were crowded into the heart of Him who spoke. All He had been forever had consummated itself at last. The long yearning to let men know what a love waited for them in the heart of God was satisfied. The light was kindled on the mountain-top, and already the quick ear of Divinity heard the stirring in thousands of valleys, where men, hopeless before, were gathering up their burdens and with the inspiration of an unfamiliar hope were starting to struggle up with them, determined not to rest until they cast them down into the shadow of that unseen cross. What cry like this has the world ever heard? Not even that first utterance of calm creative power, "Let there be light," had greater meaning or sublimity than this last agony of love that burst from the lips of the satisfied Redeemer: "I have been lifted up. I shall draw all men unto Me. Now it is finished."

The truth we are to learn to-day, then, is the truth that sin may be forgiven. It is brought with enforcement to every part of our nature. It is presented to the conscience side by side with the enormity of sin, as growing out of the same nature of the same God, who is both Condemner and Forgiver. It is urged upon the intellect as the clear revelation of Him alone who has any right to announce the sinner's destiny. It is laid close upon the heart with all the pathetic appeal of suffering, and emphasized with the terrible power of divine pain. It is the truth our souls need. Everything you have ever done that was wrong—the great and small transgressions of your life, your sins against yourself, your sins against your brother, your sins against your God—they may all be forgiven you. Your impieties and doubts, your omissions and commissions, your tamperings with truth, your wicked thoughts and words and deeds—you need not carry one of them one step farther. They may all be forgiven and swept away, and buried so deep—so deep—that neither your own self-reproach, nor the malice of your most powerful enemy, nor the judgment of the offended law, shall find them out. Better than this, the wickedness of which they sprang, the sinfulness of which these sins were but the utterance, the evil heart, that too may be taken utterly away and your soul stand pure and reconciled—not like a soul that never sinned, but with the deeper love of a soul sin-stained and washed—before the face of your forgiving God. Of all this there is no condition but the simplest—repentance and faith! You must be sorry for your sins, and you must believe this truth of their removal. You must stand up and look back into eternity and see how, ages before you sinned, there was in the perfect Godhead this eternal Christ, already rich in provision for the coming woe. The sight will not make you presumptuous, as if the guilt whose cure was ready before it was itself in being were a light and trifling thing. It will fill you with a large and glowing love, standing in wonder before a mercy so far-reaching, so eternal, and so deep. All must be lighted by the manifest Redeemer lifted up upon His cross. You must be drawn to Him, and leaving your own life behind, you utterly pass into His life and be a new creature in Him henceforth forever!

Do I state as a necessity what has been long the craving desire of your anxious soul? Do I say you must repent and trust, when this trust and repentance is the very thing that you have longed to be allowed to do? Do I say you must be drawn, when your whole nature has been hungry with the desire to be allowed to rise and run to such a gracious God as this? Then let me put the duty back and spread the new, great, certain privilege of faith before your eyes. Lo! it is finished. Nothing remains to hide or hinder your perfect open way. Whoever you are that listen to me now, there is not one of you who, if he will hate his sin and put it away from him, may not come to God with a perfect assurance that God will forgive him, and introduce him through the gate of forgiveness into a better and diviner life, and lead him on from holiness to holiness, and bring him at last to untold glory. That is the message of the cross, and God grant that some of you may hear it and be comforted and saved.

XVIII.

EASTER DAY.

"That I may know Him, and the power of His resurrection."—
PHIL. III. 10.

THIS was the Easter prayer of Paul, and his Easter prayer was the prayer of all his life, for he peculiarly lived in Easter all the time. The only one of the disciples who had not known Jesus in His earthly life, to him the spiritual life of the risen and ascended Jesus was most especially near and dear. "If Christ be not raised," he cried, "your faith is vain; ye are yet in your sins."

The Easter prayer of Paul was that he might know the power of this resurrection of Christ. He was a man who was not satisfied to know a truth unless he also knew its power; unless, that is, he felt its influence upon himself. For there are different sorts of knowledge. Every fact has its outer form and its inner power, its visible shape and its invisible meaning. Something happens and I hear of it. That is the slightest sort of knowledge. The mind simply receives and registers the incident. But let me find that that something has a relation to me—that it must influence my action and change my life; let me feel this deeply, and then I know the power of the fact. It is not the mind alone, it is the whole man, who knows it. It is one thing to stand on the shore and see the great waves and say, "There is a storm;" and it is a very different thing to be out in the midst of those waves, tossed every way by them, fighting for your life. On the shore you know of them; in their midst you know them, you know their power. The first is information, the second is experience. Some men are content with knowing facts; other people will be content only with knowing powers. An unfelt fact is nothing at all to these last. There is no truth to them that does not take their nature and their lives into its hands and change them. Of this last class was Paul, who prayed that he might "know the power of Christ's resurrection."

And Paul's prayer must be our prayer to-day. To make our Easter perfect we must come begging and trying to know in our own lives all that it means; to put ourselves into the power of Christ's resurrection and be possessed and formed by it. What shall we say, then, is this power? How does this event, past so long ago, lay hold of and govern and change the lives of men living now? What new life does it lift them to; what new spirit does it fill them with? Let us see if we can approach at all the answer to these questions.

We celebrate on Easter Day the rising of our Saviour from the tomb. For that the whole aspect of our thought and worship changes. Our sober churches burst out into flowers, our hushed voices break out into songs of praise, our whole religiousness puts on another robe—exultation instead of sorrow, "the garment of praise for the spirit of heaviness." And we go about with one another, heart saying to heart everywhere, "Christ is risen." And what makes that such a glad greeting is the assurance that is hidden in under it and is heard up through it: "We too shall rise." It is the assurance of our immortality bound up with Christ's, the certainty that because He rose we shall rise also, that makes the resurrection such a message of gladness to us all.

But is this all? Is this simple assurance of continued existence, that we are to rise from the dead and go on in some future state of existence—is this what Paul means by "the power of the resurrection"? It seems certainly evident enough that Paul meant more than this—that it was some great powerful change to be worked in and on him himself. On him—not merely on things about him. It was not simply that by Christ's death and resurrection the tyranny of the old law of decay had been broken, so that instead of living seventy years his life was to stretch out into eternity and never to end. It was evidently that the quality of the life itself was to be changed, that he was to be something new and different, and not that he was just to be the same old thing a little or a good deal longer, when he should know the power of the resurrection. This was what he prayed for.

Indeed, there are not many of us that would or ought to count the revelation of immortality so very great a boon if all that it meant were simply the infinite continuance of life. Merely that an eternity should be opened up, out into which we should see stretching infinitely these poor, purposeless lives we live; that we should be told that we were to keep on struggling and grudging and envying and crawling, misunderstanding one another, and blundering about in our half-knowledge; just to be told that we need not fear an end of this—that a revelation had come to tell us that it might last forever. Would this be such a joyous message? Would it not rather be terrible? This life of ours does well enough, we think, for a little time; but magnify it into an eternity and it is simply horrible. A "power of the resurrection" which could do only this for us, and nothing more, it would be far better that we should not "know," for it would condemn us to helpless disgust with our own life, which we must yet go on living for ever and ever.

This was not what Paul prayed for, and this is not what we want, then—not mere immortality. This opening of new prospects is no blessing unless there be promised some new capacity to fill them. The new world is no satisfying message unless there comes also some tidings of a new man who is to occupy it. The promise of resurrection finds its consummate satisfaction only in close union with the other promise of regeneration. The two must go together—the new world and the new man.

This, beyond all doubt, is the idea of Paul. Mere eternity of time, an endless renewal of the mere fact of life forever, would have been nothing to him—less to him than to almost any other man that ever lived—if there were connected with it no spiritual renewal, no infinity of spiritual life. He puts it all in one verse to the Romans: "That like as Christ was raised up from the dead by the glory of the Father, even so we also should walk in newness of life." There is the whole power of the "resurrection"—a new man for the new world. In every respect in which Easter opens a new prospect before man it must open also a new character in man. Until it has done that, man has not really "known its power."

In order to understand this it is necessary for us to see that Christ's resurrection has effect upon us not simply as a prophecy. It does not simply promise us something that we are to hope to reach when we have crossed the line of death and entered on the future world. It was not simply the announcement, "After you are dead another life will begin; therefore live now in hope." On the contrary, it was a new value and color given to this life; it was a change in the purposes and ways of living now that it introduced.

Indeed, the work of Christ in rising from the dead was not, properly speaking, a revelation of the human immortality. Men had known that before. The Pharisees believed in it completely. Christ made it surer, certainly—He made it perfectly sure; but His great work was done in bringing that future life, before so vague, so dim, so far away, into close oneness with this present life. The two had been two and He made them one—one in their government, one in their purposes, one in their one great, pervading, embracing responsibility. He "brought life and immortality to light," as Paul says. He put them where they could be motives; and just as, when you hold before your child the prizes of his coming manhood for temptations, you change his view not merely of the life he is to live when he is thirty, but also of the life that he is living now at twelve, so Jesus, when He made eternity clear and familiar to us by letting us see Him close as He passed into it, by opening its door wide and letting its golden glory stream back on the world on Easter Day, altered, transfigured, not merely that world which before had been to the most hopeful of mankind nothing but "Hades," "the unseen," but also this whole present world, which is the preparation for it, and must share in the changes of its character.

I often think that there is some faint echo of the power of Jesus' resurrection when for the first time the death of a dear friend comes into a man's life and makes it thenceforth different, never again what it has been before. I do not mean the mere soberness and solemnity which the whole thought of living from that hour assumes; I do not allude to the mere sadness of bereavement, but I speak of that new sense of reality in the world beyond the grave which comes to all of us when for the first time we can think of one who has been intimate in our interests as having gone there and sat down in the intimacy of its interests, which have heretofore been so foreign to us and so far away. Heaven has at once an association with us. We have a relation there. One name is known in its mysterious streets, and so its streets become less mysterious and remote to us. It is somewhat as when a mother in some little country village sends her boy to the great city, and at once feels familiar with the great city because somewhere, lost in among its hurrying thousands, her boy is there. His familiar life, transported to it, seems to make it familiar. She feels as if she knew all about it. She talks of it with a kind of affection, as if it were almost her home, because it is the home of one she loves. She catches every mention of it as if it were a message meant for her. To go there is the constant dream of her life, and she feels as if when she came there she would know at once the streets in which her heart has had its home so long. So when a dear friend dies and goes to heaven, heaven at once catches and naturalizes into itself all our love for him. We read about it as if we knew it, and when we think of going there ourselves we think of it as going home, because our heart has had its home there so long.

Is it not evident, then, from this what it was that Jesus did for all the world, and what it was His desire to do for all of us, by His resurrection? First, by His life and death He had made the closest appeal that ever has been made to the human heart. He had taught man to love Him. He had called out the deepest and tenderest affection. With all this He passed down into the grave. We saw Him go in at the black door. We watched and waited after He had disappeared, till at last from a region that before had been to us like a land of ghosts, the region beyond the grave, the land of those who live again, we saw Him come out, still clothed with our affection, still bearing our hearts with Him. At once that strange land lost its ghostliness. He was there, not changed, but still such a one as we could love. His life there made it all real to us. We understood Him when He said, "I ascend unto My Father, and your Father; and to My God, and your God." They were ours as well as His. We knew them as ours by knowing them as His. Already, just as the mother in her village lives yet in the great city, and her life is different because her child is there; as the friend lives in heaven while he is still on the earth, and his life is altered and is happier and higher because his friend has gone to bliss, so the true Christian lives in the spiritual world in which Christ is, even while he lives still in the body. His life is different this side the veil because his heart has passed through with his risen Saviour to that now familiar realm of life that lies beyond. In Paul's wonderful words, he is "risen with Christ." In the words of our collect for Ascension Day, which have the whole truth in them, "Like as he does believe our Lord Jesus Christ to have ascended into the heavens, so he also in heart and mind thither ascends and with Him continually dwells."

This is the power of the resurrection. You see it is no far-off promise. It is a present gift. It is not the offer of a meager hope. It is the joy of Christian possession. It is the power of regeneration. "Except a man be born again, he cannot enter into the kingdom of heaven." Just as soon as a man is born again by the power of God's Spirit, he has already entered into the kingdom of heaven which Christ opened when He arose from the dead.

And more than this. As the first power of the resurrection is the power of regeneration, as a man begins to be under the influence of the eternal life that is held out before him only when he begins to have eternal life abiding in him, so it is not only in the beginning, but all through the new life. The life of a true Christian seems to me to be continually full of Easters; to be one perpetual renewal of things from their lower to their higher, from their temporal into their spiritual shape and power. This is the true meaning of the self-sacrifice and self-denial with which the Christian's life is filled. You are called on to give up a luxury, and you do it. The little piece of comfortable living is quietly buried away underground. But that is not the last of it. The small indulgence which would have made your bodily life easier for a day or two, or a year or two, undergoes some strange alteration in its burial, and comes out a spiritual quality that blesses and enriches your soul for ever and ever. You surrender some ambition that had exercised a proud power over you; in whose train and shadow you had hoped to live with something of its glory cast on you. You send that down into its grave, and that too will not rest there. It comes forth again with its old vigor purified and spiritualized, but made more strong and vigorous—a holy desire in place of an eager passion, as different as was the risen Christ who gave His "peace" to His disciples from the yet uncrucified Christ as the populace fancied Him, when they thought that they could "take Him by force and make Him a king." You surrender a dear friend at the call of death, and out of his grave the real power of friendship rises stronger and more eternal into your life. So the partial and imperfect and temporary are always being taken away from us and buried, that the perfect and eternal may arise out of their tombs to bless us. So our life is like the life of a tree, which is always full of immediate apparent failure, which is always dropping back after each rich summer to the same bareness that it had last winter, which keeps no leaves or fruit, and stands again and again stripped of every sign of life that it has put forth, and yet which still has gathered, as we see when we watch it with a larger eye—has gathered all those apparent failures into the success of one long, continuous growth; has not lost the strength of those old summers, but gathered them into its own enlarged girth and sturdier strength. What seemed to perish and die has really been only grown in, and makes the mature life of, the noble tree. And so it is with our hopes and plans and endeavors and resolutions and thoughts, which seem to fade and perish, but which, if we have the Christian vitality about us, have been really grown in and make the new life, which is not merely a thing of the future, but a thing of the present. They are not simply taken away to be kept—the child that you saw die, the dream that you saw fade—to be kept in some future state till you shall be fit to come and get them—

"Kept over your head on the shelf."

They are here all the time; not to be had by and by, but to be had now. They can be had in their spiritual return to you by and by only as you first have them and keep them spiritually now. You must carry their presence with you into the future state or you cannot receive them there. And so, as we said, the power of the future resurrection is all along a power first of present regeneration. The things that God promises He will give us there He first does give us here, and so fits us to receive them in their completer giving. The new life which is held before us is first wrought out by the new birth creating the new man within us.

In this view, how very slight a thing is death! How very easy it becomes for us to understand the Bible story that Christ, by His death and resurrection, killed death and took away its victory and sting! If the new spirit is formed in men here, if you and I may have eternal life abiding in us, clogged, hampered, and blinded, indeed, by the constraints of the poor body that we live in, and yet genuine and vital even here, and if death be nothing but the breaking down of the body to let the spirit free, then how clear it is! The word of summons comes and the soul leaps to answer it. The eternal life in us answers to the eternal life beyond the grave, recognizes it, flees to its own. There is no violence of transfer. It is a continuation of the one same life. The grave is only the moat around the inner castle of the King, across which they who have long been His loving and loyal retainers on the farther side enter in, sure of a welcome to the heart of His hospitality. Far above any morbid or affected, unnatural, unhuman pretense of a wish for death there towers this calm Christian confidence, ready to die, yet glad to stay here until the time comes; knowing that death will be release, and yet finding life happy and rich with the power of the resurrection already present in it; counting both worlds God's worlds, and so neither despising this nor dreading the other. That is the Christian light on the dark river and the fields beyond, that streams forth only from the opened door of Jesus' tomb.

I have dwelt thus long upon the truth of the new man for the new world, the regeneration for and by the resurrection. That, be assured, is the great Easter truth. Not that we are to live newly after death—that is not the great thing—but that we are to be new here and now by the power of the resurrection; not so much that we are to live forever as that we are to, and may, live nobly now because we are to live forever.

And this great truth of Easter will decide and fix the whole character of the religion that grows up about it.

1. In the first place, it will establish the preëminent and necessary joyousness of true religion. Easter Day, rightly considered, makes the religious life the happiest of all lives, and insists upon our always treating it as such. For the happiest of all conditions is that in which one is the partial possessor already of a hope that promises its own completion. The child's life is so very happy because it already has enough of the real, conscious manly character in it to prophesy more for itself. And the true man never outgrows the child's joyousness, because he keeps always a future before him of what he is to be, suggested, promised, and in part realized by what he already is. The two unhappy and joyless conditions would be, one the utter absence of hope, and the other the possession of a hope that was only hope, that had no real existence in the present. So a religion that opened no eternity, or a religion that offered no beginning of eternal life until the other world was reached—either of them would be unhappy; one with despondency, the other with restlessness at the postponement of the soul's worthiest ambitions. But once admit this power of the resurrection which we have seen; let the new eternal manhood, formed within us now, begin to promise us in every hope and dream and glowing picture of holiness what the new man is to be and do forever, through those undivided ages where only by the growth of love and worship the eternal souls shall know that eternity is growing older;

let present imperfection be at once consoled and stimulated; let every dissatisfaction with the present be made, not a discouragement, but an inspiration, by the continual consciousness of the great law of eternal growth; let the everlasting Saviour be always speaking out of every language of outer and inner life to the immortal soul, "Thou shalt see greater things than these;" "What thou knowest not now thou shalt know hereafter"—and then can such a religion be anything but one continual joyousness? The whole life is recast. Every new hindrance or delay becomes either the proof or the occasion of some new love. Fear, which is always partial and superficial, is cast out, and the nature is submitted utterly to the great profound sway of love. Worship springs, not out of duty, but out of eager willingness. It becomes the heart's own glad registration, by one "Ebenezer" after another, of the progress through which it has been already led. The joyousness as well as the holiness of eternity begins within us even now.

At least, to-day, my friends, let us remember this: that religion is, not by accident or chance, but by its own very nature, the happiest of all lives. Just so far as it ever grows sad and gloomy, it grows irreligious. This is the true index of the power of the resurrection.

2. And this same joyousness and hopefulness must extend itself and cover our fellow-creatures and all nature. That man ought to distrust his Christianity very deeply who finds that when he has become a Christian he takes no more large and hopeful and charitable view of his fellow-men and their lives than he did before. The glory of a revealed immortality is

that it exalts into struggle for a purpose that which seemed to be only the restless tossing and heaving of mere discontent. You have a neighbor, for instance, whose whole life dissatisfies you. There is no symmetry about it. It seems to be made up of mere tiresome tossing hither and thither, back and forth, under the power of mere passion. He is neither good nor bad, you think. He does good things, but they are done with no persistency. He thinks a high thought sometimes that surprises you, but you cannot see that it has any place or meaning. It seems to have wandered in like a comet, and to have no real place in the system of his mind. He does kindnesses, but his kindness is all fitful and unreliable, broken up by moods of bitterness or gusts of temper.

And what you see in him in the little you see on a larger scale in the great world—poor fitful efforts after goodness, broken and distracted; a mere unrest and moral turmoil everywhere. What can interpret it except the great opening of an eternity, and the sight of the power of that eternity working even here? With that in view, we come to a large and tolerant suspense of judgment that is good for us. Who can say how much of this which seems purposeless restlessness is really purposeful struggle? The wild, confused waves are going somewhere. We grow to a sure conviction that very much of what seems bad is only good unformed and struggling under the power of the resurrection to its full development and exhibition. This, I do believe most deeply, is the true Easter view of our disordered world.

I am not preaching any mere feeble optimism. I

am not weakly calling that good which is evidently and finally bad, of which there is abundance in the world. I would not, just for the sake of mental and moral relief to ourselves, claim that the world is going right, when so evidently and in so many ways it is going wrong. Even on Easter Day the world is very bad and irreligious and untrue and impure. But I count him a poor Easter Christian who does not feel the power of the resurrection filling him with hope, who does not gather from the victory of Christ a firm assurance that the good is stronger than the evil, and who does not rejoice to know that some at least of the doubt and bewilderment about us, some at least of what seems the decay of mere corruption, may be the fermentation of new life slowly ripening for the purposes and under the power of that immortality which Jesus brought us.

I wish we had time to point out also how this power of the resurrection, this new eternal manhood once created in us, transfigures and changes not merely all internal, but all external things. The world itself, even material nature—trees and fields and skies, noontimes and mornings, sunsets and midnights—cannot be the same when they are found to be the education-place, the school-room, of a being with a destiny such as the resurrection of Jesus Christ makes known for man. We cannot think of them as made only to feed us and to warm us and to shelter us—to have relation only to our bodily wants. They must have moral uses. They must bring moral meanings to that soul which this new truth of immortality exalts to be the monarch of the world. You say that this is poetry. But is not all religion poetry? Is not every Christian by the very necessity of the case a poet? There is no poetry on earth like the Christian's faith, that most noble of all creative powers, "the substance of things hoped for, the evidence of things not seen." And so it is the commonest Christian consciousness, belonging not only to a few exalted minds, but to all Christian minds in their several degrees, that to them, with their new life, the whole world of nature became new too, had new words to speak to them of God and of eternity, and that all through their lives there are times when the enlightened universe becomes vocal and its visible realities impart to them

"Authentic tidings of invisible things,
Of ebb and flow, and ever-during power,
And central peace subsisting at the heart
Of endless agitation."

But most of all this power of the resurrection, this present apprehension of an immortality, transfigures the whole morality of our lives. What is it to do our duty? Ah, how many of us know the slavery and bondage of long days and years, when with no enthusiasm to inspire us, with no love for the hard tasks that were laid upon us, we have just tugged away at things that we knew we ought to do, under a vague and dreary instinct, discouraged and disheartened by the continual sense of how poorly we did them after all! Ah, all that is changed as soon as the Easter truth of the new man is shown to us—a new man, made in the image of Him that created him, of Him who rules him. So that henceforth there is not merely a submission of the soul to the law, but a sympathy of the soul with the Lawgiver, which turns morality into fidelity, which breaks the hard mask off from the mere doing of duty and turns it into the loving service of the Saviour. There are many great and exultant moments in our lives; moments in which some new, heretofore unfelt motive takes us into its power, when some new work for us and some new power in us starts forth and makes life seem fresh and green, like a spring morning that forgets all the stains and storms that have gone before it. But among all such moments there is none that can compare with that in which duty passes into love—when morality, reaching itself out into eternity, asserts its sameness of nature with the service that the glorified nature is to render to God in the heavenly city, so that the obligation of honesty in our bargains is seen to rest on the same sanctions and to be lustrous with the same beauty now that will belong to the singing of the everlasting songs and the casting of the crowns before the Saviour's feet—the moment when our life thus knows Christ and the power of His resurrection.

I have tried to tell you what that power is. It is the power of a realized immortality, the power of a personal regeneration, the power of a present Christ.

What can I do, then, but invite you all to know that power by earnest self-surrender, by patient prayer, and by a childlike faith that willingly takes into its loving life the willing, living, loving Christ of Easter Day? O fellow-believers, let us hope that at His table now we may meet Him and feast with Him, and deeply know Him and the power of His resurrection.

XIX.

ASCENSION DAY.

"And a cloud received Him out of their sight."—ACTS i. 9.

"Then we which are alive and remain shall be caught up together with them in the clouds, to meet the Lord in the air: and so shall we ever be with the Lord."—1 THESS. iv. 17.

LAST Thursday was Ascension Day. Then we remembered how the Lord, whose story we have once more followed through the months of this winter which is now past, mysteriously at the end departed from the sight of men, and called upon their faith to follow Him and recognize His power still at work even when they could not see Him. These two texts which I have chosen for to-day contain the story of the Ascension. The first describes the fact of Christ's departure. The second tells us what His departure is to be to His servants; how, even in that last and crowning experience of life, they are to have some fellowship with Him.

As to the first of these, the story of what actually took place upon the Mount of Olives, I have always felt that the Ascension of Jesus was the event, of all that are recorded of Him in the Gospels, the most difficult to present to the imagination in any picture of its possible methods or circumstances. We cannot follow it out at all in its details. We have to rest, I think, in the mere fact of His departure in some way unlike the old familiar way of death. Something which had been foreshadowed in the mysterious departures of Enoch and Elijah was fulfilled in the disappearance of the Lord who was so vastly greater than His servants who had gone before Him. It could not be that, once having died and then arisen from the dead, He should at last by a new death have yielded to the power which He seemed to have subdued. It could not be that, again living among men, He should just live on forever, so never letting His ministry pass beyond the imperfection of the visible, always drawing the hosts of believers to Jerusalem, instead of lifting them up purely to His spiritual home, in holiness. And so there came a disappearance which was not death; a disappearance strange and mysterious, but not more wonderful than had been the life and character of Him who so departed. I think that any man who had watched Jesus' life and understood its wondrousness, and then stood watching to see what would be that strange life's final scene, could have asked nothing more, could hardly even have cared to know the details of method—how this marvelous body had gone, where it had gone—but would have accepted and acknowledged the perfect fitness of the story, when the disciples with calm and solemn faces came back into Jerusalem and only said, "While He blessed us He was taken up, and a cloud received Him out of our sight."

It is not, then, the physical meaning of the Ascension of Christ that I want to speak of. What does it mean spiritually? What does the mysterious going away of Him who for three and thirty years had lived such a marvelously human life upon the earth mean for us whom He has won to His service by the life that He lived here? And the first thing that it means, I think, is the assertion of the necessarily infinite and transcendental character of Christ, the establishment of the vastness and magnitude of the relation between Him and the world. See what I mean. Imagine the life of any one of the disciples of our Lord. First he had been a Jew. He had worshiped God. Far off, enthroned in mystery and majesty, God had been true and real to him. He had knelt in the temple at Jerusalem. He had listened in the synagogue at Capernaum. He had meditated as he floated on the blue waters of Gennesaret. Everywhere he had known God, but an unreality had haunted all his knowledge. He had struggled to find God, but God had eluded him. He knew Him, but he could not make Him real. Then had come Jesus. Wonderful had been the months that they had spent together. Beautiful and solemn had been the gradually growing certainty that God was real. The commonest things had been interpreters of Him. The baked bread, the penny for the taxes, the fishing-net and fishes, the water-jars at the wedding—all of them had seemed to be right in the hands of God, warm with His divine touch, bright with His divine smile. We can understand that. We can see how beautiful it was. Can we not also see a certain danger that must have been in it? As a child is always in danger of coming to think about his father as the provider of the household, as the willing furnisher of food and clothes and shelter to his children, and to forget the real heart of fatherhood, the care for the character, the wish for spiritual helpfulness, so may it not have been with these disciples? The arrest and death had violently broken the spell, indeed. The disciples had wakened from their dream that this sweet life with their Master could go on forever—the pleasant walks across the breezy hills and in the quiet lanes; the ready table spread in the great desert place; the happy sight all through the long day of this kind, loving face. That was all gone with the awful night when Judas led the soldiers to Gethsemane. But even after the Resurrection, Jesus had sat with them at table at Emmaus, and He had met them by the familiar lake and multiplied the draft of fishes. Still their souls clung to the lower forms of company, and even to the material advantages that His presence would bring them. But then came the Ascension. He disappeared. All the constant sight of Him was over. They had to lift their eyes, to lift their hearts. The dear familiarity which they had gained with Him never could be lost again. But now the mystery, the majesty, which they must have lost sometimes came back again. They could no longer think of Him as the multiplier of bread solely or chiefly. The higher purposes of His being filled in behind His special acts. The greater life of their souls with Him, keeping all the intimacy of their special earthly intercourse, began. Peter and John and Andrew and Bartholomew worshiped the unseen God in the memory of their own dear Jesus, and loved their Jesus with all the profound worship which they paid to God. Life, duty, love, and prayer became large and solemn, while they still kept the reality and personalness of the Incarnation.

And now is not that something perpetual? Is it not something that comes back to us with ever-new freshness as we come back ever anew to the wonder of the Ascension? There is a constant tendency of religion to belittle itself. As it becomes real to us the ends for which it exists seem often to grow small. This always appears in men's relations to Christianity and Christ. At first God seems to us very dim and far away. And yet there is a certain awe and reverence in all our thought of Him. We speak with bated breath. There comes a seriousness into our faces at His name. Then comes the blessed revelation of the Gospel. Christ the Incarnate, close here by our side, tells us that God our Father is not far away. He teaches us that all that interests us interests Him. He tells us that we may ask God for everything we want. He encourages us to lay our most homely burdens at His feet. The merchant may call to God in his perplexity of business; the school-boy may ask for help in his hard task; the sick man may cry out for health; and no appeal for safety from any poor frightened man or woman shall go unregarded. This is the glory of the Incarnation—the intimate, personal God. But is there no danger? Once, when Jesus was on earth, an eager, passionate man came running to him, hot with a fiery grievance, and crying out, "Lord, speak to my brother, that he divide the inheritance with me." Once, as the Saviour sat with a woman at a wellside and made her feel how near He was and how strong He was, she broke out at last and cried, "Sir, give me this water that you speak of, so that I need not come hither to draw." Once, when the Lord had won His disciples' trust entirely, two of them came to Him one day and asked Him to promise them that they should be kings in the kingdom which they thought that He was just going to establish. All these are illustrations, I think, of the way in which men even now come to a belief in Christ—catch something of that idea of the nearness of God which is involved in the Incarnation, but apply it only to the lower order of things, and are inclined to deal with the Christ in whom they have learned to believe only upon the earthly ground. One man believes in Christ, and thinks that His religion is the only safeguard of good government. Another man believes in Christ, and to him the Christian faith seems to be almost provided that it may be the bulwark of his favorite conservatisms. Another man never seems to get beyond the prayer for daily bread, though he never could have prayed that prayer with the beautiful and childlike trust that fills it now if it had not been for the way in which Christ has made manifest to him the all-providing Father. One believer can never get his thought of Jesus large enough to transcend his own little set or denomination of mankind. Another, though he looks beyond the line of death, and talks much of what Jesus is going to do for him in the other world, has really made that other world only an enlargement of this, as earthly as the earth itself, and thinks of Jesus there only as saving souls from pain almost as material as that from which a brave fireman plucks the child whom he rescues from a burning house. Now all these men are believers who are using Christ in His lower offices. They are following Him like the multitude who ate of the loaves and were filled, and then came hurrying across the lake that they might still be with Him when the famine should fall on them again. What hosts of Christians such as these there are! The Master does not turn them off for the imperfection of their knowledge, for the earthliness of their needs, and for the lowness of their appeals to Him. But then His soul longs to have them meet Him upon higher ground, to have them ask Him for the heavenly things with which His nature aches in His desire to give them away to those He loves. As a father gives his children bread and waits for the day when they shall ask him for knowledge, for sympathy, for hope, for inspiration, for noble ideas, and for strength to meet temptation, so Jesus guards your house for you, makes your business prosper, holds up your head in sickness, builds you the pleasant companionship of His Church, and promises you happiness forever, and all the time is looking anxiously to see your face glow with the higher desires which He most loves to satisfy—with the desire of holiness, of a divine unselfishness, of the communion with Himself.

But now imagine that the Incarnate Life had never passed into the heavens. Think of Jesus here on earth. Can we imagine anything but that the lower uses of His life would have usurped men's attention?—just as in those days of the Gospels a thousand would have flocked to Him with gaping curiosity or selfish greediness for one who came with a soul eager and hungry for His holiness, a thousand would have clung to His strong hand for one who craved admission to His heart, a thousand would have stood amazed at His power over the stubborn forces of the earth for one who lived with Him in the heavens, where His soul was living all the time. But now the Ascension came. It did not break the spell of the Incarnation. None of us believers in the Lord treads the most fresh and unexplored new soil of any Western prairie without feeling that it is the same earth which has been consecrated through its utmost length and breadth by the divine feet of Jesus. The Incarnation keeps God forever near and real; but when we cannot find the God incarnate still visible on the earth, but must go forth into the heavens to seek Him, that effort must forever help us, however we still dare to tell Him of our very lowest and most humble needs—that effort must forever help us to seek Him most for that which He most loves to satisfy, the need which the unseen part of us has for the unseen part of Him, the need which our soul has for His soul, the need of being made holy and heavenly.

I think I see in the balance of wants which lies in the completest Christian's heart and finds expression from his lips, in the way in which he freely asks God for the smallest things he wants, and yet is always drawn away from these petitions to sublimer prayers, the rich and ripe issue of a faith which has in it a Bethlehem and a Mount of Olives—an Incarnation and an Ascension: an Incarnation so that we may always pray with perfect trust and confidence, and an Ascension so that we may always pray with loftiness and spiritual aspiration. In such a faith Christ is always coming to us here upon the earth, and we are always, as St. Paul promised us that we should be some day, even now being caught up in the clouds to meet the Lord in the air.

Is there not something that corresponds to this and lets us understand it in the history of every friendship which has grown strong and familiar here upon the earth and then has been stretched by the death of one of the friends until it reaches all the way from earth to heaven and bridges all the gulf between? You used to see your friend every day. You talked with him of little things. You grew familiar over trifles. The fields under your feet, the merchandise that passed from hand to hand, interpreted you to each other. The commonest chat over the newspaper made you more truly friends. And then death came, and none of that treasured familiarity is lost in all the years that have passed since you looked into his face for the last time. He is as near to you as ever. He is with you on the earth. And yet you think of him more loftily, you seek his inspiration more solemnly, you invoke his memory as a more sacred spell than you ever were moved to look for in his daily presence. You feel your impurity and baseness when you think of him now, as you did not when you used to sit with him by the fire and walk with him in the streets. He is the same to you, but greater. He is as real, but far more lofty. He has not ceased to meet you on the earth, but now you also meet him in the air, and so he influences both the least and the greatest part of you. You dress yourself as he used to like to see you dressed, and you try to think and see things as he must see them now as he stands before God's throne.

Let us try, if we are really Christians who believe that Christ our Lord has "ascended into heaven," to enter into His heavenly life by the largeness and loftiness of the prayers that we bring to Him. God forbid that we should so misread His exaltation that we should hesitate to ask Him for the very smallest things; but the things that belong to our peace are what He wants to give us. The things that make this world and its interests seem small when we think of them: the forgiveness of sin, the perfect purification of our souls, the driving out of selfishness, the disregard of comfort in pursuit of duty, the care for brethren more than for ourselves; not comfort, not spiritual rest, not freedom from pain here or hereafter—not these, but the chance, the power, the will to glorify God our Father in our lives as He, the perfect Son, did in His—this we may ask if we believe in the Ascension and have understood the heavenly life of Him who is still our Brother and Saviour.

Another suggestion which comes to us with the story of the Ascension of Jesus is that of the true association of our humanity with the vastness of the universe. I have already said how difficult—indeed, impossible —I think it is for the imagination to draw any picture of the details of this wonderful event on which our minds are fixed. No man can even imagine for me what was the fate of that dear flesh and blood which, having suffered on the cross and lain in Joseph's tomb, disappeared from the disciples' sight upon the Mount of Olives. Where it was carried, what changes it underwent, no man has ever known. It is all so far past our knowledge that no man's guesses have the slightest value. We do not wish to hear them. But yet the story makes this fact clear: that a true human life, still truly human, passed forth beyond our human conditions and found itself a place in the sublimest regions of the universe. I cannot trace it, but that body of Christ yet lives somewhere in some mysterious and unknown region of this vast creation in one little corner of which we live. Humanity, then, so the Ascension tells me, may be at home somewhere else than on the earth. It has nobler kinships than with the brutes. It may enter into the welcome of larger hospitality than any that the stateliest mountains or forests can extend. The Resurrection had shown that humanity might relive here upon the earth, even after the catastrophe of death, that seems so terribly the end of all. The Ascension showed that out beyond the earth, wherever the vast system of existence is held as a unit in the hand of one Creator who is Lord of all, out to the end of all things over which God reigns, this humanity, which seems to be shut in to one small planet, may go and find a home and kindred beyond the farthest star.

Is that a gain? If every enlargement of the general life of the race is a boon to the weakest and poorest being who bears the human nature and who comes in sight of the larger outlook of his kind, then surely this great light thrown on the range of human existence is indeed a gain to any poor, depressed, and struggling man who comes to believe it. The slave learns that the master who is to him like a god is a man like himself. A humanity like his own sits in those stately halls and walks over those broad fields. A struggling student learns that his humanity has risen to the height of David's song or Newton's insight. A country boy becomes aware of the stupendous distances to which men like himself have explored the globe, and of the strange transcendent regions in which they have planted their human homes. A self-respect, a noble ambition, a consciousness of freedom and of chance, must come. A great, vague, but strong call must sound out of the distance. This dream of being something must gather into a vision and the soul leap into the heaven of new hopes.

I turned to write this sermon from the reading of a remarkable article in the "Atlantic Monthly," in which a most intelligent and observant writer has told the story of the operatives in a New England factory town exactly as it is going on to-day. It is a terrible tale; not for the suffering of which it tells, not for the conscious misery of the people—that is much less than perhaps, in our sentimentality, we are apt to think— but for the blank limitation of life, the utter earthliness, the absence of high thoughts and hopes, the dreariness to which humanity has been reduced. That is what makes it terrible. To turn from such a story to the everlasting record of how once a human being passed beyond the cloud, still human, and those who watched Him saw Him no more, but there came back to them certain assurance that He still lived and had been welcomed in the central splendors of the universe—it is like being present at the sunrise, when the dark earth finds herself full of glory, and partner in all the greater glory in the midst of which she swims. The soul that truly believes the story which it reads may be still deafened by the clatter of machinery and crowded in by the squalidness of the low town, still jostled in the dingy streets and blinded and choked by the dust of earth, but it has gained the freedom of its own self-consciousness. It is proud with the pride of an imprisoned king. It has gone forth after Christ. It meets him in the air. Fettered and fastened down in body, yet when it knows that the human Christ has ascended into the heavens, with its human heart and mind it too thither ascends, as the collect so nobly prays, and with Him continually dwells.

No man can fully comprehend all this without the whole aspect and thought of death being changed to him. For a human being to go out from this earth is a dreadful thing if it is only with this earth that humanity has any known relation. No wonder that he would rather fret himself against the wharf than cast adrift upon a sea that has no other shore. He goes into the outer darkness. He leaps off from the precipice where all the millions have leaped before him, and he knows no more, for all the millions that have gone before him, where his leap will carry him. But now let us believe in the Ascension. Once a human being, the best and completest of all human beings that have ever lived, the human being whose humanity was perfect by its very union with Divinity, has gone, still human, out of the sight of men—gone, evidently, all alive. We cannot trace His course. The cloud received Him. But yet we know that somewhere out beyond the limits of our little earth that true humanity of His has found a home. Still we may long to know a great deal more; but, knowing that, do we not know much? Humanity can live beyond the earth, can keep broad live relations with the universe. The man who goes to-day, then, goes still into the dark, but the darkness into which he goes is pierced now by a path of light, and at its heart there is a home of light to which he goes. For His humanity has claimed its place in the great universe. The humanity of Jesus has gone before and makes the vast unknown not unfamiliar. Around our thought of it our thoughts of the men we have seen die, our thoughts of our own coming deaths, can gather into confidence and calmness.

A great man died yesterday—a man great in philanthropy; a man who has passed through all the tributes by which men identify and own their heroes: through hatred and scorn first, through respect and honor afterward; a man whose name for years was a taunt and byword on many a white man's lips, while it was hope and music in the ears of the trembling negro; a man whose noble career will forever mark, more than any other man's, the progress of our country out of the sin and shame of slavery. He was a man of genuine and true humanity, a man whom those who, in the days we well remember, hated him most, to-day will name with cordial honor. The great deep changes of these twenty years could find no more striking illustration than the fact that there are not many men through all the land, North or South, who will not stand in reverence beside the grave of Garrison.

When such a man dies, when a great human soul goes forth from this familiar earth, we little know how much of the assurance with which our hearts still follow it, and think vaguely, but assuredly, of the congenial work to which it will be set in some new region of the universe, comes to us from that sight which our faith has beheld on the Mouut of Olives, as we have watched the humanity of Jesus pass out to its eternal life beyond the narrow limits of the earth.

And yet this is not all. We must not talk as if it were the mere glorification of the general humanity which we behold in the Ascension. Man was exalted then, but it was a Man—one whom we know, one whom we understand and love, one who is everything to us, one whose humanity is all the more dear and true because He is vastly more than man—it was a Man like this who passed into the heavens and made the heavens forever intelligible and near and sweet to us. Let us come round to this before we close. If on some hitherto unexplored and uninhabited island far away in the seas a man goes to live, whoever he may be—the poorest and least interesting of our race—he clothes the island with intelligibleness. I can understand and realize its existence when I know that a human foot has been pressed upon its sandy beach. If he is a great, strong, notably manly man who goes there, carrying with him a large share of our humanity, then he gives the island more than intelligibleness. He gives it dignity. It is full of interest. We all wait to hear what he is doing in that now much-regarded land. But if the man who goes there is my friend, and if before he goes he tells me that the island is ultimately to be his and mine, that he is going to make it ready for my coming, that he will come back again and take me to it by and by, then how that island burns for me—the one live, real, shining spot in all the world! It is the goal of all my thoughts, the lodestone of my hopes. I think of it until the familiar house in which I was born, and where I am living still, seems strange to me compared with that one shining spot that has become so real. My friend's love makes it all glow and burn before me as if I myself already saw the sun shining on its mountain-tops and flashing on the surface of its rippling streams.

Can anything like that come to us with regard to the unknown heaven to which our Lord has gone? O my dear friends, if He is indeed our Lord, all that must come to us. Heaven is not only real because His humanity is there, not merely glorious because His greatness is there. It is dear because His love is there —the love which filled His earthly life, the love of the miracle and of the wayside teaching and of the cross. The nearness and the glory might be there and yet heaven not lay hold of our hearts. We might be well content to stand far off and gaze. We might not want to go there. We might not listen for messages, nor send our feeble voices forth in prayer. But now our Christ is there, our Saviour, what wonder if the earth a thousand times seems dull and wearisome, and always gets its best brightness from that other world in which He is, of which this is the vestibule! What wonder if we listen, and know that He must speak to us! What wonder if we want to tell Him all about our life, and our hearts know that He can and will hear us! What wonder if the hope that He will some day take us to Himself abides calm and constant behind all the transitory hopes of life, which are lighted and go out again and again, while that hope remains always as the deep sky remains behind the coming and the going of the stars!

All this the Ascension does for us. "A cloud received Him out of their sight." Into mystery and a darkness to which His going there alone gives any true light our Saviour goes. But oh, my friends, when by and by our way leads also into mystery and darkness, when truth becomes covered with doubt, and joy with sadness, and life begins to feel the waiting death, what can help us like the faith of the ascended Jesus? The way into the cloud may be a way up and not a way down, a way toward Him and not a way from Him. Doubt, sorrow, death—these may be, these to the true soul must be, like the clouds over the Mount of Olives through which the Son of God went up to the right hand of His Father. "We which remain shall be caught up in the clouds, to meet the Lord in the air: and so shall we ever be with the Lord. Wherefore comfort one another"—comfort yourselves too, comfort and strengthen yourselves and one another—"with these words."

XX.

WHITSUNDAY.

"The communion of the Holy Ghost."—2 COR. XIII. 14.

THE great benediction of the Christian Church never grows old and never becomes monotonous. It is like the sunshine, which rises on us every day of our lives with a fresh beauty; or like our truest friendships, which are forever new. "The grace of the Lord Jesus Christ, and the love of God, and the communion of the Holy Ghost, be with you all." Among the blessings invoked in it is this last: "the communion of the Holy Ghost." Upon how many ears has the invocation of that blessing fallen! How many souls have felt the peace and assurance that was in it descend upon them as if it fell out of the opened heaven! And yet how vague to many of those who love it most is the full meaning of the phrase! It is well, I think, that we should study it to-day. For to-day another Whitsunday is here. Again the door stands open, and we look into the chamber where the pentecostal grace was given to the Jewish peasants which made them the teachers of the world. Again we see the tongues of fire burning over the disciples' heads. Again we witness the true birth of the Christian Church in the gift of the communion of the Holy Ghost. It is good for us to draw near reverently and try to understand the wonder as we may, for the power of which the Church was born is the power by which it has lived ever since and is living now. And for us, as for those apostles, there is no blessing more continually needed than "the communion of the Holy Ghost."

We go, then, first to the perpetual and universal facts of human life, for Christianity always uses them and is in harmony with them. And one of the deepest of these facts is man's perpetual need of intercourse and fellowship. A life of solitude is never satisfactory to a truly healthy man. He needs some fellowship. And for his whole satisfaction he needs various fellowships: with those above him, on whom he depends; with those beside him, who are his equals; and with those below him, whom he helps. All three of these relationships furnish the life of a completely furnished man. And the essence of all these fellowships is something internal; it is not external. It is in spirit and sympathy, not in outward occupations. It is communion and not merely contact. This goes so far that where communion is perfect, where men are in real sympathy with one another, contact or outward intercourse may sometimes be absent. I said no man was satisfied with a wholly solitary life; but a man may be satisfied with a very silent life. If he can be assured of sympathy with other men, can know that he shares their feelings and that they share his, he can be content that very few words should pass between them, conscious all the while of a communion that lies deeper than communication. What a man really needs, then, is a true understanding of other men, community of intelligence producing community of sentiment, interest in the same things producing the same feelings. This is communion. And then the second fact is that the communions or fellowships of men are seldom direct, but come about through a medium. They are not the mere liking of men for each other for qualities directly apprehended, but they are the result of a common interest in something which brings the men together and is the occasion by which their sympathy is excited, the atmosphere or element in which their communion lives. Is not this so? Two children in the same family grow up in cordial love for each other; but their love is a love of and in the family. They did not deliberately choose each other for friends, but their hearts were drawn out in the same direction, toward the same father, the same mother, the same home life, and so they met and came to know each other. So two scholars find their element of communion in their common study. Two business men reach each other and become friends through their common business. Two artists learn and love each other's natures through the interpretation of the beautiful work in which they are both engaged. Two soldiers' hearts beat together in the throbbing heat of the same battle. And two reformers enter into each other's life in the indignation or enthusiasm of a common cause. In every case you see the union of men is made through a third term, an element into which both enter, and in which they find each other as they could not without it. This is the way in which men come to be gathered in those groups which make the variety and picturesqueness of human life. The men of business are gathered in that mutual understanding which is born of their common occupations; their personal sympathies are presided over by and are included in the communion of business; the scholars are gathered in the communion of learning, the artists in the communion of art, the philanthropists in the communion of philanthropy; while men, as men, as separate from all the other orders of beings which fill the universe, hold their personal relationships all included in, all under the sanction of, their common human nature, all embraced in and sealed by the great communion of humanity.

Now it is in the application of this same idea that there lies, I think, the key to this phrase, "the communion of the Holy Ghost." Once more there is an element, an atmosphere, in which men are brought close together—brought together as they come under no other auspices, in no other way. That element is God. Men meet each other, when they meet in Him, with peculiar confidence, dearness, frankness, and truth. Just as there is a certain character which belongs to the intercourse of men who are met as the pursuers of a common business, and so are met in the communion of that business; and there is another character which belongs to the intercourse of men who are met as the disciples of a certain study, and so are met in the communion of that study, so there is yet another deeper and completer character which belongs to the fellowship of men who come to have something to do with one another as the servants of God, and so whose communion is the communion of God. Not directly, not simply for the apprehended and appreciated qualities which they perceive in each other, but two men, both of whom love and are trying to serve God, even before they know anything more about each other, are united in that fact, and all their later union and the gradual mutual understanding which grows up between them grows up within that fact and is all filled by it. All their fellowship is a fellowship by and through God. Their communion is the communion of God.

And now take one step farther. Who is the Holy Ghost? I do not want to talk to you theologically this morning. I want to speak of the Holy Ghost purely with reference to this one work, the communion which He makes between men. But who is the Holy Ghost? He is the effectively present Deity. He is God continually in the midst of men and touching their daily lives. He is the God of perennial and daily inspiration, the Comforter to whom we look in the most pressing needs of comfort which fill our common life. He is the God of continual contact with mankind. The doctrine of the Holy Ghost is a continual protest against every constantly recurring tendency to separate God from the current world. A God who made the world and then left it to run its course under the tyranny of force and law; a God who redeemed the world eighteen centuries ago and left it to be blessed by or to miss the blessing of the redemption which He had provided— neither of these ideas of Deity can comprehend the truth of God the Holy Ghost. A present God, an ever-living God, an ever-pleading, ever-helping, ever-saving God—this is the God whom Christ told of and promised, the God who came in the miracle of Pentecost and is forever here. And now add this idea to what we said before. Wherever the fellowship and intercourse of men has a peculiar character because it is born of the presence of God among men; wherever men's dealings with each other, or men's value of each other, is colored with the influence of the truth that we live in a world full of God; wherever our communion with each other takes place through Him, the sacredness and usefulness of what we are to each other resulting from what He is to all of us, then our communion is a communion of the Holy Ghost.

Do I make this plain? Here are two groups of men. They both hold together in their own ways. But one of them is united by the mere liking of individual for individual. The other is bound together by common allegiance to a principle. One is like a mass of sand crowded and pressed together so that particle clings to particle and a show of solidity is presented. As soon as the sand grows dry the cohesion disappears and the whole mass falls apart. The other is like a gathering of iron-dust about a magnet, where each particle holds fast to its neighbors by the pervading power of the magnetic influence that fills them all. Then, if you substitute a person for the principle, and make gratitude and loyalty the power that holds the men together, you come nearer to the idea. Who has not seen and felt the beauty of a company of men held into brotherhood by their enthusiastic affection for one central man who overtopped them all and dropped his bounties into all their lives? His name became the watchword of their union. Their whole great company seemed to be filled with and repeat his character. And then, if for all lower persons you substitute God, and think of men as bound together and doing all good things to one another because they are His children and receive alike His daily goodness, then, in a world of men whose principle of unity is a forever-present Deity whom they all love, you have the communion of the Holy Ghost.

Or see it in an illustration of it. You go into some foreign land, where men are very different from what you have known them here. You find men there—men with the common human form, and, as you come to know them, with the common human characters and passions. It is not in our human nature not to feel a fellowship with those human beings. Simply as atom to atom, your humanity is drawn to theirs. With an interest such as no brute inspires, they take hold of your life. There is the communion of humanity between you. But suppose, as you go on and know them better, you find that among them there are some whom God has touched, and who are drawing toward Him, loving Him, trying to do His will. It may be very blindly, it may be through a heavy mass of brutal ignorance, or through the tortuous channels of some fantastic superstition, but in some way they are showing the power of a present God. The Holy Ghost has reached them. They see dim streaks of spiritual light. They make vague flutterings of spiritual desire. Or suppose the other extreme. Suppose these souls you find are lofty, pure, wise souls—souls far above you in spiritual light and vigor. In either case, do not you, a man who, in your own degree, are living in the power of a present God, find yourself drawn into the fellowship of these kindred souls, whether they are higher or lower in the spiritual life than you are? Your soul recognizes a servant of the Lord it serves. He may be above or below you in the household, but he serves the same Master. Through that Master you are brought together. In your common search for holiness under the care of Him from whom holiness proceeds, you meet each other. It is the communion of the Holy Ghost.

I doubt not there is a deeper philosophy in this than we can understand. The Bible truth is, we have declared this morning our belief, that the Holy Ghost is "the Lord and Giver of life." The power of life is the power of unity everywhere. It is the presence of life in these bodies of ours that keeps them from falling to pieces. The moment that life departs dissolution comes. Health is the true and close relationship, the happy ministry, of part to part. And so life, which is the gift of the Holy Ghost—nay, which is the presence of the Holy Ghost in society or in the soul—is the power of unity in society or in the soul. The society in which there is no presence of a living God drops into anarchy and falls to pieces. The soul in which there is no presence of a living God loses harmony with itself, becomes distracted. Sin is incoherent and disintegrating. Goodness is the power of coherence. No mere compact of man with man or nation with nation can ever bring about reliable and settled peace; no mere aggregation of selfishnesses in treaties and confederations can ever obliterate the awful fact of war—nothing but a common love of God and obedience to His laws and enthusiasm for His will; not a communion of policy, or a communion of good nature, or a communion of unambitious indolence, but a communion of the Holy Ghost.

Again, our idea finds its illustration in the different characters of different households. I think that all of us must be able to see it there. Lift the curtain, if you will, from two homes, both of them happy and harmonious, neither of them stained with vice nor disturbed with quarrels. One of them is a household of this world altogether. The domestic relationships are strong and warm. The loves of husband and wife, of parents and children, of brothers and sisters, are all there. They prove themselves in all kind offices. Each helps the other, and there are no jealousies, no strifes. There is the best picture of the communion of the family affection. Now look into the other home. All is the same, but with this difference: that here there is an ever-live, strong, vivid, loving sense of God. As real as father or mother, as real as brother or sister, God is here. No act is ever done out of His presence. He is felt in the education of the children. The children are His gifts. The love of each member of the household for the rest is colored all through with gratitude to Him. All of that love is deepened because each desires for each sacred and spiritual mercies. My dear friends, there are such households; not households where the family affections have been crowded out by religious feeling, but where they have been deepened and transfigured by it; where parents love their children better, and children love their parents and one another better, because they all love God; where the common intercourses of home are signs of something deeper, and really signify the communion of the

Holy Ghost. What does it mean when religion enters into a family, when over all the home life is stretched out the hand of God, and all a household is converted? I do not know how to tell the story of what happens then—of the deep, sweet, solemn change that comes over all the family experience—except by just this phrase: that the communion of natural affection has passed into the communion of the Holy Ghost. All these loves which were there before move on still, but they are all surrounded by and taken up into one great comprehending love; and he who enters in at the door of that converted house hears them all in deepened, richened music, the same strains still, only full of the power of the new atmosphere in which they are played.

And so it is with friendship. Two men who have known each other for years become together the servants of Christ. His spirit comes to them. They begin the new life of which He is the center and the soul. How their old friendship changes! How it is all the same, and yet how different it is! It opens depths and heights they never dreamed of. Where they used to do so little for each other, now they can do so much. Where they used to touch only on the outside, now their whole natures blend. They have taken friendship and planted it where it belongs, in the soil and air of the divine love; and it opens its essential richness as the tropical flower which has been living a half-life in northern soil tells its whole sweet and gorgeous story of itself when it is carried to the bright skies and warm ground for which God made it.

One of the most valuable changes which comes to a human friendship when it is thus deepened into a communion of the Holy Ghost is the assurance of permanence which it acquires. There is always a lurking distrust and suspicion of instability in friendship which has not the deepest basis. No present certainty answers for the future. Present kindness only bears witness of present regard, and each new moment needs its new proof. How we have all felt this!

> "Alas that neither bonds nor vows
> Can certify possession!
> Torments me still the fear that love
> Died in its last expression."

This must be so to some degree with an affection where each is held to each only by the continuance of personal liking. But when friendship enters into God, and men are bound together through their common union with Him, all the strength of that higher union authenticates and assures the faithfulness and perseverance of the love that is bound up with it. The souls that meet in God may well believe that they shall hold each other as eternally as He holds each and each holds Him.

And the same power which insures the perpetuity of friendship must also secure a wider range of sympathy and fellow-feeling among men. The more the associations of men come to consist in what is essential, and not in what is merely formal, the larger becomes the circle of a man's fellow-creatures with whom he may have relations of cordial interest. So much of our communion with men is a communion, not of spirit, but of form. We associate with men because we happen to be thrown in with them in the mere circumstances of our lives; because we live in the same circle of society, and so our habits are the same; because we are seeking the same ends of life in the same kind of actions. And very often our sympathies are bounded by the same narrow lives which limit our associations. But the communion of the spirit, the communion of the Holy Ghost, is something deeper, and therefore something wider, than that. Wherever any human soul is loving the God whom we love, feeling His presence, trying to do His will, though it be in forms and ways totally different from ours, the communion of the Holy Ghost brings us into sympathy with him. There is no influence of the Christian life more ennobling, more delightful, than this. The more you come into communion with God, catch His spirit, understand His life; the more quick your eye becomes to detect the spiritual life of other men, though it be hidden under the strangest forms, the more broad your heart grows to embrace it. Coming to love God is like climbing a high mountain. It takes you out of the low valley of formal life. It sets you upon the open summit of spiritual sympathy, close to the sun. Thence you look out into unguessed regions of noble thought and living, with which you never dreamed that you had anything to do. Oh, upon Whitsunday that all seems so plain which sometimes seems so dark and difficult. It is not by working away upon our forms and organizations and trying to make them coincide that the present miserable divided condition of Christendom is to be outgrown. It is only by the perception of one another's earnest spiritual purpose underneath their different methods that Christian sects like those that divide our Christian world can come to anything like sympathy or union with one another. And they can come to know one another's spirit only as they come to know God, and to understand how much more is the spirit than the form to Him. It is the communion of the Holy Ghost in which Christians must meet. If they could only meet in that high atmosphere they would make very short work of these terrible differences of form and organization which trouble them so much now. They would no more quarrel about them than two soldiers meeting on the wall of an enemy's citadel to capture it would quarrel about the different patterns of the sealing-ladders by which they climbed there.

But meanwhile is it not a very lofty and inspiring ambition to offer to a man, that the more he knows and loves God the more he shall see the noble and the good in all his brethren? We should like to believe in men so much more than we do! We are almost ready to give up in despair; the meanness, the foulness, the cruelty of humanity crowd on us so. It is a great promise to make to a young man when you say to him, "If you will earnestly try by obedience and love to enter into communion with God, these brethren of yours, who are like sealed books with stained covers, shall open to you, and you shall see goodness, nobleness, truth, devotion, all through them." It is a promise which, if he takes it, may be his salvation from wretched cynicism and despair. There never was a man who really tried to serve God who did not have his sympathy with his fellow-men widened thereby.

Here is the difference between religious and secular philanthropy. Secular philanthropy loves and helps men directly, for themselves. Religious philanthropy loves and helps men in God. Secular philanthropy has often a tendency to despise the people whom it helps. Its pity is streaked with scorn or disgust. Religious philanthropy is always growing, as it becomes more religious, more reverent toward the beggar whom it feeds, or the sick man whose bed it smooths. Secular philanthropy is always dwelling on the duty of charity. Religious philanthropy is the overflow of brotherly kindness, the communion of the Holy Ghost. There is much of so-called religious philanthropy that never gets above the secular spirit, and much of so-called secular philanthropy that is loftier and finer and more religious than it knows; but these are the distinctions that lie between the help which men give to one another for themselves and the help which they give to one another for the love of God, whose love inwraps them both.

It is time for me to stop, for here there waits for us the sacrament of the holy communion, which shall illustrate to us, as we receive it, all that I have said. I have not dwelt upon all of the great work of the Holy Spirit, whose manifestation at the Pentecost we celebrate to-day. I have not tried to tell of that transforming work upon the soul by which He makes it anew into the image of Christ. I have dwelt only upon this: that as we come to Him we come to one another; as we come to God the Holy Ghost we come to one another. He is the constructive principle and power in human life. By Him every society of good men is bound together. By Him the Christian Church rises into the sky of God's grace like a majestic tree full of all precious fruit. By Him the family wins a new sacredness, and every friendship of men who are trying to serve God is bound into indissoluble union with an unseen but strong compulsion. If you are afraid of yourself as you find how you are drawing away from your fellow-men and growing into a more and more selfish life, you must come to God; you must enter into the communion of the Holy Ghost. If you have a quarrel which you hate and know is miserable, but which holds you fast, your only freedom from it is in the communion of the Holy Ghost. Come there and your quarrel will break and scatter as the ice melts when you bring it into the sun. If you are conscious of narrowness and of inability to sympathize with men whose forms of life or faith are other than your own, still it is in the communion of the Holy Ghost that you must find the broader spirit. It is the communion of a common forgiveness and a common inspiration. As in an old village men and women gather from their several houses to drink of one common fountain and meet one another there, so they who need the help and pardon and comfort of God, coming to get them from the everlasting Comforter, meet one another in Him.

May we so meet in Him this morning, and the blessing which has rested upon so many generations rest once more on us, making our communion a true communion of the Holy Ghost.

XXI.

TRINITY SUNDAY.

"Again, He sent other servants more than the first. . . . But last of all He sent unto them His Son."—MATT. xxi. 36, 37.

THIS is Trinity Sunday, and Trinity Sunday is in some sense the day of faith. It is the day of the soul's aspiration and ambitious desire to know all that it can know about God. There are two questions which it is possible for the believing man to ask about his faith. The first of them is not ambitious. It is overcome by the presence of difficulty and doubt and disagreement. It tries to reduce Christianity to the lowest and simplest terms. It asks, "How little may a man believe and yet rightly call himself a Christian?" There is a time for such a question. When the soul, puzzled about many of the details of its belief, still longs to keep hold of the sacred name, or when, aware that souls may doubt and differ much on special points and yet be one in spirit, we desire to feel ourselves in fellowship with just as many devout and earnest hearts as possible—at such times as these this question comes rightly enough: "How little may a man believe and yet be truly called a Christian?" It is the invalid's question: "How low can I let the fire of life burn down and yet not totally go out?" The other question strikes another note: "How much does my Christian faith give me a right to believe and know concerning God?" Do you not feel the difference immediately? That is an aspiring and ambitious question. It is a question full of force and hope. It is a question that opens a future. It is the question, not of the invalid upon his bed, but of the strong man with his armor on. However the first question may claim certain conditions for its own; however it may properly recur on some dull days, perhaps in some long, dull periods, of Christian life, evidently the true question for our faith to ask is, not that, but this other. Only in the struggle and desire to know all that we can know of God must lie the hope and satisfaction of mankind.

I have wanted to begin my sermon of to-day with such a plea as this for the ambitiousness of faith. There is a great deal of danger of our forgetting that to believe much, and not to believe little, is the privilege and glory of a full-grown man. There will come times —and upon such a time our lot has fallen—when men are led to sing the praise and glorify the influence of doubt. Assuredly it has its blessings, but while we magnify them we ought never to forget that they are always of the nature of compensation. The blessings of doubt are like the blessings of poverty, not to be chosen for themselves, but to be accepted thankfully when they come in to mitigate the unnaturalness of the condition into which a life, missing of its true purpose and success, has fallen. There do come times when you must cut a tree down to its very roots in order that it may grow up the richer by and by; but a whole field of stumps is not the ideal landscape. The forest, with its wealth of glorious foliage, is the true coronation of the earth. There is a great deal of danger lest the tendency to dwell upon the blessings and culture of doubt may come to make a full and rich faith seem to be almost a burden instead of a treasure; a thing for a man to be pitied for, and not to be congratulated upon. It is, I think, no very unusual thing for men who believe little to look at one who lives in the richness of a large, full faith with something almost like commiseration, somewhat as there is a tendency in settled invalidism to count exuberant health a somewhat gross and vulgar thing; and their feeling is very apt to communicate itself to the believing man himself, and make him half ashamed and mistrustful of his own belief.

Against such a tendency we want to warn one another and to warn ourselves. Seek faith—as full and rich a faith as you can find. Try to know all you can about God and your own soul. Count every new conviction which is really won a treasure and enrichment of your life. There are dangers in accumulation of every sort—danger lest the thing accumulated should lose some of its value as it becomes more plentiful; danger lest the sense of possession should lose for us some of the discipline that can only come in search— but these dangers are nothing to the danger of the despair of faith, the terrible danger of coming to think that God is darkness and not light, the terrible danger of ceasing to hear His perpetual invitation to His children to come on and in, into ever more trustful and certain knowledge of His purposes, of His love, and of Himself.

TRINITY SUNDAY. 321

If all that I have said be true, then there can be no loftier study with regard to man than the attempt to trace his progress into richer and richer faith; to see how humanity becomes the recipient of revelation after revelation of God, until it stands in the full light of the New Testament. Upon this Trinity Sunday, when we especially recall the great statement of truth in which our faith culminates, I want to make that attempt. Let us try to trace in briefest outline the growth of faith, and see how branch adds itself to branch until at last there is the glory of the perfect tree.

1. Faith begins when a man becomes aware of his own soul. We must go back as far as that. We picture to ourselves (although no man has probably identified it in his own experience, and no historian has ever put his finger on it in the record of the world)—we picture to ourselves a deep and solemn moment when man, having known himself thus far solely in his most external nature, as a being of the senses and of the flesh, becomes aware of the mysterious spiritual life which lives within. He comes to know of keener pains and more exquisite pleasures, of duties and responsibilities and hopes and fears which are not of the body, but of a truer self which lives within the body, and which, when he has once found it, becomes to him his only real, true self—the he who really lives his life and owns the only essential and intrinsic character which he possesses. That is the beginning of all faith. In that faith in his own soul man for the first time becomes capable of belief in unseen spiritual existence anywhere. Unless he had that primary knowledge of

spirit in himself, all evidence of spiritual being would come to him and pass away from him as uselessly as the south wind blows across a stone. That first faith comes by self-consciousness. A thousand voices come to whisper assurance to it when it has once begun to know itself, but its birth is out of the bosom of the human self-consciousness. A man knows his own soul, knows that he carries a spiritual life, and in that knowledge faith begins.

2. But faith, once born thus in the consciousness of spirituality, cannot lie unobservant in its cradle. It lifts itself up and looks abroad upon the world. Just as the child, grown conscious of its own intelligence, searches in all things for an intelligence correspondent to his own, and finds it in the parental providence which protects and rules his life, so man, believing in his own soul, searches the world in all its higher regions for the evidence of soul, of spiritual nature, correspondent to his own—the evidence of thought and will and love—and finding them abundantly, attains the faith in God. Next to the faith in soul there comes faith in the Father-soul or God. That faith precedes all Bibles, all recorded utterances of God. Man does not learn from any book the first truth of the existence of Divinity. The utterances of the Books of God, when they come, confirm the faith and make it large and rich, just as, when he whom we have known of with a perfect certainty for years comes into our presence at last and speaks to us, the perfect assurance which we have had of his existence grows yet more sure. So, when God speaks in revelation, we do not merely know what He wills, we know with a new kind of certainty

that He is; but the first certainty came before He spoke, except in that speech which is inarticulate, unrecognized, but real, the speech of nature to nature, of the highest and original nature of any sort to the lower and derived natures of the same sort, the speech of the fountain to the stream, the speech of the father to the child. In that speech comes the faith of God into the soul of man, and man believes in God.

3. This, then, is the genesis of faith. Man has believed in his own soul and he has believed in God. But this is only the genesis, only the birth and the beginning. So far all is solitary. Each man has known nothing yet of God but what his own personal consciousness and experience can tell him. How natural the next step is! Here are these hosts of men around him. Here are these generations of men stretching back behind him. They too had souls. Each in his own individuality, and then together in the groups in which they have lived, they have had spiritual natures and spiritual interests in which they too have been related to God and have drawn forth the utterances of His spirituality. As soon as we see this, then, all the spiritual history of man becomes the subject of our study. That God whose life and ways we have found reflected in our own experiences—which experiences, when we have once come to know Him, we begin to call His treatment of us—behold all the ages, all the nations, in proportion to the seriousness of their life and the momentousness of their purposes, become mirrors of Him, telling us things concerning Him which the range and depth of our own personal life was too limited to show. All human history is a store-

house for our faith. Out of it all comes knowledge about God.

4. And then in the midst of that history of all the peoples, each showing us something of God, there shines out one peculiar history, the history of a peculiar people. With greater issues, with profounder life, the story of the Jews stands out, not, as it sometimes seems to be described, as if God had used their national life as a mere set of ingenious pictures to tell men things which were not real in their day, which were not to be real for years and years to come. Not so! The history of the Jews gets its perpetual interest from the fact that, being the most conscientious and spiritual of all peoples, the Jews had deeper things to do with God than other races, and so God showed things concerning Himself in His relationship with them that He did not show—that He could not show—when He was dealing with the Roman or the Greek. There is the first and deepest value of the Old Testament, which tells their history; there is the fundamental fact which makes the belief in that Old Testament a real addition to and growth in faith.

5. But the Old Testament is something more than the history of a religious people and of God's relationship to them. Whoever reads it carefully finds a new idea coming in—the idea of direct communication from God to man. Through chosen men there are perpetually arriving messages from God, telling His people directly and distinctly what is true and what they ought to do. Abraham, Moses, David, Isaiah—all the way down to Malachi the long line of the prophets runs, God speaking to each of them, and through them

speaking to His listening people. I will not pause to say how naturally the expectation of some such power of communication from God to man follows upon the faith in God's existence; how almost impossible it seems to be for men to keep any faith in a wholly silent and uncommunicative God. I am not trying now to prove the faith, but only to show you how stage by stage it grows to its completeness. All that I want you to notice, then, about the prophets is what a great new life comes into man's belief when their voices really break upon his ears. Man has believed in his own soul. He has believed in God. He has believed in a government of God, and learned something of what God is by seeing how His government proceeds. But everything so far has gone on in awful silence. Now God speaks! "Thus saith the Lord," declares His prophet. Is it not almost as if the tree had grown to its full stature without foliage, all its branches perfect, but all bare, and now at last they all broke forth into leafage in one glorious moment? It is not simply what the prophets say. Certainly it is not the glimpses of yet unborn history which they sometimes give us— what in the narrower and stricter sense we often call prophecy. It is that in them God has spoken—spoken with such a voice that the conscience and the heart of man can hear.

6. If this were all it would be very much indeed; but there is something else. At last I come now to the text, which I have not yet mentioned. In the chapter of Matthew from which it is taken Some One is telling this same story which I have tried to tell—the story of the gradually ripening provision for the faith

of man. And He has reached this point. He has just recounted the story of the Hebrew prophets. A Master has sent His servants to the workmen in His vineyard to secure their loyalty and service. The mission has not done its work: " The husbandmen took His servants, and beat one, and killed another, and stoned another. Again, He sent other servants more than the first: and they did unto them likewise." There is just the point that we have reached—the mission of the prophets. And then the Speaker goes on and declares another new act of the Master of the vineyard: "Last of all He sent unto them His Son." Just see what we have here. Jesus is talking about Himself. He is telling about His own coming into the world. He is declaring what came before Him and compelled His coming. And He declares that with His coming there was a distinct change, a clear step forward from one method of the revelation of God to man to another method of the revelation of God to man. That seems so clear. God sent them servant after servant, but by and by He stopped the stream of servants and sent unto them His Son. Fix your mind clearly and simply on these words. Can they mean anything else than this: that there was a distinctly new method of communication, a distinctively new kind of revelation, when Jesus Christ, the Son of God, came, which had not been in the coming of Isaiah or of Moses? They were servants. This was a new being with a new name. This is the Son.

Nor is it hard to discover, with these two names before us, what was the nature of the change which the coming of Jesus brought about. If you can picture to yourself a father who has sent message after message to his wilful boy, assuring him of love, and begging, tempting, commanding his obedience; if you can think of him at last, when all of them have failed, gathering up all the affection and majesty of his fatherhood and going himself, that with the look of his own eye and the outreach of his own hand he might bear living witness of that which no messenger could tell, then you can feel the difference which Jesus means to describe. If you can picture a king whose armies are insulted and despised going himself and putting his own life trustfully into the power of his rebellious subjects, that he might show them all his heart, again you see the difference. It is the everlasting difference between selfhood and its power, as distinguished from the closest and most intimate of messengers. A being's knowledge or authority that being may impart to a servant, and that servant may communicate. But a being's self can be handed over to no hired stranger, however loyal and obedient and devoted he may be. There is a mystery and depth of power in a man's self which is all his own. Now try to state to yourself what was the distinction that Jesus drew between Himself and the prophets who had come before Him, and you will find, I am sure, that it lies just here. They brought God's messages; He brought God's self. They revealed God's plans; He opened God's heart. They told men what God wanted; He showed men what God was. That inner incommunicable soul of selfhood which none can manifest but he whose it is—nay, none save he who is it—that was what Jesus came to show men concerning God, and it was His power and prerogative to show that which He declared when He said that He was different from all that had come before Him; that while they were the servants He was the Son of God.

If we believe what Jesus said about Himself, my friends, and earnestly desire to receive Him and to treat Him according to the nature which He declared and claimed for Himself, does it not seem very clear that it is as the Son of God, not as the servant of God, that He must be received? Not as another Moses with a purer law, not as a new Isaiah with a loftier inspiration, but as one who in a different way brings us the very life and heart and nature of God Himself; therefore not only with intelligent docility, but with adoring love, with loving adoration—so He is to be received.

This is the real truth of the divinity of Jesus Christ. Its value to us, its whole relationship to us, indeed, resides in this: that it involves in Him a power to bring the very being of God close to our being, in a way purely His own. If the New Testament, if Christ's own words, are full of the joyous and confident assertion of that power, then they are full of the assertion of His divinity. That is the way in which you ought to question your New Testament to see whether it declares the divinity of Jesus: not by the hunting out of proof-texts and single words of Christ, but by the broad survey of His whole mission as He Himself conceived of it, and then the serious asking of yourself this question: Did He or did He not think of His mission as intrinsically different—different in kind—from the missions of all the great teachers of the race? And, if so, where was the difference? Could it have lain anywhere else than in the fact that He manifested not simply God's truth, but God; that He made the life, the heart, the love of God to be present among men, in their affections and their homes? And if He had wanted to state just this difference in the clearest words, could He have put it more clearly than this: "God sent to the world servant after servant, etc."?

I see that certain teachers, with a partizan alacrity, have said that the New Version of the New Testament has established Unitarianism and abandoned the divinity of Jesus because it has changed the English of several verses, and notably because it has left out one text which every scholar of the least information has known for years was not originally part of the book in which it stood. The truth of the divinity of Jesus, of the distinct difference between Him and every other savior, of the supreme manifestation of the life of God in Him, does not hang on a few verses. If it did it would be weak indeed. If it did we may almost say that it would not be worth questioning those verses for. No; that truth shines through all Christ's thought about Himself. It breaks forth in every description of the work He has to do. It burns as the soul of His enthusiasm. It makes the deep solemnity and the awful joy that fill His life. He gathers it around Him, with the most touching reverence for the mystery of His own nature, whenever He calls Himself the Son of God and takes up with hands conscious of a new kind of power the work which the servants of God had failed to do.

And now suppose that this divinity of Jesus becomes part of a man's faith. Think what that means. Suppose that in addition to all that a man has believed before—in addition to believing that he has a soul, and that there is a God, and that God rules in love, and that God has spoken in the messages of the prophets—suppose a man really believes that, entering into our human life, God has been here upon the earth. What shall we say of that belief; what will it be to him who holds it? Will it be some great burden which he will carry about groaning and wishing that he could get rid of, haunted by it perpetually, looking back with longing to the sweet and simple days when no such awful intrusion of Divinity had broken the snug compactness of his human life? The question answers itself. If to believe in God is a glory and delight, the nearer the God whom I believe in comes to me, the more glorious and delightful grows my life. To tread an earth which He has trodden, to think thoughts and to feel emotions which, just as I think and feel them, in their human shapes, He the eternal God has thought and felt—this is assuredly a marvelous enrichment of my living. I have gone out and up into a new world with this new faith—a new world, yet the old world still; the old world teeming and bursting with new meanings, radiant with new light, sacred and beautiful all through with the remembered presence of the Son of God. Surely no man who has once known what it is to live in that world can ever turn his back upon its richness.

7. Shall we go on? Is there yet something further before the possibilities of human faith shall be fulfilled? Indeed there is. All this revelation which has come to us has been revelation about God. We have gone on and up until we have come to believe in Christ. He is the Son of God; in a supreme, peculiar way making

TRINITY SUNDAY.

God's nature known where every other revealer has only been God's servant, bringing men His messages. But evidently the revelation cannot stop there. If Christ does indeed show God to man, then He must also show man to himself. The sunbeam reveals to the flower not merely the sun, but the flower; and so he who sees God in Christ sees also himself, and learns his own capacity as he receives the God whom Christ makes known to him.

Little would be any faith which did not culminate and round itself with faith in our own spiritual capabilities. To lie like a stone and see the stars sweep over us across the sky, and have no movement, no response in our own hearts—there is no blessing in that. But to find that when Christ shows us God our natures recognize the Divinity with love, and strive to repeat in themselves the image that the Son of God has shown to us—that opens infinite joy and hope.

Is there any recognition of all that in the New Testament? Certainly there is. When Jesus comes and says, "I am the Son of God, distinct and separate, so holding that name solely by Myself that all His other messengers are servants and not sons; and yet you to whom I bring Him in your native power of response to Him are all His children, and I can bring Him to you only in virtue of this essential belonging to Him which is in you as His children"—when Jesus says that, He is declaring just this completeness of His work which I have been describing.

And Jesus does say that. He calls Himself the Son of God and He calls us God's sons. There is no confusion. His Sonship stands above our sonship always.

Not one of us may say, as He says, "He that hath seen Me hath seen the Father." And yet all of us, because we are able to see the Father in Him, know ourselves truly sharers of His Sonship.

Not many years after Christ had ascended into heaven, the greatest master and scholar of His truth, the man who above all others had fathomed its meaning and wrought it out in his experience—the great St. Paul—declared this final fact about what Christ had done. "Because we are sons," he wrote, "God hath sent forth the Spirit of His Son into our hearts, whereby we cry, Father." The manifestation of God in Christ completes itself by the manifestation of God in us. The dispensation of the Son who descends from above is fulfilled in the dispensation of the Spirit who occupies our souls and gives us perpetual divine light and help, and makes our life part of the life of God.

Again I say all previous faith would be but worthless to us, however sure and certain it might be, if it did not come up at last and complete itself in this. To believe in the sun and not in the eye; to believe in the sweetness of the honey and not in the power of taste; to believe in the God over us and around us and not in the God within us—that would be a powerless and fruitless faith. But to believe in God the Son and God the Spirit too, in the divine capacity within us answering back to the divine offer around us; to believe in ourselves through the divine presence which we are capable of receiving and containing—that completes the faith of man. He may unfold that faith more and more, he may fathom it deeper and deeper and bring up richer and richer treasures, but he can add nothing to it. He has sailed around the globe of possible belief. He has attained the complete faith by which a man is saved.

And now in one last moment let us look back and repeat to ourselves what is contained in this completed faith of the full Christian man. Let us see how branch after branch has added itself to this growing tree of faith before our eyes, until at last the tree is perfect. First man believes in his own soul; he knows that he is spiritual. Then he believes in God; he knows that his spirit is but an echo of the central and eternal Spirit which is over all. Then He believes that God rules the world; all history becomes His work, and one especial history stands forth—the history of a sacred people—in which God's hand is most peculiarly manifest. Then he believes that God has spoken to mankind; the voices of the prophets bring messages from Him. Then, doing what those prophets failed to do, behold, there stands forth One who bears God's nature and is God's Son. And in the presence of that life of Christ the man's own life opens its possibilities and becomes filled with an ever-present power of Divinity, with the helping, inspiring, comforting Spirit of God. As if one stood and saw the meager stalk enlarge and open its spreading branches and clothe itself with leaves and at last complete itself in the glory of its golden fruit, so grows this full rich faith before our eyes. It is the faith in God and the faith in man, in the fullness of God's strength making the completeness of man's possibility. We call it the faith of the Trinity; but I have wholly failed in what I have tried to do to-day unless I have made you see that this great faith is no one single dogma which men may prove or disprove by an ingenious argument, but is a great conception of the universe, and of the Power which rules it, and of the place of man within it, into which a man can only enter by the experience of life. It is the story of the life of God and the life of man in fullest and openest relation to each other.

About this faith, the faith of all the Christian centuries, the faith to which our Church is consecrated, the faith to which this day belongs, let me say one or two things before I close.

First, it cannot be a matter of indifference and unconcern to any living man whether that faith be true or not. Say that you believe it, say that you disbelieve it—both of these declarations are intelligible; but to say that it is a thing of no consequence, to say that you do not care whether it is true or not—that proves either that you do not know what it really means, or that you are wantonly careless about the things which above all others deserve the thought and care of every intelligent and earnest man.

And second, to come back to where this sermon started, if a man does believe the doctrine of the Trinity, he ought to rejoice and glory in his faith as the enrichment of his life. Not as a burden on his back, but as wings on his shoulders, he ought to carry his belief. To cease to believe it would be, not welcome liberty, but incalculable loss. For a new soul to come to believe it is not, as men have often foolishly talked, the putting out into a sea all dark with mists and fogs. It is the entrance into a luxuriant land where all life lives at its fullest, where nature opens her most lavish bounty, and where man has the consummate opportunity to be and do his best.

I rejoice with you to whom that faith is real. Measure this great tree in your own life and see how large it has grown there. How much of this complete faith of God and man do you believe? That means, How fully are you living? Not how many doctrines do you hold, but how much of the life of God have you taken in to be your life? May we to-day rejoice anew in all the faith which God has given-us; and may He help us by obedient lives to make what He has already given us ever more and more deeply ours, that so it may be possible for Him to give us richer and richer faith forever.

XXII.

THE TRANSFIGURATION OF CHRIST.

"And Peter answered and said to Jesus, Master, it is good for us to be here: and let us make three tabernacles; one for Thee, and one for Moses, and one for Elias. For he wist not what to say."—MARK IX. 5, 6.

IN that book which is known as the Second Epistle of St. Peter, the apostle, now grown into old age, is heard recalling the event of which the story is told in this chapter of St. Mark. "And this voice which came from heaven," he says, "we heard when we were with Him in the holy mount." He is remembering the Transfiguration. Through all the busy and burdened years which have come in between, Peter has never ceased to hear that voice which on the mountain had declared Jesus to be "the beloved Son of God." As he looked back to the whole scene he must have been thankful that his impulsive suggestion, spoken in the confusion, when "he wist not what to say," had not been accepted by his Lord. The event which he remembered had been so much more to him than if its outward form had been made perpetual. It had passed into that glorified world of memory, where its spiritual meaning and radiance had shone out from it. It had become sacred forever with the manifestation of its spiritual truth.

THE TRANSFIGURATION OF CHRIST. 337

This is the best thing which can happen to the events of life: that they should pass into the region of exalted memory, where their true light may shine out for the illumination of all the life which we have yet to live. Less and less, I think, do we desire that the mere conditions and circumstances of life should be maintained. More and more do we dread that the events of the past should be lost out of our memory. Richer and richer seems to be that illumination in which they are set when they are spiritually remembered and we can see the fullness of their meaning. It is not always pleasant to see still standing on the street-side the house in which you lived when you were a boy. Other people have come and lived in it, and their lives, mixed with yours, look out upon you from its windows. But your boyhood itself—that goes back from you into a realm of light and eternity, winning clearness and interpretation as it goes, and takes its place there, glorified, not distorted, revealed, not falsified, pouring out power and illumination upon all your life. As the great men of the world walk sometimes with great labor and distress along the common streets of life and then pass off into a world of undying fame, where they stand close and clear forever to the heart and the intelligence of man, so the great events of our lives have their world of undying influence, whence their power comes forth to touch and shape the life which is made up of the procession of less illustrious events.

I want to speak to you to-day of the power of the most exalted moments of our lives. The Transfiguration had been the most splendid moment in the life of Peter. Part of his life had been lived in the commonplace labor of his trade as fisherman. Part of it had been given to the loving and puzzled study of his Master's nature, trying to find out the secret of this wonderful power. One long stretch of it had been clouded with his mean and wretched sin. Many years of it had been given to the patient, faithful labor of his missionary life. In the midst of it all there shone forth one experience of unmixed and certain glory. Out of this confused and undulating land stood up one mountain-top which never lost the light. Once he had seen Jesus in apocalyptic glory. Once he had felt the very fire which burns in the robes of the everlasting purity and power. Once every doubt, every darkness, every delay, had disappeared, and he had been in heaven for an hour. The splendor of that moment never faded. The old man died rejoicing in the memory that it had once been his, and feeling sure that in it was the promise of all the glory to which he was going.

To many, if not to all, men's lives come such splendid moments as came to Peter on the mountain of the Transfiguration. If I could uncover the hearts of you who are listening to me this morning I think that I should find in almost all—perhaps in all—of them a sacred chamber where burns the bright memory of some loftiest moment, some supreme experience, which is your transfiguration time. Once on a certain morning you felt the glory of living, and the misery of life has never since that been able quite to take possession of your soul. Once you knew for a few days what was the delight of a perfect friendship. Once you saw for an inspired instant the idea of your profession blaze

THE TRANSFIGURATION OF CHRIST. 339

out of the midst of its dull drudgery. Once, just for a glorious moment, you saw the very truth and believed in it without the shadow of a cloud. Do not you know some of these experiences? I am sure you do. And often the question must have come, "What do they mean? What value may I give to these transfiguration times?" So much depends upon the answer which we give to that question that I may well ask you to study it with me awhile.

And, first of all, the impulse must be right which gives to these highest experiences of our lives a prophetic value. The first instinct is to feel that they are not complete and final; that they point to something which is yet to come; that they are the premonitions, the anticipations, of a fuller condition, in which that which they manifested fitfully and transiently shall become the constant and habitual possession of the life.

What a mockery there would be in these supreme ecstatic moments of life if they did not meet with this instinct and claim their interpretation from it! Once to have been brought up out of the dungeon and shown the sunlight and then be carried back again, and, with the memory of it still in our eyes, to hear the bolt driven and the key thrown into the depths, so that we never again could be released one moment from our darkness—what wretchedness could equal that! Once to have seen for a moment what it is to believe, and then to feel the stone of unbelief rolled hopelessly to our tomb door—all the convictions of the human soul stand up against a cruel mockery like that! It cannot be!

And these convictions of the human soul find manifold support in what men see on many sides. There are abundant instances in which some splendor which is by and by to become fixed and habitual shows itself first in a sudden splendid flash of light, which disappears the moment it has showed itself to the man's astonished eyes. When was ever any invention made which ultimately was to take its quiet place in the midst of the prosperous industry of humankind, but first it showed itself as a dream and vanished like an impossibility before the eyes of some amazed, ingenious youth, who hopelessly begged that it would stay with him, and wist not what he said? The motive which by and by, with its steady pressure, is going to move all our life is felt first like a wayward gust out of some transcendental, unimaginable world. The friend who is to be our life's unfailing solace appears to us first in some garment of light, which we can only reverence at a distance, and can never dare to touch. It is the most familiar testimony of all truly thoughtful men. That which is ultimately to become the soul's habitual support comes first in some supreme exceptional manifestation, which, even though it disappears, still leaves behind it in man's instincts a memory that is full of hope, a deep conviction that it has not gone forever, and so a strength to watch and wait and hope for its return.

It seems to me like this: A traveler is going through a country by a long straight road which leads at last to a great city which is his final goal. At the very beginning of the journey the road leads over a high hill. Up on the summit of that hill the traveler can clearly

THE TRANSFIGURATION OF CHRIST. 341

see the spires of the far-away city flashing in the sun. He feasts his eyes on it. He fills his eyes with it. And then he follows the road down into the valley. It loses the sight of the city almost immediately. It plunges into forests. It sounds the depths in which flow the dark waters which the sun never touches. But yet it never forgets the city which it saw from the hilltop. It feels that distant unforgotten glory drawing it toward it in a tight straight line. And when at last the traveler enters in and makes that city thenceforth his home, it is not strange to him, because of the prophecy of it which has been in his heart ever since he saw it from the hill.

If we read rightly, thus, the method by which God brings His children to their best attainment, it is certainly a method full of wisdom and beauty. First He lets shine upon them for a moment the thing He wants them to become, the greatness or the goodness which He wishes them to reach. And then, with that shining vision fastened in their hearts, He sets them forth on the long road to reach it. The vision does not make it theirs. The journey is still to be made, the battle is still to be fought, the task is still to be done. But all the time, through the long process, that sight which the man saw from the mountain-top is still before the eyes, and no darkness can be perfectly discouraging to him who keeps that memory and prophecy of light.

A memory which is not also a prophecy is terrible. Better to forget than to remember only as a thing that is past and finished forever. You recall the happy days of an old friendship. Unless it is a perpetual revelation to you of the perfect friendship of the perfect life it comes to be a torture.

> " 'Tis better to have loved and lost
> Than never to have loved at all;"

but the true blessedness is reached only when you know that that which you have seen plunged into the fiery furnace is to come out again, the same, but finer, purer, holier, more worthy of the child of God!

When we have really grasped this truth, then how interesting and impressive becomes the sight of the life of our fellow-men! Many and many of these men whom we see plodding on in their dusty ways are traveling with visions in their souls. Nobody knows it but themselves and God. Once, years ago, they saw a light. They knew, if only for a moment, what companionships, what attainments, they were made for That light has never faded. It is the soul of good things which they are doing in the world to-day. It makes them sure when other men think their faith is gone. It will be with them till the end, until they come to all it prophesies.

Childhood, coming at the beginning of every life, is in the lives of many men this time of vision and of prophecy. We live in those first years in which it seems easy to do and be great things. We are full of the sense of God. We are surrounded by an atmosphere of faith. And then come doubt and hardship and the falseness of men. Tell me, who is there of us that could live through it all if we had not been upon the mountain-top first and seen and believed? There is not the skeptic who once prayed as a little child that

THE TRANSFIGURATION OF CHRIST. 343

is not to the end of his skeptical life the better for that prayer. There is not the cynic, despising and despairing of his brethren, who has not at the bottom of his heart the seed of a better hope, kept from the days when as a boy he trusted them and knew that in every one of them was a capacity of goodness.

If we go a little deeper into the philosophy of this power which belongs to the memory of our best moments, if we ask ourselves why it is that God has appointed such a treatment as I have been trying to describe for His children, I think we are not wholly at a loss. May it not be that in this way a condition or conviction which in the first place took its shape under special circumstances may best become an independent spiritual possession of the soul, to be used in all the various circumstances of the life? You cast a tool of iron in a mold. Then you break the mold and throw it away; but the tool which first took shape in it stays in your hand and is yours for a hundred uses. So, suppose that years ago there came some crisis in your life which taught you the necessity and the glory of being brave. It was some mighty day of God with you. With lightnings and thunderings God scattered your timid fears and made your whole masculine vigor to come forth. You dared to fight because you dared not feebly run away. It was a revelation of you to yourself. What then? The crisis past, the lightnings faded and the thunders hushed, you came down from the mountain. Ever since that you have walked on in quiet, level ways. But many a time, in simple tasks which had not power of themselves to bring you such self-revelations, you have found yourself able to be brave with a bravery whose possibility you learned in that tremendous hour. If, had your life continued in that tumult, you would have come to think that bravery belonged to tumult and was only possible in the stress of battle, can you not see why God caused the sky of your life to clear, and would not let you build your tabernacle on the mountain? Now you are brave for any lot. Your courage, summoned by some petty struggle of to-day, does not even recall the first awakening which came to it in that long-past exalted hour. Men are meeting the petty enemies of the household and the street to-day with a fortitude and a fearlessness which they learned thirty years ago on the battle-fields of the Rebellion. Men are bearing little disappointments with a patience which was born in them while they stood by the death-bed of their best beloved and watched the hopes of all their life slowly sink under the rising flood. It is good that the power which is first born under exacting and peculiar circumstances should then be set free from those circumstances altogether and become the general possession of the life, available for all its needs. The cloud forms about the mountain-peak; but once formed there, it floats away and drops its blessing upon many fields.

Closely resembling this is the way in which the qualities of great men become the possession of the world. Great men are in the world what the most enlightened and exalted experiences are in the life of any man. They are the mountain-tops on which the influences which are afterward to fertilize our whole humanity have birth. There stands out some great pattern of unselfishness; some martyr-life which totally forgets itself and lives in suffering self-sacrifice for fellow-men. About that man's life gathers an utterance, an exhibition, of the glory of self-sacrifice—of how it is the true life of mankind, of how in it alone man becomes truly man. Does all that abide in him, live and die in his single personality? Does it disappear forever in the withering flames which consume him at the stake? Does not that fire set it free, cast it forth into the atmosphere of the universal human nature, and make it the possession of all mankind? Have not you and I the power to live more unselfishly to-day because of the unselfishness of the great monumental lives of devotion?

What is the power of the cross of Jesus? Manifold, I am sure; more manifold than you or I, or all the sinners who have been saved by it, or all the theologians who have devoutly studied it in all the ages, have begun to know or tell. But certainly one part of its power lay here: it was the loftiest manifestation of man's power to give himself for duty and for fellowman that the earth has ever seen. In Jesus our humanity went up into the mountain and was transfigured. It shone with light there on the cross. Thenceforth, into whatever depths of selfishness it might descend, it carried the power of that transfiguration with it. In its certainty that He who suffered there was one with it and really bore its nature, it knew that not to be selfish, but to be unselfish, was its true life. That is the reason why so wonderfully, through all the years of miserable self-seeking which have come since, souls everywhere have come out under the power of that cross and let themselves be crucified for fellow-men, and why the dream of a world glorious with mutual devotion has never been lost out of men's hearts.

Those lives of self-devotion, however humble and obscure they seem, have always themselves the same power which belongs to the sacrifice of Jesus. They too throw light on darker lives. They are lesser hilltops grouped around the great mountain. Such lives may we live in any little world where God has set us!

The most interesting and suggestive groups in the world are always those in which identity and contrast are most fitly mingled. A scene of nature gives us the best pleasure when it is like and yet unlike some scene which we have seen before; not its mere duplicate, and, on the other hand, not so entirely different from it as to suggest no comparison. Two men call forth our interest when they both are evidently human, making us feel the humanity which is common to them both, and yet each has his distinct peculiarities and personal characteristics. Is not this the principle which really is at the heart of our relation to the exalted and triumphant moments of our past life? What is it that makes a man plodding along through regions of prosaic doubt remember always one shining day of years ago, when all the clouds of doubt parted and swept away, and for the time he thoroughly believed? It is because of the sense of identity and the sense of contrast both, which the remembrance of that day brings with it. In the midst of all his bewilderment he feels sure that he is the same man who lived that glorious, ecstatic day. It is not another man's. It is his. And in all the exultant sense of its possession he is all the more terribly aware how far he has

THE TRANSFIGURATION OF CHRIST. 347

departed from it now. It fills his present life with shame. These two together blend into the longing regard with which he looks back upon it, into the eager tenacity with which he treasures it. If there were no sense of contrast with the present, that long-past day of loftier experience would fade away, and the man would live in the mere satisfaction of immediate delight. If there were no sense of identity the degenerate present would seem to be the soul's only condition. The happier past would seem to belong to some other man, and so no hope would flow out from it to the prostrate life, promising it better things.

Is not this so? Years, years ago, it may be, God gave you a day of exalted communion with Himself. Perhaps in connection with some particular event of suffering or joy, perhaps entirely apart from anything which happened, as if God gave it directly out of His opened hand, God sent you a longer or a shorter period of calm, profound, spiritual peace and joy. It was full of assurance. God seemed very real and very near to you. His truth was not only easy to believe, you hungered after more of it. You went seeking for more that you might know of Him. You did not need to seek for Him; you found Him everywhere. Christ and His light shone out from everything. As you remember those days you have no doubt of their reality. They are the realest days of all your life. They keep a hold on you which will not let you go. And are not these the two hands with which they hold you —the identity and the contrast of your present life? "I, I, this same I, am the man who once lived near to God;" and "Lo, how far from God, in what a desert of worldliness and selfishness, I am living now!" The past, our own best past, holds us with these two hands and will not let us go.

No doubt there is a deeper truth about it all. Follow out this truth, and it is impossible for us to stop short of that idea of our self which is in the heart of God and with which He made us to conform. That is what really holds us. It is that from which we cannot get away. It is our identity and our contrast with that which, mingled together, makes the restlessness, the shame, the aspiration of our lives. That "purpose of God concerning us," underlying our lives all the while, breaking forth like subterranean fire at the thinnest spots, taking possession of our consciousness at its most exalted points, as the flame pours out from Vesuvius—that is what really declares itself in our transfiguration times.

That idea of them makes those times most gracious in our history, and perfectly explains the fascination for us which they never lose. They are the utterance of our highest, truest possibility. They are not brilliant unaccountable exceptions. They are our normal life. They are the type of what we always might and ought to be. For the exceptionalness of an event is not properly measured by its rarity. The exception is the departure from the law of life, whether it comes rarely or comes often. If the law of a man's life, the standard, the ideal of it, is that he shall be true, and ninety-nine times to-day he lies and only once he tells the truth, those ninety-nine times are really ninety-nine exceptions. Once, only once, he has been his true self, conformed to his law.

It is really the feeling of this—to put the matter in a little different way from that in which we have put it before—it is the feeling of this truth that our best moments are not departures from ourselves, but are really the only moments in which we have truly been ourselves, which has made the memory of men's best moments hold them with such power. Those moments became the rallying-points of all their struggles after better life. Every enterprising experience turned to them as to a burning light, drank from them as from a living fountain. They gave unity to all the scattered struggles. This and that effort to resist temptation was not a solitary thing, sure, in its solitariness, to fail and disappear. They were signs of the nature struggling for its true destiny, the destiny which had been declared and recognized as its truest in that one supreme experience.

All this must have come to Simon Peter. Between the Transfiguration time and the time of his Epistle he had lived in the struggle for holiness and usefulness. Sometimes he had succeeded. Whenever he had had success in any degree, that success must have realized itself in the light of his great memory. Whatever he did that was true and brave must have most easily naturalized itself, so to speak, in virtue of the revelation which had come to him upon the holy mount, that not darkness, but light, not evil, but good, not uselessness, but usefulness, is the true and native condition for a human soul.

If all the world could know that, what a great change would come! If we could all be sure that our best is our most natural—that it is the evil which is most unnatural; if I knew man simply in his intrinsic nature, nothing at all of this long dark history of his, I think that nothing he could do would be so good as to surprise me. It would be his wickedness that would seem strange. To keep that feeling about him, in spite of this long history of his—that is the triumph of the truest faith.

The best men are the truest men. This patience, this courage, this spirituality which makes my friend's life or the world's hero's life sublime and glorious, is not a departure from humanity, it is a realization of humanity. When we look at it we want to say, not, "How strange that a man should be this!" Rather we want to say, "How strange that any man should be anything but this!"

"Christ is the perfect man," we say. When we say that we ought to mean that Christ is the only absolutely true man that has ever lived; that all men, just as far as they fall short of Christ, fall short of humanity; that not that Jesus should be sinless, but that every other human being who ever lived should be a sinner, is the real moral wonder of the world.

Here, and here only, can come the real meaning of the sinfulness of sin. Let me go about always saying to myself, "To err is human!" and what chance is there that I, being conscious of and rejoicing in my humanity, should think it terrible to do what I believe no man can be human without doing? Somebody meets me and says, "Christ!" "Ah, yes," I answer; "but then, you know, He was a peculiar sort of man. He was not just man like us! We cannot think that we can be what He was. That would be to degrade

His divinity and to depreciate His work." So we talk with a false show of reverence, when really just the opposite is true. Really we disown and misinterpret Christ when we refuse to see in Him the true type of man, once seeing which no man has any right to be satisfied or rest until he comes to be like Him. That is the real power of His redemption.

The best man is the truest man. It is in our best moments, not in our worst moments, that we are most genuinely ourselves. Oh, believe in your noblest impulses, in your purest instincts, in your most unworldly and spiritual thoughts! It is the moment when the idea of your profession flashes on you through its dry drudgery—that is the moment when you see your occupation the most truly. Believe that, O mercenary merchants, O clerks and shop-boys overwhelmed and stunned by the clamorous detail of business life! You see man most truly when he seems to you to be made for the best things. Believe that, O cynics! May God show it to your blinded eyes. You see your true self when you believe that the best and purest and devoutest moment which ever came to you is only the suggestion of what you were meant to be and might be all the time. Believe that, O children of God!

This is the way in which a soul lives forever in the light which first began to burn around it when it was with Jesus in the holy mount!

Sermons. First Series.
25th Thousand. 12mo. 20 Sermons. 380 pages. Cloth, $1.75. Paper, 50 cents.

"Humanity, and not sectarianism, is built up by such sermons as these. Mr. Brooks is a man preaching to men about the struggles and triumphs of men."—*N. Y. Tribune.*

"We emphatically apprise our readers that if they overlook this volume they will miss some of the freshest, most fervent, most truthful, most quickening, most comforting and helping religious discourses which life is likely to bring them. If all preaching were to be like this how we should all wish that great were the company of preachers."
—*Literary World.*

Sermons. Second Series.
THE CANDLE OF THE LORD, etc. 20th Thousand. 21 Sermons. 378 pages. Cloth, $1.75 Paper, 50 cents.

"Dr. Brooks is wonderfully suggestive in opening men's thoughts in directions which give to life fresh meanings."—*N. Y. Times.*

Sermons Preached in English Churches. Third Series.
12th Thousand. 14 Sermons. 320 pages. Cloth, $1.75. Paper, 50 cents.

"He has a message to deliver, it is from God; he believes in its reality, and he delivers it earnestly and devoutly, and his hearers catch the enthusiasm of his own faith."—*Churchman.*

Twenty Sermons. Fourth Series.
12th Thousand. 378 pages. Cloth, $1.75. Paper, 50 cents.

"Mr. Brooks brings to the pulpit the mind of a poet and the devout heart of a Christian, with a very large and generous human personality."—*Independent.*

The Light of the World, and Other Sermons. Fifth Series.
12th Thousand. 21 Sermons. 382 pages. Cloth, $1.75. Paper, 50 cents.

"Because he reveals to men with force and beauty their true and deeper selves, meant for all good and right things, Dr. Brooks preaches a word which they ever rejoice to hear, and having heard, can never go away unprofited. His larger parish will cordially welcome these twenty-one sermons."—*Literary World.*

Sermons. Sixth Series.
7th Thousand. 12mo. 20 Sermons. 368 pages. Cloth, $1.75.

"How shall we describe these twenty sermons? They take the old stories told in the Hebrew narratives and fill them with a life that throbs and glows with the breath and blood of to-day. Simplicity and power seem to be the attributes of this preacher. . . . Gladly we welcome this new vial containing the life-blood of a master spirit."
—*The Critic.*

"These sermons, in their spirituality of temper, their breadth of sympathy, their insight, and their beautiful literary quality, are quite on a level with any earlier sermons from the same hand. . . . Like its predecessors it is full not only of consolation, but also of spiritual stimulus."—*The Outlook.*

Sent by mail, post-paid, on receipt of price.

E. P. DUTTON & CO., Publishers, 31 W. 23d Street, New York.

By the Rev. Phillips Brooks, D.D.

THE INFLUENCE OF JESUS.
THE BOHLEN LECTURES FOR 1879. Fourteenth Thousand. 16mo. 274 pages. Cloth, $1.25.
LECTURE I. The Influence of Jesus on the Moral Life of Man.
" II. The Influence of Jesus on the Social Life of Man.
" III. The Influence of Jesus on the Emotional Life of Man.
" IV. The Influence of Jesus on the Intellectual Life of Man.

" It is written with an open heart toward the thousands who are seeking to find the secret of the fascination which men have in Christ as Man, and will be welcomed in much the same quarters as those in which 'Ecce Homo' found a hearing ten years ago. It is a strong and healthy book, which has grown out of the life of a strong and healthy man."—*N. Y. Times.*

" The ringing keynote is the Fatherhood of God to all mankind, the favorite idea of this distinguished preacher, and one which he here develops with all his characteristic energy, eloquence and hopefulness."—*The Literary World.*

TOLERANCE.
TWO LECTURES addressed to the Students of Several of the Divinity Schools of the Protestant Episcopal Church. Fourth Thousand. 16mo. 111 pages. Paper, 50 cents; cloth, 75 cents.

" Mr. Brooks's two lectures in eloquence, sweetness, and literary charm are what he always is when at all equal to himself. For their substance they lay down a doctrine of tolerance which would at a touch bring all sections of Christendom together on the basis of a tolerance which carries in it the promise of spiritual unity."—*Independent.*

" They are marked by the broad and catholic spirit of Dr. Brooks, and are to be commended to all students, and with especial earnestness to seekers after the unity and union of Christians."—*N. Y. Observer.*

" It is a book for large-minded men and women of whatever creed or no creed. . . . To appreciate these lectures fully they should be read from the first line to the last. One clear-cut and finely polished sentence follows another in such natural sequence, illustrating each the other, that they form a harmonious and inseparable whole."
—*Home Journal.*

" In this his latest contribution to religious thought the eloquent Rector of Trinity Church appears at his best. The subject he has chosen, equally with his mode of treating it, are characteristic of the man."—*N. Y. Times.*

BAPTISM AND CONFIRMATION.
Fifteenth Thousand. Paper, 10 cents.

THE GOOD WINE AT THE FEAST'S END.
A Sermon on Growing Old. Paper, 25 cents.

A CHRISTMAS SERMON.
Paper, 25 cents.

AN EASTER SERMON.
Paper, 25 cents.

THE SYMMETRY OF LIFE.
An Address to Young Men. Paper, 25 cents.

THE LIFE HERE AND THE LIFE HEREAFTER.
In attractive paper covers. 25 cents.

LETTERS OF TRAVEL.

By PHILLIPS BROOKS.

*14th Thousand.   Large 12mo.   392 pages, cloth, gilt top, $2.00.
White cloth, full gilt, with cloth cover, $2.50.*

CONTENTS:
First Journey Abroad. 1865-1866.
In the Tyrol and Switzerland. 1870.
Summer in Northern Europe. 1872.
From London to Venice. 1874.
England and the Continent. 1877.
In Paris, England, Scotland, and Ireland. 1880.
A Year in Europe and India. 1882-1883.
England and Europe. 1885.
Across the Continent to San Francisco. 1886.
A Summer in Japan. 1889.
Summer of 1890. Last Journey Abroad.

" Few, if any, of the books of 1893 will attract or deserve more attention. The volume embraces letters to his father, mother, brothers and other relatives. . . . To many of these letters a peculiar interest attaches, in that the writer regarded them somewhat in the light of a private journal, and, reclaiming them on his return, preserved them for the pleasurable reminiscences which they awakened. . . . His biography is in course of preparation, but we are confident that there will be nothing in it which will more accurately reveal the grandly simple character of this great man than do these letters. Here he opens his heart without reserve, and without any thought of being misunderstood."—*Boston Daily Advertiser.*

" We owe a debt of gratitude to the family who have consented thus to open the door and let us sit by Phillips Brooks's side and hear him talk in familiar conversation."—*The Outlook.*

" There could be no better memorial of the beloved and eloquent preacher than this volume. It is thoroughly characteristic of the man, and therefore thoroughly delightful. It is full of bright sayings, kindly reminiscences and gleeful, even boyish, talk. Phillips Brooks would never have grown old had he lived a hundred years. His mind and heart were always fresh, and he had such a hopeful way of looking at things that you could not help breaking into happy laughter as he talked. We have enjoyed the volume intensely."—*N. Y. Herald.*

" They abound in everything which can make such a compilation attractive—pleasing scenes and incident, good company, a light, dignified and vivacious style, and the strong personal charm of a very unusual man driving the quill."—*The Independent.*

" Thousands will read the letters with as much eagerness as if they were written to themselves."—*N. Y. Observer.*

" These letters present a new and winning side of Phillips Brooks's character. They prove that he was at once an acute and sympathetic observer of men and things, that he had a keen sense of the ludicrous, as well as a large fund of bubbling and spontaneous humor; and that in spite of all the honors that came to him, his heart remained as simple as that of a child. We know of no letters to children published during the present generation more delightful in every way than those included in this volume. In flashes of unexpected humor, and in their genuine and unstudied humanness, they are charming."—*N. Y. Tribune.*

" But to cite all that is pleasant in the book, all that reveals, without any effort at revelation, what was pure and kind and faithful in Bishop Brooks's nature, would be to cite the book entire. . . . From the first letter to the last we feel in the reading that we are learning, perhaps, the most valuable side of a valuable life, and that we are being shown the anchorage of that warm and large heart, to which thousands did honor after it had ceased to beat, in the narrowing home circle where Bishop Brooks was brother, son, uncle and friend."—*N. Y. Times.*

" His letters are a treat. . . . They bring their readers into a contact with one of the greatest souls of the ages—a contact which cannot fail to benefit any one who feels it."—*The Interior* (Chicago).

Sent by mail, post-paid, on receipt of price.

LECTURES ON PREACHING.

Delivered before the Divinity School of Yale College in January and February, 1877.

BY THE REV. PHILLIPS BROOKS.

Twelfth Thousand. 12mo, 281 pages . . . $1.50.

"Unlike Robertson, Phillips Brooks continually reminds us of him. He has the same analytical power; the same broad human sympathy; the same keen knowledge of human nature, toned and tempered and made the more true by his sympathies; the same mysterious and indefinable element of divine life, so that his message comes with a *quasi* authority, wholly unecclesiastical, purely personal; and the same undertone of sadness, the same touch of pathos, speaking low as a man who is saddened by his own seeming success,—a success which is to his thought, and in comparison with his ideals, a failure. No minister can read carefully these lectures without getting a profounder sense of the true grandeur of his work, and a clearer conception of at least some of the secrets of success in its prosecution."— *Harper's Magazine.*

"No one in our country has had more continuous or more conspicuous success in preaching than Mr. Brooks; and the book he has given us points directly to the principles which underlie his power. No one can read it and go on repeating the proverb, 'as dry as a sermon,' if only sermons shall be conceived and delivered in the moral and intellectual atmosphere with which these lectures surround the subject.

"The teaching in these lectures is of necessity full of vitality. It is to be compared not so much to a treatise on tactics or an exhortation to enlist, as to a strain of martial music inspiring the enthusiasm of a soldier. It is withal very noble and very genuine. No theological student could ever read it and doubt that character lay at the bottom of his success. Full of inspiring suggestions as it is, no one could glean from it any comfort in trusting to inspirations and neglecting work and study."— *Scribner's Monthly.*

"The enthusiasm for the profession which this book displays has contagion in it, because it is not expended on that which separates the profession from other occupations, but on that which it shares with them. Throughout the book runs a single thought never lost sight of,— the greater the man the greater the preacher; and again and again, when discoursing of practical methods, the lecturer returns in some form to his golden text, that it is the man behind the sermon which makes the sermon a power. It is because the lecturer, holding this truth firmly, addresses himself to the living facts of a preacher's profession rather than to the mechanism or elaborate organization in which he works, that his words will be life to the living and glittering generalities to the moribund."— *Atlantic Monthly.*

"We do not hesitate to say that they are of more practical value than any work of the sort we have ever seen. . . . . It is a book to be read for the feeling it awakens, but feeling so lofty that it is one with wisdom and truth."— *Literary World.*

"Nothing of the kind can be superior to his first four lectures They might be truly described as an analysis of the elements of Christian manliness, and as a statement of the conditions on which men who preach can hope to win other men. Nearly every page contains something over which the reader lingers with delight."— *New York Times.*

"No man, lay or clerical, who likes bright thoughts and clear, artistic expression, can afford to neglect this volume."— *New York Sun.*

"There is a noble breadth and height and depth to each of these lectures. They are both roomy and full. Of all the courses which have been given on this foundation, we remember none that are more vital, fresh, and inspiring. One does not need to be a minister to read them with great satisfaction and great improvement."— *Boston Advertiser*

"It would be very easy to fill columns with fresh, sagacious, subtile, *true* observations from these pages."— *Boston Evening Transcript.*

For sale at all bookstores, or sent by mail, post-paid, on receipt of price.

E. P. DUTTON & CO., Publishers,

Phillips Brooks Year Book.

SELECTIONS FROM THE WRITINGS OF THE

Rt. Rev. PHILLIPS BROOKS, D.D.

By H. L. S. and L. H. S.   16mo, 372 pages, gilt top, $1.25.

"I am so much impressed with its wonderful insight and the spiritual fitness of the quotations that I desire to express my personal gratitude to the editors for the spiritual help which they have given to me and to thousands of others, by the rare discrimination and excellent taste which they have shown in their happy work. No complaint can be made to the effect that this book does not fairly represent Bishop Brooks. It gives us a great many of his best thoughts, his communion with the Master, his spiritual insights, and his highest aspirations."

"One of the richest and most beautiful books of the year in point of contents. . . . It would probably be impossible to find in any volume of this size, drawn from distinctively religious writings, a richer fertility of spiritual resource and intellectual insight than is to be found in these pages."—*The Outlook.*

"The thoughts are so deep and grand and uplifting, the beauty of the language so great, the selections so varied and so wonderfully chosen, and the poetry as if written for its place in the book! Your country owes you a debt of gratitude for stringing the pearls and arranging the gems so as to bring out their greatest beauty and make apparent their intrinsic value."—FROM AN ENGLISH LETTER.

"In looking these over, one is impressed that the compilers must not only have known what was appropriate to select, but must also have been intimately acquainted with the great preacher. We see, even more clearly than we would in reading through the complete volumes of his sermons and lectures, the man and preacher himself."—*Zion's Herald.*

"The stuff out of which the book is mainly made is royal purple, and it is like the sound of a trumpet or the rush of many waters, as one opens his ear to the impassioned voice that speaks in these pages."—*Atlantic Monthly.*

"The fitness of these passages is evident at once, and it must be confessed that this work, in the beauty of its selections, in the fitness of its type, and in the simplicity of its binding, is the beau ideal of what a year book ought to be. It is as choice and as delightful as one could wish. Such a work as this will go into thousands of hands and find immediate response, and it is calculated to do a great deal of good. In it Bishop Brooks will still preach to the multitude, and he will lead to heaven and guide people in the right way."—*Boston Herald.*

"Those who have known and loved Phillips Brooks, those who have listened to his glowing words and seen his illumined face, and those who have merely been able to trace his thought in print, will take a tender pleasure in turning the leaves of this "Year Book" compiled by loving hands. It will be a help from day to day; for the ringing sentences, the wise counsellings and the inciting to a higher life, strong in themselves, seem almost sacred now one feels impelled to heed them."
—*Boston Transcript.*

Sent by mail, post-paid, on receipt of price.

E. P. DUTTON & CO., Publishers, 31 W. 23d Street, New York.

A VALUABLE SERIES OF SERMONS.

PREACHERS OF THE AGE.

The volumes are uniform in size, appearance and price, and each contains some twelve or fourteen Sermons or Addresses specially chosen or written for the series. They are issued in 12mo size, cloth extra, at **$1.25** each, and contain fine **Photogravure Portraits** reproduced, in most instances, from **unpublished** photographs.

"An excellent series."—*N. Y. Evangelist.*

1 **Living Theology.**

By EDWARD WHITE BENSON, D.D., Archbishop of Canterbury. 13 Sermons, 236 pages. Portrait. $1.25.

"Dr. Benson displays three traits at once—elegant and critical scholarship, philosophic thought, and deep spirituality."
—*Christian Union.*

2 **The Conquering Christ,**

And Other Sermons. By ALEXANDER MACLAREN, D.D. 14 Sermons, 212 pages. Portrait. $1.25.

"Dr. Maclaren has no superior, perhaps no equal, in the British pulpit in the analysis of Scripture in his deep searching for the hidden riches on which he is to build."—*Independent.*

3 **Verbum Crucis.**

Being Ten Sermons on the Mystery and the Words of the Cross. To which are added some other sermons preached on public occasions. By WILLIAM ALEXANDER, D.D., Bishop of Derry and Raphoe. 14 Sermons, 206 pages. Portrait. $1.25.

"These addresses on the seven sayings will be found very useful for those clergy who wish to give their people on Good Friday a service of devotion, and yet are too crowded with work to prepare their own material."—*Churchman.*

E. P. DUTTON & CO., PUBLISHERS, NEW YORK.

4 Ethical Christianity.
A Series of Sermons by HUGH PRICE HUGHES, M.A., of the West End Wesleyan Mission. 14 Sermons, 190 pages. Portrait. $1.25.

"We are convinced that there is no American minister who will not be wonderfully stimulated by reading these fourteen discourses. .... He has got a message from his heart, and he tells it in simple, tender, straight, heart language."—*Zion's Herald.*

5 The Knowledge of God,
And Other Sermons. By WILLIAM WALSHAM HOW, D.D., Bishop of Wakefield. 17 Sermons, 220 pages. Portrait. $1.25.

"Marked not only by the Bishop's well-known power of putting difficult truths into 'plain words,' but by that loving and persuasive spirit which gives him his great charm as a preacher."
—*London Guardian.*

6 Light and Peace.
Sermons and Addresses. By HENRY ROBERT REYNOLDS, D.D. 13 Sermons, 224 pages. Portrait. $1.25.

"Dr. Reynolds belongs by long possessed rights in this series. He is an English Congregationalist, since 1860 Principal of Lady Huntingdon's College, Cheshunt, Herts. He has been prolific with his pen in many directions. The sermons in this collection are elevated in theme and treatment. They touch the noblest themes in a noble manner, and with much imaginative power and eloquent force."—*Independent.*

7 The Journey of Life.
By W. J. KNOX LITTLE, M.A. 11 Sermons, 226 pages. Portrait. $1.25.

"The friends and admirers of the Rev. W. J. Knox Little, Canon of Worcester, will welcome this collection of clever sermons from him. The sermons all bear on some phase of the solemn thought suggested in the title, and bring up practical points which Canon Little knows well how to handle in a direct, wise and helpful manner."—*Independent.*

8 Messages to the Multitude.
By C. H. SPURGEON. 12 Sermons, 318 pages. Portrait. $1.25.

"This volume shows the great preacher at his best in the treatment of the Divine Word, and it will be, with the lifelike portrait of the preacher, a valuable memorial to the multitudes of his admirers."
—*N. Y. Observer.*

E. P. DUTTON & CO., PUBLISHERS, NEW YORK.

9 **Christ is All.**
Sermons from New Testament Texts, on various Aspects of the Glory and Work of Christ, with some Other Sermons. By H. C. G. MOULE, M.A., Principal of Ridley Hall, Cambridge, England. 18 Sermons, 248 pages. Portrait. $1.25.
" Devout and thoughtful expositions which cannot fail to be helpful."—*Interior.*
" They breathe the very spirit and power of the Gospel."
—*Church Bells.*

10 **Plain Words on Great Themes.**
By J. OSWALD DYKES, D.D., Principal of the Theo. College of the Presbyterian Church of England. 15 Sermons, 224 pages. Portrait. $1.25.
" These discourses are full of freshness, spirituality and genuine power. Young preachers especially might study with peculiar profit the chief characteristics of these sermons. We can hardly recommend too strongly."—*Advance.*

11 **Children of God,**
And Other Sermons. By the Rev. E. A. STUART, Vicar of St. James's, Holloway. 20 Sermons, 246 pages. Portrait. $1.25.
" A collection of brilliant, dramatic and effective sermons by one of the rising preachers in the English Established Church."
—*Independent.*

12 **Christ in the Centuries,**
And Other Sermons. By A. M. FAIRBAIRN, D.D., Principal of Mansfield College, Oxford. 13 Sermons, 232 pages. Portrait. $1.25.
" They are fresh and striking in thought, noticeably choice in diction, and instinct with the wisdom of human experience and the spirituality which is the fruit of close and tender fellowship with Christ. . . . No man in England to-day is more thoroughly representative of English Congregationalism than he."
—*Congregationalist.*

13 **Agoniæ Christi.**
Being Sermons on the Sufferings of Christ, together with Others on His Nature and His Work. By WILLIAM LEFROY, D.D., Dean of Norwich. 11 Sermons, 234 pages. Portrait. $1.25.
" Eleven thoughtful, solemn, often profoundly tender and always deeply impressive sermons on the deity, humanity and sufferings of Jesus."—*Congregationalist.*